Valuing Diversity®

New Tools for a New Reality

Lewis Brown Griggs

Lente-Louise Louw

Editors

McGraw-Hill, Inc.

New York   San Francisco   Washington, D.C.   Auckland   Bogotá
Caracas   Lisbon   London   Madrid   Mexico City   Milan
Montreal   New Delhi   San Juan   Singapore
Sydney   Tokyo   Toronto

Library of Congress Cataloging-in-Publication Data

Valuing diversity® : new tools for a new reality / Lewis Brown Griggs
    and Lente-Louise Louw, editors
        p.   cm.
   ISBN 0-07-024778-1
    1. Minorities—Employment—United States.   2. Multiculturalism—
United States.   3. Personnel management—United States.
I. Griggs, Lewis. II. Louw, Lente-Louise.
HF5549.5.M5V35   1994
658.3′041—dc20   94-22295
                                         CIP

2 3 4 5 6 7 8 9 0 DOC/DOC 9 0 9 8 7 6 5 4

ISBN 0-07-024778-1

*The sponsoring editor for this book was Betsy Brown, the editing supervisor was
Ruth W. Mannino, and the production supervisor was Pamela A. Pelton. It was
set in Palatino by McGraw-Hill's Professional Book Group composition unit.*

Printed and bound by R. R. Donnelley & Sons Company.

Contents

Preface

Over the past decade, pioneering organizations and individuals have led the way toward a new appreciation of cultural differences among employees, customers, suppliers, and the many others who hold a stake in managing diversity. As the world's workforce grows ever more diverse, our ability to manage these demographic challenges will determine whether the United States, and other nations, can compete globally. We see diversity, in its broadest meanings, as this century's greatest challenge to organizational life worldwide.

Many organizations that have been pioneers in learning to value and manage diversity have invited managers to discuss the challenges organizations face. Out of such discussions have emerged a major finding: Capitalizing on diversity provides a distinct personal, interpersonal, and organizational advantage. This becomes truer every day, but many organizations still "don't get it."

Valuing and managing diversity remains, in 1994, a relatively uncharted journey. As a manager of one of our client organizations remarked in the 1980s, "We don't know what valuing and managing diversity will look like, but we've begun the journey of learning." Those who started the journey in the eighties are now ahead in the race to ensure that *no potential is lost* in the diverse workforce of the nineties and beyond. Those who have risked in this area, choosing to plunge in and learn by their mistakes, have been richly rewarded. They have discovered that differences in culture, ethnicity, gender, race, perspectives, personality, style, values, and feelings need to be honored and encouraged, not merely tolerated. They know that out of differences come more than multiple perspectives or added value—that the real value of a diverse workforce is that it nurtures synergistic interactions across difference. It is this synergy that produces unpredictable consequences in terms of breakthrough and results (productivity, innovations in service or product development and operations, and more collaborative teams).

These results don't come easily or quickly. Interactions across differences present real challenges and demand commitment and investment of resources along with a willingness to begin a complex journey. Valuing and managing diversity is not something to be left only to so-called experts. Diversity programs are also not "cognitive" exercises that can be mastered by taking a crash course. They demand real-life experience, falling down and pulling yourself up along the way, learning to become self-aware, to acquire new skills, and to apply these skills in the workplace. And they must be seen as an ongoing process rather than a one-time event.

The purpose of this book is to create awareness of the role and importance of valuing and managing diversity and relationship, to encourage looking at pitfalls and challenges that can lead to promising future directions, and most importantly, to encourage and inspire you to begin your own journey. The book begins with focus on diversity and ends with focus on relationship but, as suggested in Chapter 8, the two concepts are really inseparable, and you will notice that each contributing author seems to make or presume such a connection.

Knowing that the only experts on these issues are those committed explorers who simply set forth on the diversity journey with no compass, we were clear that we wanted this book to introduce you to experienced consultants in the diversity field with whom we have worked professionally: Steve Hanamura, Francie Kendall, Percy Thomas, Rafael Gonzalez, and Tamara Payne. They are dedicated to their work, as you will read in their biographical statements, and they speak honestly and passionately from their diverse perspectives. They use different styles and approaches to tackle the issues on which they have chosen to focus, but they share with each other, and with us, a common vision: Every individual in the workplace must be free to be fully herself or himself and to be in working relationships that are satisfying as well as creative and productive. As authors, we also share the belief that, with our common humanity as a given, it is our *differences* that distinguish us and through which we learn from each other.

Because of our vast diversity, this book was not edited to be "seamless"—that is, to present a unitary view, tone, or style. Some of us define diversity more broadly than others. Some use case studies, some personal experiences, some use *I*, some use *we*, some use *one*, and some talk to *you*. Some use *minority* and some don't. Some use *Hispanic*, some *Latino*, and so forth. We also address you, the reader, whether you are a manager, a supervisor, or a leader, as a working member of your organization, who regardless of title must deal with these issues in a very personal way.

We hope that the final impact of our presentations will spark greater awareness as well as provide you with useful and practical guidelines you can use to effect change in your organization. But this book is not intended to be a trainer's manual, and it decidedly does not provide hard-and-fast answers or solutions. We ask you to read and think about our ideas and experiences, to discuss them among yourselves and throughout your workplace, and, finally, to take the risk of developing strategies and processes that work for your organization.

Lewis Brown Griggs
Lente-Louise Louw

1

Valuing Diversity®

Where From...Where To?

Lewis Brown Griggs

In the beginning, for each of us, is self. As infants, our egocentrism helps us stay alive. We focus only on self and getting our own needs met. As children, we expand our boundaries to include a slightly broader sense of self-interest that includes not only self, but family. Over time, we expand our boundaries beyond family, to a circle of friends and the immediate community. Generally speaking, we continue as adults to feel safest and most comfortable with people *like* ourselves at those three levels. Our "comfort zone" of relationship may be within our socioeconomic class or our culture, language, race, age, gender, ethnicity, or any of the special groups we might join—a class studying a certain subject or a functional group at work, for example.

The point is that we're constantly organizing ourselves around a group of individuals with whom we have something, if not most things, in common. In fact, identifying those things we have in common with others is a natural, healthy stage of development. It helps us form our own identity and, more so, to establish the sense of self we need if we are to recognize and include others in our world. Imagine a time before there were mirrors when it was *only* through others that we learned to understand who we were and to learn that what we saw to be true about others confirmed what was true about ourselves. Then imagine a time when we lived in small, closed communities and felt a need to be cautious about "outsiders" until we were able to establish a sense of safety with them.

The origins of our discrimination need not be objects of shame or blame. To be "discriminating" in the positive sense is what allows us to sort through sources of information to learn the roots of our attitudes and prejudices and, ideally, decide in each new situation confronting us whether the circumstances require us to protect ourselves. There are many situations in which the circumstances do indeed require us to discriminate between who's safe and who's not or what behavior is appropriate and what's not. It's important to understand that context, or situational specificity, is a factor we must always consider—that what's safe, irrelevant, or even positive in one situation may not be in another.

When each of our various groups of immigrants arrived in North America, even though they had chosen to leave behind oppressive religious, economic, or political situations in order to seek freedom, independence, and the right to self-expression in one form or another, they found themselves among a group of such diverse people that a first pressing need was to look for commonalities. The most obvious way to go about it was to find areas of similarity with the dominant culture that greeted their arrival. Historically, it might have been any group, but in the North American case the dominant culture was English and Northern European. For each new wave of immigrants, this continued to be the case, so that the common denominator soon became the English language and English and Northern European customs. The same process would likely have gone on had the original wave of immigrants been Asian or African or Latin.

Because of this fact of our history, the intention to have full and free expression and individuation, which is the written and unwritten value behind our customs and laws, was often subverted in favor of an unwritten and unacknowledged requisite to become as *similar* as possible to those already here—to blend into this new culture. And so, anything that made them stand out as different was put aside, in some cases rather abruptly. Many families, for example, chose to stop speaking their native language even in their own home and to abandon the customary dress and behavior of their native culture so as to appear, if not become, what they perceived as American, and to do so as quickly as possible.

In spite of all other differences, one of the things that most of these newcomers did have in common is that they all chose to come here. Obviously, this free choice does not apply to the early influx of African-Americans, who did not elect to come here, nor to Native Americans who were already here. All other newcomers to America, however, had clearly chosen to venture into new territory, whether to seek relief from something oppressive in their homelands or to reach out for something this new country promised. And so there's something about the personality, and, ultimately, the gene pool of these immigrants to North America that is held in common. Combined with the common language immigrants quickly acquired and, of course, the basic human similarities we all share, this need to accommodate to the dominant culture had the effect of discouraging the expression of even superficial behavioral differences and diverse cultural styles. In those early times, the discomfort of being different was the greater problem to be solved.

Interestingly, many people today reject diversity training with the argument that people are more similar than dissimilar and so we should not waste time focusing on our differences. I like to point out in response that it is precisely the comfort of knowing that we are mostly similar that should enable us to look at our differences without fear that we will lose anything—either our own identity or the bonds we share with others as human beings. Faced with this argument, what I must stress in reply is that it is not our similarities that cause our problems—like it or not, it is our differences. Sometimes the difference is the result of a false perception that can be corrected, and sometimes it is quite real, but in any case it is our differences that cause problems.

If employees or managers want to improve their ability to function in the workplace or marketplace, then they must start by uncovering the differences—in attitude, in style, in ways of being and doing—that triggered the decision to seek improvement in the first place. If differences among individuals keep a manager from finding the right employee, from noticing equal competence, from communicating in an interview, from trusting an applicant enough to hire, from understanding enough to train, from valuing enough to promote, or from seeing differences as benefits, then it's clearly the case that a greater knowledge of *differences* is needed in order to break through the barriers thought to be caused by the presence of differences.

Even when the need for greater knowledge of differences is confronted and understood, many continue to defend against actually *valuing* those differences. Instead, they make the point that even though we are different when we come to this country from our place of origin, in time we become increasingly similar and, the longer we stay, the more effectively we melt into the general population. Therefore, the logic goes, why not just wait until people complete their melting process, and, in the meantime, hire those who have already assimilated?

Here, I like to call upon the analogy of the floating iceberg whose tip breaking the water's surface, as we all know, belies the often enormous breadth of its base, hidden beneath the water. As icebergs increase in number and/or drift into close proximity to each other, they are likely to clash at their bases, even though, from our vantage point at the water's surface, there is no visible contact.

In the context of the workplace, a similar dynamic often occurs; that is, because we speak a common language and dress and act in common ways, we seem to work together "above the table" without any apparent friction. And then, having learned to act in a conflict-free mode, at least superficially, we believe that we have learned all we need to know about accommodating each other's differences and recognizing and rewarding our similarities so that the task at hand can be accomplished. Below the surface, however, our behaviors—manners, communication style, listening attitudes, and so forth—represent the deeper and broader base of the iceberg, the contours of which are determined by our conditioning, our history, and the values rooted in our different cultures.

The effect is that, while we appear to be communicating without apparent friction above the table, all too often we are suppressing feelings of mistrust, dislike, and irritation in varying degrees beneath the behavior we show on the surface. We really do not see our coworkers or colleagues in their fullest expression, nor are we seen in ours. Yet to be successful, all professional interactions, just like personal interactions, depend upon reciprocal recognition of competence, feelings of trust, open communication, and a shared sense of our end goals. Obviously, when we cover or deny our ignorance of or discomfort with another person's style and manner, the professional interaction is compromised and the results of our working together are negatively affected.

In other words, it is possible to reach a level of comfort doing things with people who are different, but to break through to a higher level demands more and carries with it greater rewards. Actually, this type of behavior, this appearance of getting along despite differences, has been institutionalized in America's workplaces and in our interpersonal relationships. The "rules" are both written and tacit.

Most of us have been taught to react to differences among people in one of two acceptable ways, so that our behavior won't be labeled as "discriminatory." First, when we see differences, we're taught to presume that they are false, that what we are seeing—about most white males or about black females or about those with physical disabilities, or any number of other characteristics that mark us as different—are, in fact, not so. Regardless of whether what we see or experience or believe is at least partially true, or most often true, or statistically accurate, and that acting upon our perceptions or knowledge might be appropriate, we are admonished to mistrust our judgments and/or to presume our position to be false. Real differences are lumped in the category, then, as misconstrued differences and are denied.

Second, because not all differences can be denied (such as obvious gender differences, some obvious differences of skin color and racial characteristics, and obvious differences in accents and language facility), a second-level category had to be devised so that we could maintain our nondiscriminatory policies and "liberal-minded" attitudes and behavior. Any real, undeniable differences we might encounter between us and others, in our personal, professional, or organizational life, must be considered "irrelevant." If we are to do this well, we are told, we must consider them to be 100 percent irrelevant to whatever the task at hand.

The various categories of "real" differences we are asked to regard as 100 percent irrelevant to the task at hand, if we are to be applauded as nondiscriminatory, are: race, age, gender, physical ability, religion, and, in some states, sexual orientation. In the context of the workplace, that means that employers are not allowed to consider these differences in hiring, promoting, or firing, all factors having to do with evaluating whether the person is the most appropriate person for the job.

In my view, both of these intentionally limiting practices have the effect of reinforcing rather than breaking barriers caused by discomfort with difference. It is true that when we act affirmatively and work to ensure equal employment opportunity, we do successfully avoid discriminating arbitrarily and prejudicially against those unlike ourselves; but, at the same time, we fail to develop a positive "discriminating" ability, one that is capable of fully "seeing" human beings in all their diversity. And we fail to achieve real equal opportunity in the workplace when our actions, however well intended, are rooted in denial and ignorance instead of acceptance and appreciation of individual variability. Right now, if you examine them carefully, most of our antidiscrimination efforts perpetuate denial and ignorance which, in turn, perpetuates more denial and ignorance.

Some breakthroughs do result when we act affirmatively and when we work to ensure equal opportunity, for it is possible, certainly, to gradually become more familiar with people different from ourselves and to eventually reduce whatever discomfort we once felt. But all too often, affirmative action and equal opportunity practices—when driven, as most are, by denial and ignorance—promote situations in which one group gives "equal opportunity" to the other (especially the dominant groups to the less dominant) to act in ways that make "us" feel comfortable. Or, to put it more bluntly, *equal opportunity* all too often means entering into competition with one another to see who wins the race to become bicultural enough that everyone has the illusion of feeling comfortable with differences. It is an exhausting and depleting race for anyone to have to run, to deny (as if false) and to ignore (as if irrelevant) one's own cultural and ethnographic identity. Yet for decades we have been asking people to leave their differences at the door and to apply their energy not to the task at hand but to the task of becoming bicultural.

Looking at our history of dealing with diversity actually helps us see how we are evolving, all of us at different stages. We started out, for example, from a strongly egocentric position. We then moved to ethnocentrism before coming to a prolonged period of acting "affirmatively" and ensuring "equal opportunity," only to discover, with the rapidly changing demographics of recent years, that we need to shift our course and *affirm* our differences, *accept* our differences, and, ultimately, *value* those differences.

What Is Diversity?

I believe *diversity* should be defined in the broadest possible way. Not only does *diversity* include differences in age, race, gender, physical ability, sexual orientation, religion, socioeconomic class, education, region of origin, language, and so forth but also differences in life experience, position in the family, personality, job function, rank within a hierarchy, and other such characteristics that go into forming an individual's perspective. Within an organization, diversity encompasses every individual difference that affects a task or relationship. Diversity also has an impact on the products and services developed by its workforce as well as on personal, interpersonal, and organizational activities.

Clearly, there is a benefit and a risk inherent in defining *diversity* so broadly. The benefit is that it is accurate, that it is all-inclusive, that each person is recognized as part of the diversity that needs to be valued. That's healthy. To limit the definition of *diversity*, as even much of the diversity movement itself did a few years ago, to differences of gender, race, and constitutionally protected differences, is to ignore much of the diversity that we each bring. Furthermore, such a limited view serves to maintain polarized tensions around the discussion of differences, as we have seen so often between black and white, men and women, straight and gay, politically "right" and "left," North and South, Jew and gentile. Every difference was immediately polarized in such a way that one side was made right and the other wrong. Alternatively, when we realize our individual diversity—I am white, *and* I am male, *and* I am heterosexual, *and* I am whatever, and so are you—then we can begin to realize that each of us is a rich mixture of aspects of self.

The risk to be aware of in defining *diversity* so broadly is the inclination some have to take refuge in its broad scope—that is, to avoid really looking at our own *-isms*, our own discomfort with differences in age, race, gender, and so on. When we use its far-reaching scope to hide our biases and prejudices, then we aren't moved to do the important work we need to do in uncovering our own racism, or sexism, or classism, or heterosexism, or whatever discomfort with difference gets in the way of truly seeing and valuing another person's competence and uniqueness. It is important to pay attention to whether or not we are pretending to honor *all* differences as a cover for not confronting the particular differences that cause us the greatest personal discomfort.

Why Value Diversity?

Most people don't "value" diversity until they perceive it to be in their self-interest to do so. I am talking specifically about long-term self-interest and/or enlightened self-interest, which, of course, is a value judgment. In fact, it is enlightened self-interest that constitutes the only sound reason for valuing diversity, whether at the personal, interpersonal, or organizational level. For many, the main reasons for engaging in the valuing diversity process are to reverse past wrongs, to assuage guilt, to act affirmatively or ensure equal opportunity just because it's "fair." None of those reasons are sufficient to bring us to the meaning of enlightened self-interest, however, for none of those reasons allow us to place positive value on the fact of our differences from others. And if we do not experience the real benefits that come from changing our relationships to those different from ourselves, then our fears of defeat are realized. I've indicated that valuing diversity occurs at the personal, interpersonal, and organizational level and that at all three levels there needs to be self-interest if we are to justify embarking on the diversity journey in the first place. So let's start with our personal self-interest and presume that the first difference to be valued is our own. I shouldn't need to make a case for valuing oneself; most people recognize that the qualities we appreciate in ourselves and those that others like, or love, or respect in us are likely to be those relative and/or comparative things about us that stand out in some way as being different, or even unique. It is most often the qualities that differentiate us that others refer to in describing us and that they admire in us. Even though our similarities may be prerequisites to our being liked or respected, those prerequisites are not usually the ways in which we generate the greatest love, admiration, respect, trust, or recognition.

Actually, all valuing diversity work should begin with a greater understanding of exactly who we are—culturally, demographically, and ethnographically as well as with regard to age, race, religion, gender, country, community of origin, language, sexual orientation, education, class, and so on. Most agree that an important goal in life is to become our fullest selves, to be the most we can be, which, of course, means being the most unique and different we can be—because the most I can be is very different from the most someone else can be, given our differences in life experiences, perspectives, talents, and personality attributes.

To become the most we can be, then, depends on becoming conscious of our differences and giving them energy and freedom of expression. Once we "get" that, it's an easy leap to recognize that somebody else's uniqueness also needs to be fully expressed if he or she is to be his or her fullest self, and, furthermore, that we play a part in allowing and encouraging that freedom. In recognizing that it is in our self-interest to allow others to be their fullest selves and in theirs to allow us to be our fullest selves, we come to recognize our interdependence and to feel safe in the relationship. The only limits are whatever boundaries are required to maintain each other's "safety." And these boundaries should be limited to the essential ones.

In interpersonal relationships, self-interest then becomes one of mutual fullness, where each person not only allows but encourages the other to grow, to see who he or she is, how his or her behaviors affect us, what he or she looks like from the outside, and so forth. By creating a relationship in which each person focuses on the fullest possible expression of the self, we bring to the relationship the energy required to create synergy in the space between us. (How synergistic relationships are formed and work is the subject of Chapter 8.)

In the context of the workplace, training efforts have long been devoted to getting people who are very similar to each other to work better together. Adding, if you will, $3 + 3 + 3 + 3$ (each number being an individual relatively similar to another) so that similar people complemented each other was thought to be a lot more productive than just being in the workplace together and not working effectively. With affirmative action and equal opportunity programs, the focus shifted to getting diversity into the workplace ($1 + 2 + 3 + 4 + 5$), and even most managing diversity work has been focused on *adding* those individual differences in a way that can be as complementary and result in a similar outcome.

Of course, managing heterogeneity is more difficult, at first, than managing homogeneity. But today, in most organizations, communities, and countries in this rapidly shrinking global village, we do not have the option of working in a homogeneous environment. Gradually, therefore, necessity being the mother of invention, we are becoming aware of the multiple opportunities presented by having a heterogeneous work environment. More and more individuals and organizations are recognizing that diversity is in their self-interest—that in working toward personal, professional, or organizational goals, there is much to be gained in the relationships formed with "different" others.

For organizations, there is an increasingly larger demographic talent pool from which to choose workers. More and more, organizations can remain competitive only if they can recognize and obtain the best talent, value the diverse perspectives that come with talent born of different cultures, races, and genders, nurture and train that talent, and create an atmosphere that values its workforce. One of the many rewards organizations begin to see when they establish a diverse workforce is an increased market for its services or products.

Who Should Value Diversity?

It's obvious that all of us—senior executives, middle-level managers, workers and employees, customers and clients, every individual in any organization that employs people or uses volunteers to accomplish any end, to manage or execute any internal function or external service, or to produce, sell, and/or deliver any product—have an opportunity, if not a responsibility, in our own self-interest, to gain knowledge of, become comfortable with, and ultimately value, our own and others' differences.

Both democracy and free enterprise—which I regard as the most radically progressive and "liberal" systems on earth—are intended to be fully inclusive and participatory. Neither is perfect, and neither can be left unregulated anymore than our personal freedoms can be unregulated, but each system serves us well only insofar as it garners our full participation and inclusion. I find it ironic that people devoted to business pursuits not supportive of full inclusion are thought of as "conservatives" and people devoted to participation and inclusion are regarded as "liberals." Placing high value on full participation and inclusion ought to be seen as "conservative" given that it is these factors that *conserve* the benefits that flow from both democracy and free enterprise.

Just as all of us need to participate in democracy in order for democracy to work for all of us, all of us need to participate in free enterprise, government enterprise, nonprofit enterprise, and educational enterprise if each is to be fully realized and work for all. Just as our relationships can't be full unless each individual expresses himself or herself fully in every relationship, our various organizations can't be fully productive unless the individuals within are fully themselves and the internal and external relationships are fully engaged. In the same vein, a community or a nation or the world we live in cannot be fully functional without the fullest possible participation and inclusion of all its members.

Where Should Diversity Be Valued?

Where should diversity training be done? Well again, the answer is a broad one—everywhere. On an international scale, it's easy to recognize that doing business with other countries, other customs, other languages, and other practices demands greater knowledge of the many individual differences that enter into our personal, interpersonal, and organizational relationships. In some respects, it is a "forest-and-tree" issue; clearly, one kind of forest is very different from another kind of forest. From a distance it seems almost irrelevant that each tree within the forest has its differences from the one next to it because from a great distance the similarities dominate our view.

The same metaphor applies whether we look at the differences that mark us internationally or nationally. It is an illusion to presume that on a national level we have homogeneity and need only deal with our similarities. Obviously, within our own culture and geographic boundaries each individual comes from a different group and set of groupings, as indicated previously. Without stereotyping individuals and making easy presumptions that every individual in a group shares the same values and behaviors, nevertheless, gaining some knowledge and insight about the groups from which an individual comes is useful in knowing that individual. But we need to remember to hold that knowledge in a neutral, safe place as we explore the extent to which it may or may not be true for that individual. We must allow ourselves to experience the uniqueness of that individual above and beyond and aside from all of the traits that we associate with the groups to which that individual belongs.

On another scale—in the community in which we move through our daily lives, often without knowing each other—on the bus, in the restaurant, at the airport, in the supermarket, at the post office, it is not as necessary to value each individual's diversity as long as we are valuing each person's rights. In these impersonal settings, "tolerance" of diversity is usually enough, unless serving individuals in these environments is part of our work. But when it comes to the workplace, as I have suggested all along, it is vital that we move way beyond mere tolerance for individual differences; here, there are tasks that must be accomplished, and they rely on cooperative and collaborative interpersonal relationships.

For close relationships to work, in any setting, they must be enhanced rather than depleted by our differences. In our families and in our most intimate relationships, of course, differences must be understood and not just tolerated. The degree of intimacy may be less in the communal transportation facility than in the communal work-place, and greater in the family and other intimate interpersonal rela-tionships, but it's only the *level* of intimacy that is different; the process of valuing one's own and another's differences is exactly the same. And so it is *everywhere* that we need to do this valuing diversity work.

When Should We Begin Valuing Diversity?

When should valuing diversity work be initiated? The answer is now. There is no reason not to embark on our diversity work within our-selves, within our relationships, within each and every organization in which we work, and with each and every outside customer or client with whom we interact. It is less useful to spend three years developing and refining diversity strategies than it is to simply begin by doing. A first step might be simply awareness raising as a foundation for later work; by now, we know that as consciousness expands, behavior does, indeed, change. Our programs will improve as we move forward and uncover more and different needs specific to our situations, but the need for diversity training is not likely to disappear. Think of all the phrases most of us grew up with: "Practice makes perfect." "There's no time like the present." "Any decision is better than none." "If not now, when?" "Today is the first day of the rest of your life." They all make the same point. So let us begin.

How Do We Begin?

We know that organizations today are facing complex challenges. Most of these are dynamic, interrelated, and systemic in nature; that is, they are intertwined and capable of affecting the operations of the entire organization.

More than any other challenge, perhaps, the diversity challenge affects the organization at all levels: personal, interpersonal, and orga-nizational as well as local, national, and international. The scope and direction of valuing and managing diversity programs, ideally, must be developed within the context of broader challenges facing the organization as a whole. Diversity responses, in other words, need to be well integrated into the organization's overall strategic responses. Systemic thinking is critical to diversity issues.

Yet it is situational priorities that determine how and when the organization can respond to specific diversity challenges. Obviously not all organizations have the resources, time, leadership, or consciousness to do it all, much less do it all at once. Important as the diversity challenge is, "imperfect" management of the complex interventions required is a better way to develop a strategy that works for your organization than planning for years a "perfect" strategy that never gets practiced. So let us briefly consider some issues currently being addressed in organizations and how valuing diversity and relationship are at the heart of these issues.

- *Conflict resolution.* Conflict is inevitable in any organization. However, enhancing relationship patterns among managers and employees alike can keep disagreements from escalating into conflicts.

- *Employee relations.* Employee surveys and audits provide an assessment of the work climate and point out key areas needed to improve employee relations. Focusing on diversity and relationship issues can effect significant changes in the organizational climate and bring to the surface the key problem areas employee surveys have highlighted.

- *Empowerment.* Successful organizations know that empowering employees means valuing their diversity, which brings out their creativity. The process of empowering people can begin on any of the three levels (organizational, personal, and interpersonal), but true empowerment for all can happen only when responsibility is assumed at all three levels.

- *Leadership (on all levels).* Today's leaders know that success in the twenty-first century will come to those who grasp the fundamental importance of relationship within their organizations. The days are gone when a leader of an organization achieves objectives solely through charismatic leadership or personal power. Managers and supervisors must make the transformation from technical expert to manager of people, especially increasing their personal effectiveness working with diverse groups. If organizational objectives and organizational success are to be realized, all of today's leaders, at all levels, must focus on relationship dynamics and assume facilitative and enabling roles.

- *Learning.* For learning to take place in an organization, personal, interpersonal, and organizational flexibility is critical. Individuals need to be receptive to new information, and the organization as a whole needs to constantly adapt itself. At all levels, learning is an ongoing process that depends on strong internal relationships among employees and between managers and workers, and external relationships between the organization and the customers and clients it serves.

- *Productivity.* It is important to consciously identify barriers to productivity at the organizational, personal and interpersonal levels. Managers and supervisors, as always, must demonstrate authority, delegate tasks, solve problems, be effective and innovative, demonstrate leadership, and empower employees but without resorting to the energy-depleting relationship patterns of control, manipulation, blame, denial, mistrust, racism, prejudice, and so on.

- *Synergistic teams.* Individuals face intense pressure to conform to today's team-oriented workplace. Both the team and the organization can be effective only when all the components that make the team effective work together in dynamic unity, that is, where the total is greater than the sum of the parts. Individual members of the team need to be their fullest selves and take personal responsibility. Enhancing interpersonal relationships, especially in structured teams, and obtaining total participation, commitment, and shared responsibility are what ultimately improves the creativity of the team and, by extension, the productivity of the organization. Teams typically operate within an organizational culture embedded in old personal and interpersonal relationship patterns. Depending on whether these organizational relationship patterns are energy depleting or energy enhancing, the team will or will not be effective.

- *Trust building.* Trust and trustworthiness are the foundation of effectiveness in today's organizations. As Max Depree states in his book *Leadership Is an Art* (Dell, N.Y. 1989), "Structures do not have anything to do with trust;...people build trust;...relationship counts more than structure." The critical question is how to build trust in a constantly changing and diverse workplace. We must increase our knowledge and acceptance of our differences, create awareness of relationship dynamics, demonstrate the effect of energy-enhancing and energy-depleting patterns, illustrate the power of relationship among diverse individuals in the organization, and enable employees to begin the crucial steps to build trust.

The challenge we present here is complex and time (and energy) consuming. We ask that you not be overwhelmed, that you do as much as you can with the resources you have, and that you take from these pages what you can use and leave the rest.

2

No Potential Lost

The Valuing Diversity®
Journey—An Integrated
Approach to Systemic Change

Lente-Louise Louw

The broad challenges facing organizations today—a rapidly changing technology, a global marketplace, the need for ongoing training—are dynamic and complex, perhaps overwhelming. What is important to note is that they are systemic by their very nature. For organizations to achieve their vision and meet these challenges, they must realize that managing diversity plays an integral role in how effectively the organization operates as a whole and with particular reference to their human resources. To survive, organizations must constantly ensure in their personnel practices that *no potential is lost*. To do so, they must embark on a committed, ongoing, and well-integrated change process.

Demographic Changes

A number of demographic changes face the leaders of America's corporate, social, governmental, educational, and religious organizations. For example:

- More women will be on the job.
- Fully one-third of new workers will be nonwhite.

- The average age of workers will rise.
- There will be a shortage of skilled workers.
- The American consumer base will be more diverse.

Indeed, our marketplace and workforce is becoming more diverse every day. Although some organizations may experience the effects of diversity more gradually than others, all will need to respond by finding ways to value and manage their diverse relationships both internally and externally.

A groundbreaking report from the Hudson Institute, *Workforce 2000: Work and Workers for the 21st Century*, commissioned by the U.S. Department of Labor and released in 1987, revealed how dramatically the labor pool is changing. In the report, the authors documented changes in our demographics and labor force that are affecting the way American organizations operate and the nation's ability to compete in a global marketplace. *Workforce 2000* projects that from 1985 to 2000, people of color, women, and immigrants will constitute 85 percent of the growth in the nation's workforce. By the year 2000, only 15 percent of the net increase in the workforce will be white males.

Since the Hudson Institute study, other studies have drawn similar conclusions. The Bureau of the Census projects that by the year 2000, the U.S. population will reach 275 million, a 7.8 percent increase—assuming that fertility, mortality, and net immigration remain near current levels. Let's discuss, in turn, each of the demographic changes listed above.

Increasing number of women. According to Bureau of Labor Statistics data from 1989, by the year 2000 women will comprise more than 50 percent of the workforce. With more women in the workplace we can expect more family-related demands (such as child care and maternity leave). (More than 50 percent of all married women with children are in the paid-labor market.)

Increasing number of people of color. People of color now make up one-third of all the new workers being hired. By the year 2000, African-Americans will account for 12 percent of the total workforce, Hispanics/Latinos will account for 10 percent, and Asians, 4 percent (*Handbook of Labor Statistics*, Bureau of Labor Statistics, Bulletin 2340, 1989.) By the year 2050, the Bureau of the Census states in its 1992 figures that approximately 50 percent of the U.S. population will be nonwhite: African-American (16 percent), Hispanic-American (21 percent), Asian and Pacific Islander (11 percent), and Native American (1.2 percent).

Increasing number of immigrants. The Asian and Pacific Islander population is expected to continue to be the fastest-growing group, with annual growth rates that may exceed 4 percent during the 1990s. By 2050, the Asian and Pacific Islander population in the United States is expected to expand to five times its current size, or 41 million.

Rising average age. The average age of people in the United States is rising. More people are living longer. By 2000, one in three Americans will be 45 or older, and people in the 35 to 45 age group will constitute approximately 50 percent of the workforce.

Shortage of skilled workers. More and different skills are required for future jobs. The need for manual labor is decreasing, and the need for "information workers" (people whose primary job function involves working with or processing information) is increasing.

Increasing diversity of the U.S. consumer base. People of color as a group now buy more than any of the countries with which the United States trades. African-Americans, Asians, and Hispanics alone (not including illegal aliens) are expected to reach 25 percent of the nation's consumer base by the year 2000, according to the Population Reference Bureau. Blacks, Asians, and Hispanics now have an annual spending power of $424 billion, which is projected to reach $650 billion by the year 2000.

Table 2-1 shows examples of how demographic trends might affect us personally—our work group, our organization's operations, products, and/or services, present and future markets or groups our organization serves, our communities, the national marketplace, and the global marketplace.

Part One: Major Challenges to Diversity—Systemic Response

The real challenge facing us all is to make sure that we address these demographic challenges systemically. Our ability to do so will determine America's ability to compete globally. Whereas the strength of many of the nation's competitors is their homogeneity, it is America's diversity that represents both its biggest crisis and its greatest opportunity. The question is: Can we adapt our old ways of being, the ways we have traditionally valued people as is now reflected in our organizational culture, management practices, and employee and customer relations? The real challenge is to grasp the opportunity diversity pre-

Table 2-1. Effects of Demographic Trends on Personal, Interpersonal, and Organizational Levels

					Effect of trends on			
Demographic trends	Individual	Work group	Organization's operation	Products and/or services	Future/current market	Community	National marketplace	Global marketplace
More women		Composition may change	More women managers More women in top management	May need different marketing strategies	Must address women's needs May need to change product line	More women in local politics	More women consumers	More women conducting international business
More minorities and immigrants		Need to work with more diverse people Need for better language skills	Need different recruitment strategies Need to deal with bilingual issues	May need different marketing strategies, products, or services	Must address different needs May need to change product line	More immigrants in local politics	New insights on foreign markets	Foreign markets increasing
Rising average age		Need to work with broader age range	Need different health care provisions May need retraining	May need new products and services	More people with age-related needs May need to change product line	Different community needs	Older consumers nationally	Older consumers globally
Higher job skills required		Need for better communication skills Need for better group process skills	Need for retraining Need for ongoing learning	May require higher skills	Need different job skills to meet more diverse needs	Secondary education needs change	Need for improved communication skills	Need for global communication skills

sents, the heart of which lies in the "unpredictable uniqueness" that is the product of interaction across differences.

Innovative organizations are seeing marketplace and workforce diversity as key organizational issues and are purposefully responding with strategies designed to integrate this issue into their broader strategic objectives related to products, markets, resources, and capabilities. These organizations are forward-looking in that they do not take a "thunderstorm on barren land" approach but, rather, regard such changes as a "gentle rain over time."

On the journey toward implementing an integrated diversity strategy, many organizations are beginning to recognize and appreciate that the challenge of diversity is not simply an equal employment opportunity (EEO) issue of creating awareness of multicultural changes in the workplace and in the marketplace. Rather, it is the most significant organizational challenge and opportunity of this century, and, as such, it needs the committed support of organizational leaders and employees alike. Nothing less than a committed and total organizational change strategy will succeed in the long term.

Organizations that decide to invest in preparing all levels of employees to become diversity champions will soon realize the benefits of including employees and customers previously excluded because of their differences from the prevailing organizational culture. What was once lost potential must now be converted into *no potential lost,* and it applies to CEOs, managers, and employees as well as to customers, and other stakeholders in the organization. As the CEO of a client organization remarked:

> What we are talking about is refocusing our relationships with our employees [and customers]. It is a change that holds tremendous power and promise because managing diversity well means shifting the emphasis from conforming to contributing, from limiting our aspirations to leveraging our assets, from concentrating on obstacles to capitalizing on assets.

The Complexity of Diversity

Diversity in the workforce is only one of the challenges facing organizations today, and in its complexity it competes with many other challenges facing human resource departments. Managing diversity is as dynamic an undertaking as it is complex, and it is critical that senior management grasp that the valuing diversity journey, as I think of it, is systemic in nature. Although specific strategies might well be called for in clearly defined areas of the organization, only an integrated response embedded in the context of the organization's broader strate-

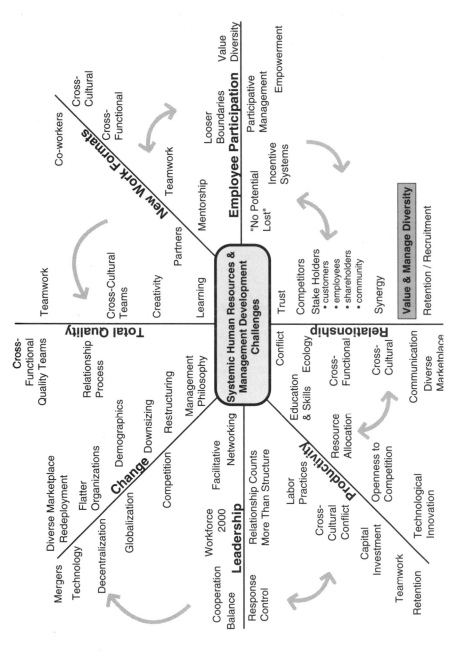

Figure 2-1. The dynamics of human resources and management development strategies.

gic challenges and objectives can achieve long-term results. A graphic representation of how deeply integrated diversity programs need to be is presented in Fig. 2-1.

Whatever an organization's specific goals may be in terms of its human resource or management development programs—for example, developing vision and leadership, assuring total quality, securing employee participation—there are underlying patterns that connect them all. *To be successful today, human resource and management interventions must maximize the potential of the total workforce in all its diversity. Whichever area is believed to be the most important entry point, any intervention must take into account the critical area of human diversity and the concomitant reality of changing relationship patterns.*

Interconnected Elements in the Diversity Journey

In working toward diversity, both management and employees must be encouraged to feel comfortable dealing with the "big picture" so that they can start to apply "systems thinking" to the challenges that face the company. Peter Senge, author of *The Fifth Discipline* (Doubleday, N.Y., 1990), explains that the essence of systems thinking lies in a mental shift: "It is a framework for seeing interrelationship rather than things, for seeing patterns of change rather than static snapshots."

The transformative work to be done must occur at the personal, interpersonal, and organizational level. There need be no concern about which element to focus on first. Because of their interrelatedness, once you begin, you'll find that action in one area will inevitably lead to action in the other. What is important is to take the first step.

Transforming People in the Organization: Personal Barriers. At this level, you are dealing with the assumptions, biases, prejudice, stereotypes, expectations and perceptions, past experiences, and feelings of the individuals in the organization.

Transforming Relationships Inside and Outside of the Organization: Interpersonal Barriers. At this level, you are focusing your attention on the dynamics of the interaction between people, the "space" between individuals. Here, you are dealing with cultural and group differences, myths, depleting internal relationship patterns (between coworkers, partners, team members, managers, and employees) and external patterns (with customers, clients, and suppliers).

Transforming the Larger Organization: Organizational Barriers.
This transformation involves working with the company culture and its
leadership, work structures, and policies and practices. Success in dealing with these dynamics requires that everyone be flexible, process oriented, and highly committed. Because organizations need to be prepared
to "hang in" for the long haul, they will need to be sure that their strategies for diversity training are well integrated into their overall strategic
plans for growth and development.

Well-known particle physicist David Bohm described the relationship between particles in a way that describes equally well the systemic nature of relationship dynamics in organizations with a diverse
workforce. He says:

> We now find that the relationships between any two particles
> depend on something going beyond what can be described in terms
> of these particles alone. Indeed, more generally, this relationship
> may depend on the quantum states of ever larger systems, within
> which the system in question is contained, ultimately going on to
> the universe as a whole.

Thinking Strategically and Long Term

Organizations have not taken their commitment to change diversity
initiatives seriously until they have asked themselves and fully understood the following strategic questions:

- What are the broader challenges facing the organization?

- What are the organization's initiatives and responses to these challenges?

- Has the organization's response to other challenges like diversity
(for example, training, innovative technology, total quality, customer service, increased communication) been dealt with in a systemic fashion (where the whole and the relationship between the
parts are more important than the individual parts)?

- Is the diversity initiative managed as an integral part of the organization's total systems change?

- Is the diversity initiative managed as an integral part of the organization's other key human resource strategies?

- How is the diversity intervention perceived by leaders and employees? As an organizational development intervention? As a human
resource intervention? As a skills development–educational inter-

vention? As a public relations effort? As a bottom-line business opportunity? As a way to avoid discrimination suits?

- What is your organization's own reason for addressing the diversity issue?

Finally, and most important,

- How consistent are these reasons with the strategic direction of the organization?

On the journey toward implementing and managing an integrated diversity strategy, the walls of personal, interpersonal, and organizational resistance will crumble as each barrier to valuing diversity is addressed and removed. When a critical mass of awareness is achieved, the great wall of institutionalize "-isms" will begin to break apart. Differences such as gender, race, ethnicity, religion, class, age, physical ability, and sexual orientation will no longer be grounds for exclusion and discrimination.

Beyond increasing the awareness of diversity, however, cross-cultural relationship skills play a key role in removing the barriers to valuing and managing diversity as well as ensuring that diversity becomes a real business *opportunity*. For relationships among employees, the organization, and customers to evolve toward a new partnership, as well as to become the basis for organizational innovation and creativity, fundamental behavioral changes must take place. As people practice new relationship behaviors and apply new-found skills of effective communication and team building, they will begin to build trust. It happens one interaction at a time. And as people learn to interact more cooperatively and productively on work teams, individuals, partnerships, and the organization as a whole can begin to reap the real opportunity diversity offers—breakthrough and creativity on every level. A more culturally sensitive and skilled workforce will enable organizations to compete in the global marketplace and to respond more effectively to the increasing diversity represented in their customers and clients.

As stated already, diversity awareness and skills training programs are effective only to the degree that they are well integrated and practically applied within the broader context of organizational goals and change strategies and managed at all levels of the organization. To achieve these broad diversity objectives, organizations must continually measure and evaluate progress. Bill Hewlett, cofounder of Hewlett-Packard, once said: "You cannot manage what you cannot measure;...what gets measured gets done." By measuring and evaluating progress against established baseline standards, organizations obtain the information needed to make necessary corrections and improvements.

Where to Begin?

The journey begins, as indicated previously, by examining the broad goals of your organization (see Fig. 2-2). At the outset, you must consciously reject the position that you or your organization operate in isolation; begin to think *systemically*. Simply put, that means you and your organization are part of a dynamic web of interrelated parts where no one part is as important as the whole and the relationship between the parts. Think of the analogy of the human body. Although textbooks will discuss one system or one organ after another, in a healthy body, all systems, fluids, chemicals, hormones, and organs are in a dynamic state of equilibrium. Beyond that, events occurring outside your body can have immediate and long-term effects on your body's ability to function optimally.

The organization in which you work is not a closed system; it is vulnerable to internal and external forces, many of which at one time or another give birth to specific challenges facing the organization. Most such challenges have a ripple effect on the lives of the employees—their attitudes, relationships, communications at all levels—as well as on the work projects for which workers are held responsible. Over time, every challenge to the organization effects changes, some subtle, some profound.

Figure 2-2. Challenges facing organizations.

In traditional companies, managers and employees alike respond to challenges by making intense efforts to intervene in some specific, limited way, often finding that the challenge has pointed up something systemic about the organization as a whole and cannot be dealt with in a partial way. It is for these reasons that I caution management and human resource personnel not to address the diversity challenge as an isolated training program; it must be regarded as an ongoing change process, integral to the larger environment within which the organization operates. As such, it will be necessary to actively examine all the complex, dynamic, and interrelated challenges impinging on its operations and to recognize in what specific ways they are affected by the diversity factor. Time invested in trying to see the bigger picture, however chaotic or overwhelming it may seem, will prevent pitfalls later on. The valuing and managing diversity journey is not orderly. Order, or stability, is a static state. By contrast, the diversity journey is not yet clearly charted and certainly not stable; it continues to demand the vision and commitment of pioneers and diversity champions. But we cannot run away from it: It has been said that complexity lies between order and chaos. The same could well be said for the diversity journey. And as a complexity theorist, William H. Roetzheim suggests in his book *Enter the Complexity Lab* (SAMS/McGraw-Hill, N.Y., 1994), "We must be chaotic enough to adapt and seek out new behaviors, but stable enough to hold onto those that work."

Initiating Systemic Change

The diversity challenge is probably the biggest human resource challenge of this century as it permeates every facet of the organization's internal functioning and the external marketplace. Initiating the systemic changes necessary to create an environment in which differences are recognized and appreciated and in which people feel valued and accepted is a priority requiring leadership and commitment. As one executive put it, "Valuing diversity must be part of the total woodwork." For any diversity strategy to become "part of the total woodwork," it must be incorporated into the broader organizational change strategy and strategic plans. This means going beyond the traditional short-sighted reactions to human resource challenges: "Quickly educate the organization on workforce change." Or "Give them some training in diversity skills." Or "Let's see what happens in other organizations."

And so let's start the process by simultaneously broadening our thinking and taking a closer look at interconnected challenges at the organizational, interpersonal, and personal levels affecting the workplace and then seriously consider how diversity might impact each of these challenges.

- Think of challenges at the organizational level and how diversity might impact those challenges:

  Competition

  Total quality

  Increasing information

  Increased risk taking

  Illiteracy in the workplace

  Flatter organizations

  Global perspectives

  Responsiveness to the total environment (including family, community, and the ecological environment)

  Alignment of goals, objectives, and overall strategies

  New technologies

  Higher entry-level skills

  Increased innovation and creativity

  Ongoing learning

  Looser boundaries and flexibility

  Full participation of the total workforce

  Ability to deal with change (mergers, downsizing, flatter organizations, new demographics)

  Building internal and external relationships

  Quality relationships with all stakeholders (employees, public, shareholders, customers, suppliers, subsidiaries)

- Think of challenges at the interpersonal level (affecting work teams, partnerships, coworkers, customer relations, and other work relationships) and how diversity may impact these challenges:

  The need for faster access to and processing of more and better information

  The need to cope with a stressful work environment

  The need to build new kinds of relationships

  The need to cope with continuous change

  The need to build trust

  The need for more authentic, genuine interactions

  The need to commit to shared goals and objectives

  The need for more open, clearer communication lines

  The need to manage conflict and power struggles

The need for better ways to manage change

The need for fuller participation

The need for increased teamwork

- Think of challenges at the personal level (affecting individual employees working in the organization) and how diversity may impact these challenges:

Coping with continuous change

Aligning personal goals with organizational goals

Taking personal responsibility

Creating a meaningful work life

Finding a balance between work life and personal life

The ability to manage conflict

The need to work synergistically in teams and new work formats

Building enhancing relationships with coworkers, managers, clients, and suppliers

The need for ongoing learning

Communicating more effectively

Setting personal boundaries

The need to develop one's career

All of these challenges are affected by the diversity factor and demand strategic thinking and commitment from the top leaders in the organization, those who usually determine organizational direction and who are in a position to see the bigger picture as well as fully grasp the systemic nature of this challenge. Full cooperation and participation of the workforce is critical, but *leaders must lead.*

Figure 2-3 depicts what goes into a holistic approach, which begins when management and employees ask themselves the kinds of questions raised earlier in this chapter:

- What are the broader challenges, including personal and interpersonal challenges, facing the organization?

- How does diversity relate to these broader challenges within the context of the organization's strategic objectives?

- What are the overall diversity challenges in relation to people, work tasks and structures, policies, systems, and practices, and organizational culture?

- What are the specific diversity challenges (for example, diverse marketplace or recruitment policy) that can be considered as priorities in the organization at a particular period of time?

Systemic Responses to Diversity Challenge

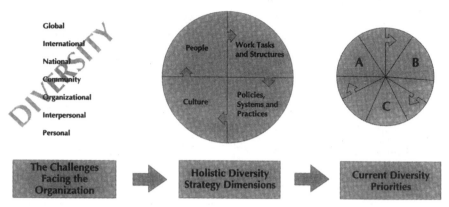

Figure 2-3. Systemic responses to diversity challenge.

Your organization's responses to challenges will depend largely on how the organization views the concept of diversity. Is it viewed as narrow or broad? Specific or general?

In the course of my work I have interviewed hundreds of individuals and organizations to learn about their understanding of diversity. I found general agreement that a broader definition of diversity is more useful than a narrow definition with its cross-cultural connotations. It is likely that your organization's responses would be the similar.

Beyond involving senior management and obtaining the full participation of all employees, initiating systemic change requires purposeful action at a number of different levels:

1. Identify the leaders in the organization who should be accountable for valuing and managing diversity (senior management, supervisors, team leaders, and so on).

2. Identify potential diversity "champions," or pockets of energy, to help drive the initiative.

3. Identify practical ways in which one can demonstrate diversity leadership characteristics on a personal, interpersonal, managerial, and organizational level.

4. Identify all the components of a holistic, integrated diversity strategy. Change plans should be initiated in several directions. All or some of the organization's vehicles for transforming inputs into

outputs can be employed, including: people, work tasks and structures, policies, systems, and practices, as well as the organizational culture.

5. Uncover major barriers and opportunities to implement a diversity strategy within the organization, and identify specific actions that could be taken to remove barriers and capitalize on opportunities.

6. Identify effective structures for managing the change process: Build on existing efforts in the organization.

7. Define the role human resources management is presently playing in the organization with regard to valuing and managing diversity, and redefine the role if necessary.

8. Identify the ways in which valuing and managing diversity could add value or provide a competitive advantage with regard to other organizational objectives (total quality, customer relations, product development, recruitment, retention, workforce empowerment, career development) and other ways of establishing more effective partnership with employees.

9. Identify specific actions that could be taken on a personal, interpersonal, and organizational level to ensure that the organization becomes a valuing and managing diversity champion.

Developing a Holistic Diversity Strategy

The primary goal of a "valuing and managing diversity" strategy is to develop an environment that serves all employees as well as the other stakeholders (customers, students, suppliers, community) and incorporates the benefits of diversity so that *no potential is lost* in achieving bottom-line organizational objectives.

As mentioned earlier in this chapter, a valuing and managing diversity strategy of any worth must be flexible (see Fig. 2-4) and initiate a change process on an ongoing basis over time. The change effort needs to be well integrated, assuring that no single part of the strategy is as important as the whole and that changes occur at the personal, interpersonal, and organizational levels.

The strategy or plan that seems to work best is one that:

- Functions over both the short and the long term
- Is developed with the participation of stakeholders
- Has clearly defined goals and objectives
- Has guiding principles or methodology

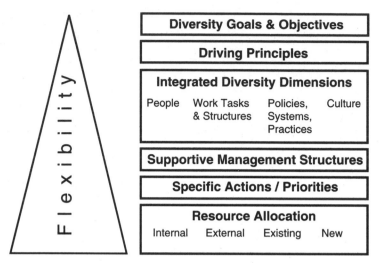

Figure 2-4. Flexible "no-potential-lost" strategy.

- Is multidimensional in its approach
- Is flexible but clear about the management structures needed to support it
- Outlines specific actions and priorities for which resources can be allocated
- Can be measured and evaluated

A successful diversity strategy is best developed by a team that is representative of the *diversity* in the organization (such as differences in race, gender, age, sexual orientation, religion, physical ability) and includes the diversity within functional groups and hierarchical levels.

A successful diversity strategy is also *multifaceted* and is always rooted in the bigger picture. As already stressed, a "systems thinking" approach or holistic model, one that addresses the *inputs* affecting the organization's overall change processes as well *outputs* the organization desires to produce, is most effective.

A successful diversity strategy is *well balanced* in terms of its inflexible and flexible parts. Once the goals and objectives of the strategy have been established, there can be more flexibility with regard to how the goals and objectives are accomplished, that is, which management structures and approaches are to be used.

Keep the following two questions in mind at every step of the journey:

- Is the organization adequately transforming diversity inputs (such as the challenges of changing demographics and market diversity) into desired outputs?

- How adequately is the organization using key change vehicles (people, work tasks, structures, policies, systems, and practices, and organizational culture) to achieve the objectives of the diversity strategy?

Phases of the Valuing and Managing Diversity Process

There seem to be five phases in the overall process of valuing and managing diversity (see Fig. 2-5). As you will see, the diversity strategy represented in Fig. 2-4 is also contained in the second column of Fig. 2-5, Phase II of the process.

Phase I: Needs Analysis. The "why, what, how, when, where, who" questioning technique in the valuing and managing diversity strategy is a simple and effective means of eliciting input from all stakeholders. These questions may be asked in various settings where the process is being initiated: special discussion groups, focus groups, advisory groups, task forces, surveys, and/or through in-depth personal interviews. Very simply, the goal is to clarify needs and set project parameters.

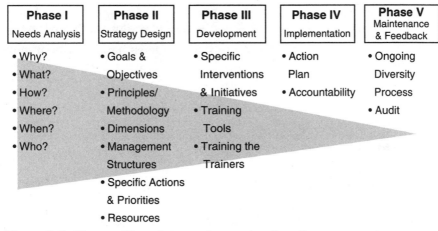

Phase I	Phase II	Phase III	Phase IV	Phase V
Needs Analysis	Strategy Design	Development	Implementation	Maintenance & Feedback
• Why?	• Goals & Objectives	• Specific Interventions & Initiatives	• Action Plan	• Ongoing Diversity Process
• What?	• Principles/ Methodology	• Training Tools	• Accountability	• Audit
• How?	• Dimensions	• Training the Trainers		
• Where?	• Management Structures			
• When?	• Specific Actions & Priorities			
• Who?	• Resources			

Figure 2-5. Phases of the valuing and managing diversity process.

By using a "dipstick" approach, each one of the questions can be probed further:

Why value and manage diversity?

What is the impact of diversity on the organization, both internally and externally, locally and globally?

What are the short- and long-term costs of not valuing and managing diversity?

What are some of the challenges, barriers, or constraints in valuing and managing diversity?

Personal	Community
Interpersonal	National
Organizational	International

What would happen if diversity were to be left unmanaged in the organization?

What biases and prejudices have been institutionalized in the organization?

What is the profile of the future workforce? What are the demographics of the supply pool?

What is the profile of future customers, markets, end users?

What is the impact of the environment on the organization (including economic, political, social, educational, technological forces)?

What is the impact of the organization's history, and the history of the community in which the organization operates, in terms of how the organization deals with the challenges of today and tomorrow?

What impact do physical and human resources have on the organization?

How will commitment to diversity, goals and objectives be achieved?

How should diversity be valued and managed? By what manner, means, methods, processes?

How does the organization change inputs into outputs?

How will the organization measure progress of the organization's work groups and individual employees? What base measures should be used?

How will the organization recognize and reward results?

Where are you right now?

Where do you want to be?

Where should diversity be valued and managed?

Where do you want to go with this initiative?

When do you begin the change process?

By *when* should diversity interventions and initiatives be accomplished?

Who should be involved? Which target groups?

Who is accountable?

Who should be communicated to?

Who are the major stakeholders?

Phase II: Diversity Strategy Design. This phase has already been touched on earlier (see Fig. 2-4). In essence, a diversity strategy that is good for three to five years should include:

Goals	Broad statements of intent related to the overall organizational strategy. A goal describes an outcome or end result that can be met through the accomplishment of related objectives.
Objectives	Clear, concise statements of desired outcomes or end results that are observable and measurable. Objectives are usually limited to a specific period of time (such as within one to two years) and are developed to address baseline measures of success.
Principles or methodology	Basic beliefs or philosophies that guide the design and development of diversity interventions and initiatives.
Dimensions	Vehicles of transformation within the organization including people, work tasks and structures, policies, systems, and practices, as well as organizational culture and climate.
Management structures	The people, positions, and work formats (such as project teams or task forces) required to implement and maintain the diversity strategy.
Actions	Specific interventions and initiatives developed to accomplish identified diversity objectives that support the overall organizational change strategy.

Priorities	The assignment of precedence with regard to short-term, medium-term, and long-term importance.
Resources	Both internal and external physical and human resources that can be committed to meeting identified diversity objectives.

Phase III: Development. Specific diversity interventions and initiatives should be agreed upon and developed using a systems thinking approach, and they should be prioritized during this phase. Training tools should be developed or adapted based on the recommendation of diversity representatives and employee feedback. The following are examples of diversity interventions that have an impact on various diversity-related areas in an organization:

Diversity interventions that impact external inputs into the organization:
- Intern programs for disadvantaged students
- Entry development programs for new hires
- Cooperation with local community colleges
- Precollegiate education programs

Diversity interventions that impact people in the organization:
- Diversity education (valuing and managing diversity competency, which includes awareness, information, skills and application objectives (the AISA Competency Chain)
- Linking diversity training to existing interventions such as leadership training, total quality management, and employee empowerment and participation
- Skills training (such as English-as-a-second-language courses, communication and interpersonal skills courses, change agent or champion seminars, sexual harassment training, enhancing relationship patterns)
- Developmental programs (such as job rotation, cross-training, short-term assignments, and task force assignment)
- Mentor programs that recognize the value of diversity in the mentor-protegé relationship
- Identification, recognition, and reward of diversity champions
- Career development programs for members of targeted nondominant groups

Diversity interventions that impact work tasks and structures in the organization:
- Job role definition
- Job processes and procedures documentation

- Performance standards documentation
- Identification of job skill requirements
- Formation of special advisory groups or task forces
- Identification of subcultures within the organization:
- Formation of cross-functional project teams

Diversity interventions that impact policies, systems, and practices in the organization:

Enhancing quality improvement programs to diversity
- Flattening the organization's management structure
- Establishing recognition and reward systems for progress toward accomplishing diversity objectives
- Linking diversity objectives to the organization's strategic objectives
- Linking diversity progress to performance appraisal
- Establishing a valuing diversity committee

Diversity initiatives that impact on the culture of the organization
- Communicating top management commitment to diversity (via video, newsletter, speeches, teleconferencing, and so on.)
- Establishing diversity networks and directories
- Defining key organizational principles
- Identifying the unwritten rules for success in the organization
- Identifying the communication channels for distributing diversity information
- Adopting more flexible management styles
- Positioning the diversity challenge as part of the organization's bottom-line business initiatives

Diversity interventions that impact outputs of the organization
- Monitoring stress-related insurance claims and turnover rate
- Monitoring productivity
- Monitoring grievances related to discrimination
- Monitoring diversity within senior management

Phase IV: Implementation. This phase includes the development of a plan that details:

- Who is involved and accountable for implementing diversity interventions and initiatives
- When the interventions and initiatives will be accomplished (by phase, if appropriate)
- Where the interventions and initiatives will be accomplished (centralized or decentralized; in functional groups, work teams, other targeted groups, or by individuals)

- How the interventions and initiatives will be accomplished (using a systems thinking approach, using broad-based participation, and so on), and how priorities will be assigned

Phase V: Maintenance. The following are the types of issues to consider during this phase:

- How to ensure broad-based participation
- How to ensure ongoing communication
- How to obtain feedback
- When and how to conduct diversity audits
- How and when reviews will be conducted
- How and when diversity efforts will be evaluated
- How to reward diversity efforts on an ongoing basis
- Who is responsible for monitoring and managing the bigger picture
- How to ensure that valuing and managing diversity becomes an ongoing improvement process rather than a short-lived training project

Challenges to Implementing a Diversity Strategy

Organizations have identified the following as some of the major challenges to implementing a diversity strategy:

- Top management, as well as managers at other levels in the organization, may not see diversity as an essential human resource issue.
- Diversity may be in competition for attention and resources with other pressing issues.
- Top management may be skeptical that demographic projections will affect the organization's ability to recruit and retain skilled workers.
- Diversity issues may be confused with equal employment opportunity and affirmative action requirements.
- The organization as a whole may not understand the complexity of diversity—that it is part of an evolutionary change process, not a packaged set of solutions.

- Insufficient fiscal resources may be committed, and insufficient and/or inappropriate human resources committed (for example, inappropriate people have been chosen to participate or are participating).

- There may be a lack of needed external resources.

- Employees may not recognize how the organization is operating from institutionalized bias and prejudice. ("We don't have a problem; we've been successful for years.")

- There may be a general widespread failure to understand the long-term costs (both direct and indirect) of not valuing and managing diversity.

- Some employees may fear a management backlash.

- Management may fail to communicate where they are going with their diversity initiatives.

- Management may fail to monitor progress toward meeting their goals.

- Management may fail to begin the process and learn by mistakes (in other words, valuing an action-research approach).

Part Two: Managing the Diversity Change Process in the Organization

Managing the diversity challenge with all its barriers and opportunities requires commitment and an understanding of the following management questions:

- What are the key differences between leadership and management activities in the diversity arena?

- Who are the leaders and who are the managers of the diversity process in the organization?

- Is there a difference between managing the diversity change process and managing other projects or "objectives" in the organization?

- Who manages the broader change process in the organization?

- What management approach will work best in this organization?

Differentiating between Diversity Leadership and Management

The following activities are based on the work of John Kotter, author of *Force for Change—How Leadership Differs from Management* (Macmillan, N.Y., 1990), and they provide the place to begin the process.

Leadership Activities	Management Activities
Defining diversity vision, direction, and values	Developing specific goals and objectives in alignment with the strategy and vision set by the leader
Setting diversity direction	
Communicating vision, values, and direction	Developing diversity plans and budgets that support the achievement of objectives in alignment with the vision and direction set by the leader
	Creating and organizing work structures that will support the achievement of the identified objectives
Inspiring and empowering people to act in a way that produces the desired changes	Empowering people—providing them with the knowledge and skills they need to do the work for which they are responsible
Creating commitment to a shared vision, set of values, and direction	Monitoring and measuring progress toward achieving the desired end result

Decide who in the organization are *diversity leaders* or *champions,* and find support for that role. Decide who are the *managers* of the process, and find support for that role. Leadership and management skills are seldom found in any one individual and a valuing and managing diversity initiative demands a team approach even more so than other human resource initiatives.

Skills Required for Managing Diversity and Change

As implied earlier, the skill set required for managing a diverse workforce and the change process is different from that required for day-to-day management. To manage diversity and the change process effectively, the following guidelines are useful:

- Use a holistic, integrated approach.

- Obtain top management commitment and accountability.

- Consciously work to integrate diversity values into the broader organizational values.

- Integrate responsibility for diversity initiatives into other management functions and initiatives such as continuous performance management and self-directed work teams.

- Integrate diversity efforts with existing strategic objectives and programs such as Total Quality Management (TQM).

- Expect resistance to change, and take steps to minimize it.

- Use a participative management approach.

- Be instrumental or facilitative rather than charismatic or autocratic in leading this initiative.

Facilitating Relationship: The Key to Managing the Diversity Process

An effective diversity leader or manager produces results by facilitating the efforts of those different from themselves. Many of today's managers, however, are not well prepared to manage such a diverse workforce. In the vast majority of cases, managers have grown up with limited experience of people of different races, backgrounds, motivations, and styles. In addition, management methods in this country have traditionally been based on the assumptions of a white-male workforce and theories of leadership and motivation that mirror a white-male manager's own experience and attitudes about work and career.

A participatory management style is preferable when managing the diversity process as it assumes that every person in the organization has the right and the responsibility to influence decisions and understand the results of those decisions. Managers need to create work environments and processes within which people can build high-quality relationships. As Max Depree, the author of *Leadership Is an Art,* stated,

> Participative management arises out of the heart and out of a personal philosophy about people. It cannot be added to, or subtracted from, a corporate policy manual as though it were one more managerial tool.

Managers of heterogeneous groups need a different skill set from those who manage homogeneous groups. Managers need to be able to value and appreciate cultural and other group differences, as well as to function effectively as part of a diverse team. To manage a diverse workforce effectively, managers must create an environment that nurtures and builds upon individual strengths. Building, maintaining, and managing relationships are the "how to" of valuing and managing diversity. High-quality relationships result when people's uniqueness is respected—when they feel nonpossessive warmth, true empathy, understanding, and genuineness.

Today's proactive organizations are addressing the diversity challenge by encouraging employee participation in focus groups and diversity networks, thereby embarking on the task of enhancing employee relationships. Focus groups and diversity networks provide a means of planning, sponsoring, and hosting various cultural events, as well as promoting outreach programs such as high school internships and scholarship programs. For example, one high-tech organization in California has five primary focus groups: African-Americans, Hispanics, disabled persons, women, and gays. These groups are proactively working to promote the hiring of a more diverse workforce.

Diversity Management Roles, Positions, and Titles

The following are examples of diversity management roles, positions, and titles. (They are based on information presented in *The Conference Board Report*, published in Report 1013 [1992].)

Roles and Positions	Titles
Manager	Cultural Diversity
Coordinator	Diversity
Director	Workforce Management
Vice president	Diversity + AA
Change agent	EEO/Diversity
Entrepreneur	Multicultural Affairs
Facilitator	Corporate Diversity
	Valuing Diversity
	People Diversity

What Is the Bottom Line?

Managing the whole diversity strategy is more important than perfecting each part. When establishing baseline measures, it is best to use a holistic or systemic approach and to consider establishing baseline measures in all of the areas targeted for change as well as the overall culture of the organization.

The New Synergy

Implementing a strategic diversity process that has been formulated at the top and translating it into reality at all levels in the organization require full employee participation. Everyone needs to learn how to move beyond basic survival strategies (characterized by "me, not you" thinking), beyond competition ("you or me"), beyond a narrow productivity focus ("me then you"), and toward full participation of all where "you and me" is the underlying theme.

But the old way of understanding "you and me" (1 + 2) is no longer enough. To face today's challenges, we need *total breakthrough*—something exponential: You *multiplied* by me *multiplied* by them, *multiplied* by us. Or to put it mathematically, $1 \times 2 \times 3 \times 4 \times 6$. Diversity strategies are based on a new kind of synergy, a synergy in which the whole is much greater than the parts. Synergistic relationships of this kind are the prerequisite for creating, for bringing something new, often "unpredictable," into being.

So how do we replace traditional concepts of survival, competition, and productivity with participation, cooperation, and synergistic relationship? We start by requiring, facilitating, and encouraging the full participation of all employees. We start at whatever level seems most applicable to the situation. If we begin at the personal level, then we must consider the full participation of all our own diverse parts: masculine, feminine, creative, analytical, intellectual, physical, intuitive, social, emotional, rational, and so forth.

If we begin at the interpersonal level, we can consider taking mutual responsibility for building enhancing interpersonal interactions, exchanges that value the uniqueness of each person with whom we work. When we do that fully and with deep commitment, we will find a surge of creativity and unpredictable breakthroughs.

At an organizational level, the same process applies to whatever body of individuals have organized for some end need.

By now it should be clear that full participation is the key to growth, development, renewal, change, and productivity at the personal, interpersonal, and organizational level. In the words of well-known physicist John Wheeler, "May the universe in some strange way be brought into being by the participation of those who decide to participate. The vital act is the act of participation."

The major challenge facing management in organizations embracing diversity and change is how to catalyze that full participation. Making changes in traditional corporate cultures, developing new strategies that are inclusive rather than exclusive, striving to see that no potential is lost in the workforce demands strong leadership, concentrated effort, a high level of commitment, and much good will. At the same time, the journey is an exciting one and the payoffs are enormous. In the beginning, you can encounter obstacles, and it is useful to be aware of the form they may take. Figure 2-6 shows a common progression of attitudes along the way.

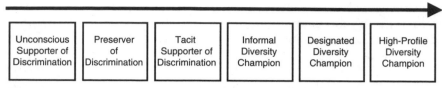

Figure 2-6. A common progression of attitudes toward diversity.

- *Unconscious supporter of discrimination.* Someone who is unaware of his or her own assumptions, biases, prejudices, and stereotypes and the impact they have on other people.

- *Preserver of discrimination.* Someone who is aware of his or her own assumptions, biases, prejudices, and stereotypes—and who continues to behave in ways that discriminate against others who are different.

- *Tacit supporter of discrimination.* Someone who is aware of his or her own assumptions, biases, prejudices, and stereotypes and who tacitly supports discriminatory behavior toward others by remaining silent. Tacit supporters choose not to speak out or act to prevent discrimination.

- *Informal diversity champion.* A change agent who is a role model for nondiscriminatory behavior and who works actively to initiate diversity-related change.

- *Designated diversity champion.* A change agent who is a role model for nondiscriminatory behavior and has been designated by the organization to play a formal role in initiating diversity-related change.

- *High-profile diversity champion.* A change agent who is a role model for nondiscriminatory behavior and who has a highly visible position within the organization. This person is a spokesperson for valuing and managing diversity within the broader context of organizational change.

Suggestions for Employee Participation in the Diversity Process

To obtain employee participation, leaders, managers, supervisors, human resource personnel, and employees should begin by answering the following questions:

- What does *full employee participation* mean in this organization?
- Why might full participation be necessary in valuing and managing the diversity process in this organization?
- How can each employee participate in valuing and managing diversity on an individual, interpersonal, and organizational level?
- What responsibility can each employee have for initiating, developing, implementing, and maintaining the change process?
- How can senior management effectively communicate the valuing and managing diversity vision throughout the organization by using a common language, testing for understanding, and ensuring relevance?
- How can each employee understand that valuing diversity has to do with the success of the organization as well as personal self-interest?

The following are steps employees can take at the individual, interpersonal, and organizational levels to become champions for diversity:

Personal level:
- Become aware of unconscious assumptions, biases, prejudices, and stereotypes.
- Become aware of personal, interpersonal, and organizational barriers to valuing diversity.
- Explore differences and similarities. Take responsibility for learning more about other cultures and groups.
- Model the behavior you expect from others ("walk the talk").
- Participate. Provide feedback and become involved in helping your organization to develop, implement, and maintain a diversity strategy.

Interpersonal level:
- Facilitate communication and interaction with people who are different in ways that respect differences.
- Facilitate unique contributions by encouraging participation with others and by sharing your perspectives.
- Resolve conflicts in a way that values and respects differences.
- Team members, partners, and coworkers accept mutual responsibility for developing common ground.

Organizational level:
- Employees participate in diversity networks and focus groups.
- They take a proactive role in promoting diversity within the organization. The drive for a more diverse workforce can be employee initiated.

- Employees are encouraged to provide feedback to work groups and the organization's management.
- Employees are encouraged to advocate changes and made to feel safe in doing so.

Employee Responsibility and Rewards in Valuing Diversity

The employee who understands and values cultural and other group differences will be better able to do his or her job and to advance in the organization. The employee who wants to advance must take personal responsibility for handling diversity challenges as well as for looking ahead, examining good role models, and asking: "What do I need to get there from here? What are my strengths and weaknesses? Do I have to change? What are the costs, and what price am I willing to pay to advance my position?"

Employees who want to do the best job must purposefully examine what is required to work well with people who are different in gender, race, ethnic background, physical ability, and so on. They must begin to know and understand the person to whom they report: become familiar with his or her goals, needs, pressures, strengths, and weaknesses and actively help this person recognize his or her own differences and how they affect his or her supervision.

In assessing those in authority in order to know the best way to approach them, it is useful to consider the following:

- How different is this person from myself?
- What are his or her strengths, and how can they be supported?
- Is this person political or nonpolitical in my organization?
- Is this person strictly results oriented? Does he or she need to see background data and evidence of effort?
- Is this person more task or people oriented?
- How does this person relate to employees who are different?

Conversely, employees can help the person to whom they report get to know *them* and their capabilities by:

- Building his or her trust in them
- Taking the initiative to present their ideas and being persistent
- Avoiding surprises

- Doing their homework before launching a project meant to impress
- Making sure they have their superior's commitment to what they are doing
- Keeping him or her informed of their progress, asking for feedback, and rewarding the feedback by reacting nondefensively

Every employee should be encouraged to make the effort to "manage up" several layers and across the organization, be prepared for changes above them, and build a constituency outside their superior's area. Employees can remain trapped in their jobs if others in the organization are unaware of their abilities.

Finally, minorities and employees with differences must make themselves more visible. Women in particular and others in nondominant groups need to be aware of the importance of image and exposure. Rosabeth Moss Kanter, in *Men and Women of the Corporation* (Harper Collins, N.Y., 1977), describes the disadvantages of solitary women and other members of nondominant groups who are often visible only as "category members." As such, they have the additional burden of representing their category, not just themselves. In these cases, any problematic situation tends to be blamed on the person as a member of the group he or she represents rather than on the individual and his or her actual situation. When women and other members of nondominant groups represent "tokens" in the organization, irrelevant characteristics overshadow ability and performance. Technical abilities may be eclipsed by physical appearances. Furthermore, because many organizations want to draw attention to their "token" employees (women, people of color, specific ethnic groups), so that the organization presents an image of fulfilling affirmative action mandates in hiring, they don't demand as much from these employees. At the same time, token employees often rise to the challenge and become, willingly or not, role models.

Employees who have a different profile from that of the traditional employee should look for a mentor who is successful, who knows the ropes, and who can provide real guidance in the complex and dynamic journey of change on which the organization has embarked.

Organizational Barriers

The valuing and managing diversity journey is a long one, and there are no easy fixes. The goal should be to commit to an ongoing improvement process and to actively manage as many barriers as possible in all areas of the organization's functioning. Managing these barriers involves both examining the organization's external and internal processes, including those processes related to the areas already referred to: people, work tasks and structures, policies, systems and practices, and the culture of the larger organization.

At the organizational level, it is important to begin by recognizing the barriers ("red flags" or warning signs) that get in the way of one's own or the organization's ability to value and manage diversity now and over time. For example:

- Assumptions, biases, prejudices, stereotypes
- Past experiences
- Future expectations and perceptions
- Feelings
- Cultural differences
- Myths
- Depleting relationship patterns
- The organization's formal and informal cultural values that do not support valuing diversity
- The organization's policies, systems, and practices that do not support valuing diversity

Barriers Related to People and Organizational Culture. In what ways can an organization's people and culture be barriers to valuing and managing diversity?

People. Individuals and teams, both internal and external to the organization, who participate in some way to produce products, services, or other end results for the organization may be a barrier to valuing diversity.

- Who has access to power and decision making? (Is there an "old-boy" network?)
- Who is included in and excluded from important meetings and/or activities?
- Who gets consulted on projects?
- Who has access to respected communication vehicles?
- With whom do people socialize?
- To what degree are people open about compensation?
- How do people compete?
- How are people recruited, and who are involved in the recruitment process?

- How are external consultants, suppliers, and experts selected?
- What are the relationships (for example, between bosses and subordinates, teachers and students, men and women, professionals and support staff, and insiders and outsiders)?
- What are the typical relationship patterns (for example, stereotyping, racism, and bias)?

The most important messages are those demonstrated through our actions.

Organizational Culture. An organization's culture is reflected in the formal and informal messages people receive. Use these questions to probe further into your organization's culture:

- How are questions asked or disagreement expressed?
- What are the work hours and punctuality norms?
- What is the dress code (both formal and informal)?
- What is the appearance code?
- What is office etiquette?
- Is there a sense of urgency or casualness?
- What are the language standards regarding types of jokes, swearing, sexist remarks, and so on?

The messages related to an organization's culture are conveyed through the vehicles shown on the following chart.

Vehicles	Questions
Stated principles (beliefs) values	In what ways do the stated values and beliefs of the organization value diversity?
	How are these values and beliefs demonstrated by the leaders of the organization?
Unwritten rules	What are the unwritten rules for success in the organization?
Mission statement	How does the mission statement acknowledge diversity's role both inside and outside the organization?
Shared vision	In what ways does the shared vision communicated by the leaders in the organization include valuing diversity?
Communication networks (both formal and informal)	How do the organization's communication networks include diversity?
Leaders' behavior	In what ways are the leaders in your organization role models for valuing diversity?

Ways in which people are rewarded and held accountable	In what ways are people recognized and rewarded for valuing diversity?
	How do managers receive feedback on their ability to manage diversity?
	How are ranking and promotions affected by one's ability to value and manage diversity?
	What are the unfavorable consequences for not valuing diversity?
Social activities	In what ways do formal and informal organizational social activities respect diversity? *Example:* If your organization were to plan an employee picnic to which spouses and family members were invited, would gay and lesbian partners be included?

Barriers Related to Work Structures, Policies, and Practices. "We've got so many complaints. Once they become formal and my boss and I look at them, we shake our heads, and say, 'This should have never gotten to our level.'" Just the simple misunderstanding of why a certain person behaves in a certain way on the work site with respect to enforcement of rules and regulations can become an issue. People have different values about rules and regulations. Some of the complaints I've read are a matter of perception: The woman or person of color may understand it one way, but the white male sees it as almost an absolute and tries to apply it, right down the line. So there's "You didn't follow the rules; I'm going to have to cite you," or, on the employee side, "Others haven't had to apply it [the rule] that way. Why are you picking on me?'"

The following questions are useful in assessing and managing these barriers in your organization:

- Do the organization's work tasks and structures, policies, systems, and rules and practices value diversity?
- Are the organization's day-to-day practices consistent with established policies and systems?
- Does the work get done in ways that value diversity?
- Is diversity valued with regard to your organization's major stakeholders?

You can better assess whether work tasks and structures are organized, structured, and managed in ways that value diversity by exploring the following:

- Are job roles clearly defined?
- Are job processes and procedures clearly defined?
- Are performance standards clearly defined?
- Are performance standards free from cultural and other group bias?
- Are the skill requirements of each position clearly defined?
- Are the levels of jobs clearly defined?
- Has job mobility, both lateral and upward, been clearly defined?
- Do work structures take diversity into account? (Are there diverse partnerships? Self-directed work teams? Project teams? Task forces? Other?)

To further assess whether the organization's policies, systems, and practices are barriers to valuing and managing diversity, ask:

- Are diversity-related policies in alignment with the organization's strategic objectives?
- Are policies and procedures applied consistently?
- Does the recruitment system take diversity into account?
- How is performance recognized?
- How are promotions determined, and who gets them?
- Is there a procedure for addressing grievances or resolving complaints with regard to discrimination?

In most cases, organizations probably have already initiated diversity interventions in at least one of the transformation opportunities offered in the organization, whether it be directly related to people and culture or to work structures, policies, systems, and practices. *The goal, however, is to facilitate transformation in each of these areas so that the challenge then becomes one of implementing and managing the different diversity interventions as "a whole"—working toward well-integrated change strategies rather than working piecemeal.*

Using The Diversity Journey Learning Map® to Manage Your Diversity Initiatives

About the Learning Map. Before designing The Diversity Journey Learning Map® (see Fig. 2-7) a group of colleagues and I asked some tough questions:

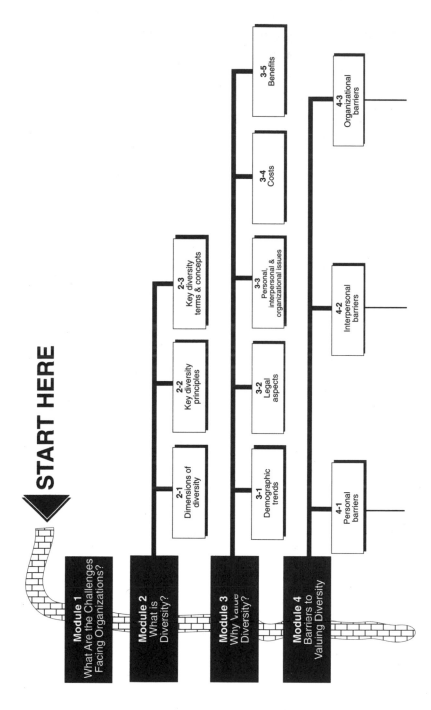

START HERE

Module 1
What Are the Challenges Facing Organizations?

Module 2
What is Diversity?

2-1 Dimensions of diversity

2-2 Key diversity principles

2-3 Key diversity terms & concepts

Module 3
Why Value Diversity?

3-1 Demographic trends

3-2 Legal aspects

3-3 Personal, interpersonal & organizational issues

3-4 Costs

3-5 Benefits

Module 4
Barriers to Valuing Diversity

4-1 Personal barriers

4-2 Interpersonal barriers

4-3 Organizational barriers

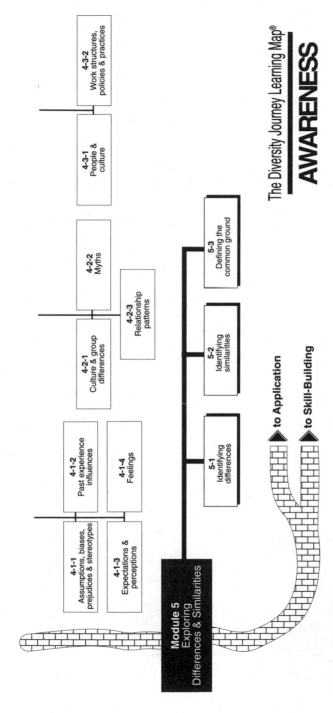

Figure 2-7. The Diversity Journey Learning Map® © 1994 Griggs Productions, Inc.

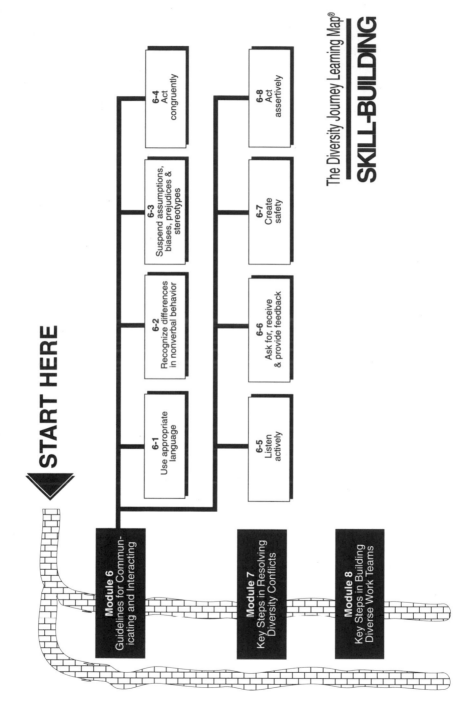

START HERE

6-1
Use appropriate language

6-2
Recognize differences in nonverbal behavior

6-3
Suspend assumptions, biases, prejudices & stereotypes

6-4
Act congruently

6-5
Listen actively

6-6
Ask for, receive & provide feedback

6-7
Create safety

6-8
Act assertively

Module 6
Guidelines for Communicating and Interacting

Module 7
Key Steps in Resolving Diversity Conflicts

Module 8
Key Steps in Building Diverse Work Teams

The Diversity Journey Learning Map®
SKILL-BUILDING

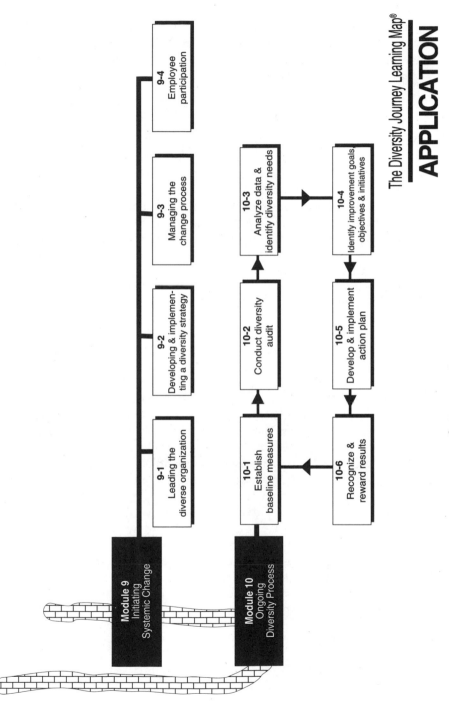

Figure 2-7. The Diversity Journey Learning Map®. (*Continued*)

- Given that the field of diversity is information-rich, and the "wealth" can be overwhelming at times, and given that the body of knowledge in the field of diversity is constantly evolving, what simple tool can we provide to help learners and facilitators process information in this area more quickly and efficiently?

- How can we make the task of seeing the bigger picture as efficient, effective, and interesting as possible?

As a result of our questioning, we developed The Diversity Journey Learning Map®. The learning map provides a means of seeing the bigger diversity picture as well as a one-step-at-a-time learning approach. No single portion of the map is, however, as important as the whole and the relationships between each part. The content related to each step on the map was developed through an extensive review of the diversity literature, interviews with approximately 80 diversity champions in 40 different organizations, as well as interviews with recognized consultants in the field of diversity. The Diversity Journey Learning Map® has been linked to the content of specific training modules developed by Griggs Productions for its Valuing Diversity® Training System.

A Road Map to Guide You in Valuing and Managing Diversity Initiatives.   The purpose of the learning map is to serve as a guide for both facilitators and participants on the diversity journey. It is a means of grasping the bigger diversity picture. Remember as you use it that no single aspect of the map is as important as the whole and the relationships that occur between learning stages. The layout of the map, for example, seems to indicate a bottom-to-top, or linear, learning sequence, but the map can and should be used in a flexible way. You will find that it is quite capable of accommodating new and ever-changing research and developments in the field of diversity.

Typically, we begin the diversity journey by increasing *awareness* of what the concept of diversity is and why it is important. Sometimes, however, organizations go directly to the *application* part of the journey and focus on developing a diversity strategy or measuring progress through a system of audits. Once they have determined their needs, they may return to the awareness and *skill-building* portions of the map or may even decide to skip skill building altogether.

The Diversity Journey Learning Map® will

- Enable you to see the bigger "diversity territory" at a glance

- Give you a method of organizing information you may already know and diversity programs you may already have in place
- Enable you to gather and analyze new information more efficiently
- Provide you with an efficient, effective *training sequence* that takes into account information and skill prerequisites.

Managing the Diversity Progress in Your Organization

Each organization should decide on the stage of the diversity journey that it believes needs attention at any particular time, as well as the context in which the intervention will take place. We have identified 10 different stages of the diversity journey. The learning map (Fig. 2-7) expands on these different stages (Fig. 2-8) and suggests the training modules that many have found useful to focus on as they navigate the diversity journey.

Decide where and when your organization wishes to begin the diversity journey and when each of the other stages will need attention. The goal should be to achieve overall competency in this area (see Fig. 2-9). Diversity managers should be clear about their organization's current goals. (See Fig. 2-10).

	YES	NO
Understanding organizational challenges		
Defining diversity		
Why value diversity		
Barriers to valuing diversity		
Exploring differences and similarities		
Communication and interaction guidelines		
Resolving diversity conflicts		
Building diverse work teams		
Initiating systemic change		
Ongoing diversity process		

Figure 2-8. Ten stages of The Diversity Journey Learning Map®.

AISA

Diversity Competency Chain

Figure 2-9. AISA: Diversity competency chain.

	YES	NO
Increase participants' *awareness* of key diversity messages		
Focus the participants on useful, relevant diversity *information*		
Facilitate the acquisition of new *skills* for valuing and managing diversity		
Application strategies and support: Identify and commit to key diversity change areas, outside the learning environment, where diversity awareness and skills can be *applied* (for example, e.g. quality teams, performance improvement, customer relationships, productivity, interpersonal communication, and leadership.) Set targets and measure progress in the context of the "real world" of work, moving beyond rigid classroom settings.		

Figure 2-10. Determining your organization's goals.

Conclusion

The scope and direction of a valuing and managing diversity initiative will be defined by the broader challenges facing the organization. Considering the dynamic complexity and systemic nature of the challenges facing today's organizations, it is likely that any meaningful diversity initiative will in itself be dynamic, complex, and of a systemic nature. Anyone taking the diversity challenge seriously will have to spend time on fully understanding

- The *dynamic complexity* and systemic nature of the *broader* challenges facing organizations today. The challenges cannot easily be understood by dissecting any one supposed symptom or cause of the challenge. The solutions to these complex challenges are no quick fix.

- The *dynamic complexity and systemic nature of the diversity challenge in itself.* It makes sense to apply Peter Senge's (*The Fifth Discipline,* Doubleday, N.Y., 1990) description of dynamic complexity to the diversity challenge. "Situations where the cause and effect are subtle, and where the effects over time of interventions are not obvious...when the same action has dramatically different effects in the short run and the long...when an action has one set of consequences locally and a very different set of consequences in another part of the system [organization],..." when obvious interventions produce nonobvious consequences, there is dynamic complexity.

- That *holistic or systems thinking* is increasingly necessary to tackle the how-to of valuing and managing diversity. Systems thinking or a holistic approach provides one with a way to see the bigger picture. In essence, no one part is as important as the whole and the relationship between the parts. As Senge states it, "It is a framework for seeing interrelationships rather than things, for seeing patterns of change rather that static 'snapshots.' "

The goal of valuing and managing diversity is to develop a practical and strategic response to changing demographics, a response that will establish effective relationships for employees and customers. The organization's ability to be a leader in its field is increasingly dependent on attracting the best people, improving team performance, and managing that performance.

Success here is directly linked to the organization's ability to value and manage the diversity of its human resources. The challenge may well prove to be overwhelming, and well-intended efforts may have very little impact unless valuing and managing diversity is seriously accepted as an integral part of the overall business strategy. Unfortunately, many organizations are still not acknowledging the connection between diversity and core business goals. They also still tend to equate diversity with affirmative action and equal employment opportunity, believing that diversity is yet another human resources program that has more to do with social investment and social work than bottom-line business needs.

The real reason for embarking on a diversity strategy is to ensure a no-potential lost outcome for the organization. The sooner the United States and other nations realize that the full participation of its diverse workforce is the most powerful competitive edge available to it in this increasingly global economy, the sooner they will be able to begin the difficult but rewarding journey. Any organization that neglects to develop an environment that embraces differences, in which all its employees are comfortable and are able to make a full contribution, is operating in a very short-sighted way. Those who are also capable of fully appreciating the marketplace opportunities that diversity offers will be the champions of the future.

Two primary questions that organizations are left to answer are: To what extent are you losing opportunities for innovative growth and development because of a culture that excludes the full participation of a diverse workforce? And: What do you believe are the keys to meeting the diversity challenge in your organization? What follows is my list; what is yours?

- Obtain commitment from the top.
- See interventions as part of a bigger picture.
- Recognize that changes are complex, dynamic, and interrelated.
- Be clear about why change is important.
- Communicate core values horizontally and vertically.
- Build trusting relationships, both internally and externally.
- Ensure full participation.
- Ensure responsibility and accountability at all levels of the organization.
- Focus on implementation—take action.
- Look for ways to balance the old and the new.
- Recognize that the concept of diversity has broadened beyond multiculturalism.
- Recognize the need for ongoing learning and continuous improvement.
- Create an ongoing change process and remember the bigger picture.
- Measure and reward progress.
- Begin today.

3

From Courage to Commitment

Steve Hanamura

A high-ranking official in the bank came out of his office and noticed that an employee was crying at her desk. He walked over to a supervisor to ask whether she knew what was happening. The supervisor explained that a customer, who had just left, made racial remarks that were very demeaning to the employee, an African-American woman. The manager returned to his office and called the customer to get his side of the story. His conversation confirmed that, in fact, the customer had been very rude by talking about the employee to other customers and to the teller who had waited on him ("What is she doing here anyway? Can she really do the job?" and other comments regarding her ethnicity). The manager then advised the customer that he should come in and close his account. Although the customer said he did not want to close the account, the manager insisted that he do so.

Two weeks passed and still no closure of the account. A second phone call was placed. "I haven't caused you any problems, have I?" the customer asked. (He had since been conducting his banking business by using the drive-through teller.) "That is not the point," the manager said, "I want you to come in and close the account, or I will do it for you." The next day the customer came in to apologize to the employee. Weeks passed. The employee waited on him a few times after that, and within a year, they became good friends.

The foregoing story is about *courage* and *commitment*. Not all scenarios will end like this. In most work settings, the feelings expressed by the customer in this story will not be demonstrated in such an open manner. Generally, people who are in opposition to diversity in the workplace know they must suppress their true feelings. Instead, they will show their resistance to racial, cultural, and ethnic diversity much more subtly—perhaps by not including some employees in a discussion or avoiding them altogether.

Furthermore, in many cases a lending institution would lose an account for standing behind its employees as the bank manager did here. His act of courage was possible because the manager was clear about what he stood for: He knew the value of preserving the dignity and worth of the employee, even at the risk of losing an account. This bank wants to be known as the employer of choice for its minority workers, and an act such as this has an impact in creating an environment where more people of multicultural backgrounds want to come and work.

Sometimes, in such situations, individuals feel powerless to do anything. It is important to note that in the bank scenario only one individual acted. We cannot assume that the overall organization is behind diversity, but when those at high levels in the organization are willing or committed to take stands like this, they can be an example to others that "each person can make a difference." An individual teller witnessing this kind of treatment of a colleague may not have the influence, as the manager did, to make an immediate change. Should other employees muster up the courage to speak out, they more likely would start by informing management of the incident in written and verbal form. The manager may or may not do something with that input. Other dynamics within organizations that are not diversity related but have an impact on how employees behave with colleagues, management, and customers are trust, communication, and safety. If these are not in place, employees may not feel that it is all right, or safe, to let management know of incidents such as this. Often, there are underlying dynamics going on within the work group that preclude actions such as those exercised in the example given.

A similar story of courage and commitment to diversity in the workplace occurred in the restaurant associated with a major golf course. Management decided to take a stand in not allowing ethnic jokes to be told in their restaurant. This decision created an extremely difficult situation for the golf course because those telling the jokes were high-paying customers and those being devalued by the jokes were high-paying Japanese patrons. The potential impact of their decision could be the loss of customers and revenue.

Accordingly, managers, consultants, and trainers may need to rethink how to position diversity as an initiative in their organizations. Employees new to diversity sometimes feel as though it is being shoved down their throats. They believe they are going to be asked to change their values. In response to these fears, some consultants will say things like, "You are not being asked to change your values, just your behaviors while on the job." But values drive what we do, and so what happens when employees are asked or told to do something in opposition to their values? As leaders, we need to take responsibility for the fact that we are asking people to make difficult changes. We are asking them to give up old ways of behaving, speaking, and doing things. We soften these comments by saying, "Just be aware before you speak of the impact your words might have on others. If you choose not to change, be prepared for possible consequences."

Any time a person takes a stand in an organization, the value system of the organization—its corporate rhetoric—is being addressed. The question of who has rights comes up in these situations. Many people are afraid to say what they feel for fear of offending someone or saying something that is not politically correct. Referring back to the golf course scenario, the golf course officials had to be clear about what they stood for: creating a comfortable environment for all their customers, not just some. The request from management to stop inappropriate ethnic jokes in the restaurant would not have been successful had not everyone been willing to do his or her part in preserving the dignity of others. The individuals who are asked to not tell the jokes may protest that they are just kidding and that the people who react to them are too sensitive, but they need to learn that respect for others—the organizational value at stake here—means that you honor the feelings of the person affected and behave accordingly.

But for everything one is asked to "give up" in the name of diversity, there are tangible gains. So that diversity is not seen as creating a different kind of animosity, it is very important for key people in the organization to equip the workforce with knowledge, skills, and training in diversity. Leadership strategies that help organizations be successful are those that create a context and establish grounds from which individual workers operate. Employees want to know: Where did these initiatives come from? Management? The CEO? The department head? Working from *oneness* provides a useful context, or base, from which to conduct diversity work. It sets the stage for using diversity as a strategy rather than an end goal.

Working from Oneness

Oneness is a state of being in which individuals and organizations are at peace with themselves and what they do. They have a vision of where they are going. If the vision is clear and the values are well in place, it becomes easier to develop strategies for dealing with resistance and/or fear. It is important to understand that resistance and fear may not go away entirely, but if we are in a state of oneness, or at least have an understanding of what that means, we can live with the uncertainties of our time.

Organizational values are really put to the test during times of downsizing, mergers and acquisitions, and globalization. During changing times, there is much ambiguity about what to expect. The more employees can know what the issues are that management is dealing with, the more they will be able to respond to changes. To be successful in working from oneness, an organization needs to examine some of the dynamics that produce a positive climate for its workers. Attributes such as feeling competent on the job, feeling included on a work team, and feeling assured of having management support all contribute to establishing a positive climate. Whereas the American culture emphasizes the need to be right and to be the best—to work hard, set goals and timelines, and "get the job done," working from oneness promotes the idea of working from a solid foundation, having a clear mission, and holding to a strong set of core values.

Valuing diversity in the workplace may be synonymous with how much trust is felt on the job. One of the most commonly asked questions prior to beginning a diversity workshop is, "Is this a safe room?" Employees concerned about whether or not they have a job do not want to risk saying anything that might jeopardize their work life—politically, socially, or personally. It is difficult to have courage when we are dealing with other forces internally, whether on an individual basis or within the system. Employees want to know that it is safe for them to explore their values in relationship to how they must conduct themselves in relating with someone who is different from themselves.

Remember, employees are being asked to deal with two things at the same time; the first is *change*—technical, demographic, and emotional. Often workers are given no time to deal with the loss of what once was but, rather, are expected to move right into what is—chaos, in many instances. The second issue employees must deal with is *differences*. The "different" worker represents part of the challenge for every organization. Values and personal styles are examples of what is different. As we continue to examine what courage is in relationship to differences among people, we must also remember that we have a lot in common; but, because our prejudices and stereotypes are so overwhelming, we rarely have an opportunity to discover our commonalities. When we discover our commonalities, we can work with our differences more easily.

Setting the Stage for Employee Readiness

When exploring the topic of diversity, we must answer some basic questions:

1. Why are we involved in diversity in the first place?
2. What is *diversity* anyway?
3. Is it like equal employment opportunity and affirmative action?
4. What are its benefits to the organization?
5. What will it cost, both fiscally and psychologically?

During the National Diversity Conference in 1991, Lewis Griggs stated that organizations enter the field of diversity from one of three perspectives:

1. *Equal employment opportunity and affirmative action.* If coming into diversity from this perspective, the organization is taking care of its regulatory or legislative needs. Management commits to doing something in diversity in order to survive or stay out of trouble. Individuals will be asked or told to tolerate diversity and differences.

2. *Diversity as a leadership or competitive strategy.* During this phase of diversity, organizations understand that by allowing for an understanding of differences, they will be tapping all their resources, not just some of their resources. The values driving this commitment may also be survival, and may include affirmative action as a motivator. Alternatively, some venture into diversity because "it is the right thing to do." For example, a hospital has on their premises a day-care center for their employees. They didn't do it because the law said they had to. Attendance and productivity increased because the employees were able to see their children on their breaks. They were then able to devote their full energy to their work because they knew their children were nearby and were being cared for.

3. *Diversity as a global or international strategy.* The drive for committing on this basis may be the need to stay current with foreign trade or to gain better products and more markets.

Before embarking on the diversity process, as an organization you need to:

- Establish what you stand for and define what values you are working from. Create a mission statement to put your core values more clearly into focus.

- Create a vision of where you are going. Vision is different from direction.

- Create a climate of readiness so employees know what to expect. Examine both the benefits and costs of conducting diversity training.

Working from oneness, creating a climate of readiness, and developing a vision are applicable not only to diversity initiatives in the workplace but to other aspects of professional life as well.

Courage

Where It Comes from and How It Takes Form

Webster's dictionary defines *courage* as the ability to face danger without fear. Courage is value driven, meaning that people will pull themselves together to do a task when something of great importance is on the line. We work from a position that something better must or will happen. Courage results from commitment—the ability to take and hold to a stand that may not be popular. Courage is a state of being or thought that allows you to take on adversity when it appears. It receives its base from strongly held values that drive you to do what is right.

Employee courage can show up in the way one receives feedback about performance. Sometimes, the feedback has to do with a misunderstanding about the meaning of words. For example, a customer in a restaurant in the East was overheard asking the waitress for "regular coffee." She was given coffee with cream. The customer, who was from the West Coast, did not know that to ask for "regular coffee" in the East would get her coffee with cream. The waitress might have been rude about it, but, instead, she had the courage to accept the feedback that coffee with cream was not what the customer meant by ordering "regular coffee."

Another example of problems arising from differences in the meanings attributed to words comes from reports of a staff meeting in England where a work group was getting bogged down on its assigned task. Someone said, "Let's table it." Almost immediately half of the people stood up to leave. "Wait a minute!" someone shouted. "Where are you going?" "Well, someone said 'let's table it,' and I think that's a good idea—we can come back later and try again." "But," said another group member, "in our country, to 'table' something means to bring it to the table right now—to put everything else aside and work on this thing until we reach resolution."

Challenges from a supervisor or peer often take even more courage to respond to than those from a customer. For example, a supervisor may ask an employee to speak up in a meeting where previously it was not safe to do so. Alternatively, a manager may be obliged to tell employees of pending layoffs. All of these situations call for courage.

In 1990, corporate America spent over $10 billion on training and education of its employees. Locally, there is a consultant who teaches a class on *how to do what we dare to know*. It is about training and acting with courage. Is it possible, for example, that some of the training we think we need would not be necessary if only we had the courage to do what we know to be the right thing: treating people with dignity and respect? Although there are things to learn about each other's culture, is it possible that some of the basic attributes of treating people appropriately are already in place? Has our world come to such a place where those behaviors are no longer taught in the home? Do we need training in how to be good human beings? It might be a "hard sell" in the corporate world to get top management to authorize a class on how to be a good person. Yet, in many cultures, business does not get done until these relationships have been well established.

Courage comes from within. Although it is usually driven by strongly held values to do what is right and just, it may also result from pain or fear. A cultural diversity workshop made up of 26 people was held in a California-based computer company. Nineteen of the participants were born outside of the United States. "Why did you come to this country?" one of the trainers asked. "To have the freedom to choose how we live," said one. "To provide for our families and make a better life for ourselves," said another. (This person sends more than half of her paycheck back to her homeland.)

Other participants had left their homelands to escape danger. In so doing, some had to leave behind other family members. One person talked about his hope to come to a free and just land, and his shock to find here that there was unjust treatment of groups of American-born people (African-Americans, Latinos and Hispanics, Native Americans, and so on). Regardless of their reasons for leaving their native countries, the many stories these participants told showed great acts of courage. For some, it was the personal courage to survive, for some to do what is right, and for some to say good-bye to family members they loved.

As individuals and workers in America, what are the challenges facing us to welcome people of all differences within our country? All Americans need to demonstrate personal and professional courage to accept people of different races, ethnic groups, nationalities and languages. On a personal level it may be necessary to reexamine the stops that keep us from allowing someone "different" to come into our world. It means looking at parts of ourselves that we may not want to discover. No one likes to learn about prejudices or stereotypes that he or she has. "Why don't they go back to where they came from?" or "I don't know how to relate to someone different" or "they aren't as smart as we are!" (Many equate a lack of ease with the language as a lack of intelligence.) At the level of work, some say: *"These people are going to hurt my chance for promotions."*

Most people do not intentionally plan to shut out others. In spite of their best intentions, many, without knowing it, say and do things that hurt those who are in any way different from themselves. Fear is often at the base of it, and there is much to be frightened about today if we let ourselves: We worry about our ability to continue making ends meet in the face of downsizing, mergers, acquisitions, product obsolescence, and so forth. It is hard to have courage when we are afraid or when we find out something about ourselves that makes us look bad.

This takes us to another place where courage is called for: relating to each other on an interpersonal level. During the first part of diversity workshops participants are often asked to share something of their background through a symbol—something that will help depict their cultural heritage and values. They are asked to talk about the impact that their cultural heritage has on the way they work on the job and how they think it influences the way others treat them on the job. During the sharing of their symbols, many are surprised to find out how much they have in common with other workshop participants—a love of family, a painful experience of losing a loved one, the desire to work and be viewed as competent. Finding they share these kinds of experiences allows them to start building trust with one another so that, later, they can begin to ask each other about their differences. The workshop also gives everyone time to learn about differing work styles and how the same work might mean something totally different to another person.

In the Griggs Productions film, *Valuing Diversity*®, Part 1, *Managing Differences,* one segment features a Native American employee who comes up with a quick way to finish a project. When the manager learns of the idea, he stops production and asks everyone to applaud the employee. A well-meaning gesture on the part of the manager, it caused great embarrassment for the employee, whose culture dictated that you not draw attention to yourself in public. She would have preferred that the manager simply put a note in her personnel file.

Productivity increases when employees familiarize themselves with the different ways each one likes to be acknowledged, and when such gestures come from a place of showing respect, not when such behavior is legislated.

Companies that are forward-thinking see the value of incorporating diversity initiatives into their trainings—some as a means of staying competitive, some to assure their economic survival, and some because it is socially and morally right to provide just treatment to their workforce. Whatever the motivator, when we take the time on a one-to-one basis to build trust and discuss possible differences in something that appears to be the same, we are dealing with diversity on an interpersonal level. As a consequence of understanding and respecting differences at this level, we find that our work teams are far more productive and that the job gets done.

Where words and labels become very important and create frustrations is in the matter of what we call members of a given racial, cultural, or ethnic group. In a historical sense, we have seen the evolution of the word *Negro* to *black* to *African-American* to *people of color*. (Among the Latin-American community, we have gone from *Chicano* to *Mexican* to *Hispanic* and *Latino* and so on). Many give up, saying "I don't know what to call people anymore, so I won't say anything. I feel like I'm walking in a mine field."

In this context, courage means not using these confusions to stop us from talking with people of other ethnic groups, nationalities, or races. Most people will be forgiving if they sense we are genuinely trying to learn what is acceptable to them.

How It Operates Systemically

A group of people assigned to a three-month team project were told they would have to work overtime—as much as 60 hours a week. One of the members said that his daughter had a school play coming up that he wanted to attend. Another team member said it was okay with him if he went to the play, but others, although they said nothing, felt he wasn't really committed to the project. The team member did attend the play, and when he returned to work the next day, he discovered that some valuable information regarding the project had been shared the night before.

The team members had not expressed openly their feelings of disappointment, of resentment, of possibly having the project slowed down, and what they perceived as their coworker's lack of commitment to the project. Although a team, they had not trusted the system, and they had not known how to communicate their attitudes and judgments. Those who had concerns might have said: "I'm disappointed that you have to go because I think it will delay getting the project done. What can we do to make it work?" or "That's okay, we'll find a way for you to give your input tomorrow." While it takes courage to communicate openly, working in teams also requires a system for working together—in this case, guidelines everyone can agree to that allow individual flexibility without compromising the work of the group. If being courageous in the system fails, it is because we, as individuals, fail to believe that we can make a difference. Someone once said that there are three types of people in the world: the few who make things happen, the many who watch things happen, and the vast majority who don't know what happened.

Building a solid foundation, being clear about the positions we are working from, and talking with others openly will help to make sure there is a systemic understanding that all individuals are contributing members of the team. This task includes helping each team member feel that he or she can voice individual concerns and still be valued as a team member.

Here are a few examples of how individuals are being challenged to make a difference systemically.

During a workshop participants began to voice concern that the workday—8:00 a.m. to 9:00 p.m.—was too long. The depth of the material and the intensity of the session made it difficult for them to process what was going on. After much discussion, company officials decided to allow some free time in the afternoon on the second day so that participants could write in their journals, reflect on what they had learned, play basketball, or engage in some relaxing diversion. One year later, company officials redesigned the course and decided to put in a very important module previously left out of the training program. The new module was put in place of the free time. The message from management seemed to be: "We want you to have balance in your day, but you have to show up when we want you to."

The solution here is for the participants to *try again*. In other words, don't give up in the face of setbacks. Even at this level, individuals can, should, and do make a difference.

A university professor and department chair was told one day by his secretary: "You are sometimes the most closed-minded, rigid person on this campus!" He was shocked by her outburst, particularly because he viewed himself as open to new ideas and willing to change but, in addition, because they had been working together over a number of years. It took him a week to digest her remark. He then went back to her and asked what she meant. "What I really meant when I said that was that I don't feel you value me on this job." Surprised, the professor asked: "What can I do to prove that I do value you?"

"Get me some business cards with my name on it," she replied. "You are busy in meetings and teaching your classes. I see incoming and prospective students, talk with people from all over campus, and hold this department together for you. I make you and the department look good, but I receive very little recognition. If I had business cards with my name on them, I could give them to students and others to pass along and say—Go to her. The added value to the department is that we could increase our FTE [full-time equivalent] students."

"That's a good point," the department chair replied. "I'll see what I can do." He made an inquiry about obtaining business cards for his secretary and was told that institutional policy does not permit any administrative office person to have cards. "If we do this for one person, then we will have to do it for everyone." Not willing to take no for an answer but not wanting to offend the university, the professor bought business cards with his own money and gave them to the secretary.

As in other settings, courage and commitment were demonstrated in this institutional environment by both the secretary and the department chair. The secretary displayed courage by being open about her personal feelings and being committed to a better working relationship with her employer. She also acted out of strong concern for improving the workings of the "system" they shared.

The department chair displayed courage in his willingness to listen to the feedback, look at his own behavior, and, at the same time, respond to the personal feelings expressed by his employee. When the university told him that it was not their institutional policy to give business cards to administrative employees, the department chair was able to look beyond their answer for a solution. For him, honoring his employee's concerns and contributing to the team superseded university obstacles.

Defining *Diversity*

I have been talking at great length about having the courage and commitment to stand up for diversity. Over a period of years diversity has evolved to become a workplace topic. With it, however, comes much confusion about what diversity is. Although I discussed earlier some of the perspectives organizations have about the meaning of diversity and why they should honor it, I have not addressed it directly. Before doing that, it may be helpful to examine its benefits and some misconceptions, or points of resistance, to diversity.

Benefits to Managing and Valuing Diversity in the Workplace

Individual	Systemic
Feel better about yourself.	Increase productivity.
Overcome personal biases and not hurt others.	Create opportunities for different groups of people.
Increase knowledge of how to work with a wide variety of people.	Develop colleagues who have a different perspective than yours.
You can make a difference in the life of another person.	Increase team effectiveness.
Add your own.	Add your own.

Misconceptions about Diversity

Individual	Systemic
I may have to change and let go of old ways.	We may lose good or potential accounts because we are using someone who is *different*.
I am afraid of not getting promotional opportunities because of these *different* people.	We cannot hire the most qualified person anymore.
I feel I have to compromise my values for what the organization wants.	We can't find qualified applicants who are *different*.
Add your own.	Add your own.

It is important that we adopt a clear understanding of what diversity is and what it is not. We need to understand the dynamics of human values and how they drive what we do. What organizations do not understand is that we must pay attention to *unspoken* behaviors and norms, for that is where obstacles to productivity start to form.

Commitment

What It Is and Where It Comes From

During World War II a Japanese-American family was sent from California to an internment camp in Arizona. They had some American friends down the street who said they would take care of their home the best they could. Their friends soon learned that their Japanese friends were receiving a diet of wieners and sauerkraut three times daily. Incensed by how their friends were being treated by the government, this family decided to deliver a chicken dinner to their Japanese friends once a week. To do so meant driving to Arizona, seven hours one way, each week.

This is an example of commitment to friendship. The American family was taking a risk: They could be criticized by other Americans, accused of being traitors, and so forth, but they were motivated by anger, pain, and concern.

The workplace connection to this story is that managers will often ask consultants: How can I motivate employees to work together? When we are working on protecting ourselves, it is difficult to be open to new ideas or to working with others. In the bank incident, described earlier, had the manager not intervened, the employee may have withdrawn or developed some self-protective behavior that would not have permitted the outcome we saw. If jokes that demean employees from certain ethnic groups are allowed to go on without check, their loyalty is bound to erode.

As stated before, commitment at the organizational level is value driven by what is important to the organization—be it survival, competition, ethics, or something else. There may be more than one value that drives its activities. By definition, an organization's commitments are a declaration of what the organization intends to do. Its timelines, goals, and objectives are based upon the commitments it makes.

Commitments should not be confused with wants or hopes. A commitment is a stand that goes beyond feelings. Commitments that are made public are more likely to be successful because those who hear them are apt to hold those who speak them accountable.

Measuring Commitment

Time and Visioning. Once a vision or strategy has been established, it is necessary to estimate the amount of time it will take to honor the commitment. One organization committed to have all of its employees go through a diversity training program over a five-year period. While they fully understood that it would be hard to have everyone go through the same amount of training, nevertheless, they committed both time and resources (money) to make it happen. Leaders went through four days of training, and occupational employees attended at least one day of training.

Visibility of Top Management. Top management needs to demonstrate its commitment by being visible to the workforce. They can accomplish this in several ways:

1. As an executive group, go through the initial work with a consultant.

2. Serve as senior faculty for all diversity training, sending an executive person to each diversity class either as a participating faculty member or an opening speaker.

3. Serve on a community task force to assist in advancing diversity efforts.

4. Speak to top executives from other organizations.

As an example, a community college in Arizona held a leadership institute for a select group of employees. Individuals, chosen 20 at a time, were selected for their ability to influence others and not just based on their credentialed status within the school. The chancellor of the college demonstrated his commitment by being visible during the institute. Not only was he in the room but any phone calls or conferences that had to be handled were handled at the site of the training. This procedure sent a clear signal that he, as the chancellor of the college, was committed to the training.

Financial Resources. This component of measuring commitment is self-explanatory. A consultant once told an organization, "Don't tell me what you want to do or what you are trying to do. Just show me your budget for it. That way I will know if you are serious about committing to diversity initiatives."

Performance Evaluation. One organization developed a performance checklist for some of its midmanagers in which each manager's pay raises and bonuses were evaluated on the basis of his or her commitment to diversity as indicated by related activities (attending training, serving on a diversity task force, volunteering in the community).

Diversified Representation on Committees and Task Forces. Organizations that make sure their committees have representation from many constituencies—those from the home office or the field, those from diverse ethnic, racial, and cultural backgrounds, and those at varying levels or in different positions in the organization—demonstrate their willingness and commitment that all groups within the organization will be heard.

It is extremely important for everyone to understand that there will be obstacles to keeping commitments—employees might feel they are being told to do something they don't want to do, they might fear the possibility of downsizing, they might be mistrustful of management's motives for any number of reasons. Those in charge need to understand the distinction between commitments, needs, and wants. Many organizations today, for example, are operating from positions of need. It is difficult to make commitments in such an environment. An organization's *needs* can be at the level of survival or, related to that basic need, a need to increase employee morale or simply to find direction. Diversity training can be useful in these situations because, by valuing everyone in the organization, morale is increased and, in turn, employees are willing to join in suggesting ways to keep their organization viable. Involving everyone is especially important during times of downsizing.

Wants, on the other hand, are just that. Wants without commitment go nowhere. We want results but often do not want to go through the process of getting them. It is important to understand that there will always be obstacles to realizing your commitments—not enough time, not enough money, employee resistance, and the fear of lawsuits.

Resistance is inevitable when people are asked to make a change, to let go of old, routine, and comfortable ways of doing things. As mentioned earlier, many trainers in diversity programs respond to employee concerns by saying, "We are not asking you to give up your values; we are asking you to change your behavior." But for many, changing behavior means abandoning values they have held for a long time. Consultants in diversity programs need to acknowledge that when you commit to something, something else must go away. If you commit to losing weight, then you commit to not eating what you used to eat—and it has little to do with what you want to do but everything to do with what you say you will do. Having support from others is vital if wants are to become commitments.

Commitments are the things you say you will do—no matter what. You do not need to be afraid if you do not always meet your timeline, but it is important to stay focused, something that is very difficult to do when everything around you is changing. You need to hold on to the vision that is driving your commitments. The worksheet in Fig. 3-1 will help you assess if you are ready to make a commitment to diversity and will show you what areas you need to work on.

Time

The amount of time we can commit to diversity is_____.

Visibility

Management will be a part of the process by:

_____Kicking off training sessions
_____Being a part of a task force
_____Participating in training
_____Supporting diversity throughout the organization

Budget

The amount of money we can commit to diversity is_____.

Representative diversity

We can enumerate the diversity of individuals represented in:

Task forces:_____
Committees:_____
Work teams:_____
Home office:_____
Field office:_____

The areas where we need to improve:

_____
_____

Figure 3-1. Diversity commitment readiness assessment.

Areas of Commitment

Commitments can be broken down into three major areas: personal, interpersonal, and organizational.

While making a career change, a man worked for a college in Oregon. The pollen in that area was so bad that he decided, in June, that he would commit to being out of that city by June of the following year. He made that declaration to a colleague without knowing where his next employment would be. In March of the following year he was on his way to a new job.

That is one example of the way personal commitment works. There are others:

1. Personal commitment is demonstrated through teaching your children about diversity. You may introduce them to people from different cultures, give them some history that is not found in textbooks, or have them view films like *Dances with Wolves, The Rising Sun,* and *Malcolm X.*

2. Interpersonal commitment occurs when you talk with someone whom you have previously excluded because of their difference from you. You may decide to approach someone who in the past has done something to offend you. (In that case, be sure to set up a climate where you can be heard.)

3. Organizational commitment takes place when you tell someone in your work group about diversity, you join a diversely representative task force, or you find out what is already happening in your organization.

The worksheet in Fig. 3-2 will help you get started.

The final act you can perform to cement your commitment to diversity is to make sure you understand the link between diversity and other program initiatives.

Commitments come from what drives us—the spoken and unspoken values we operate from personally and on the job. If employees are worried about their safety or survival, they will tend to those needs before putting time and energy into the team project or organizational structure. Systemic commitments, on the other hand, are sometimes driven by institutional policies and procedures. The government policies or legislative mandates that came about as a result of the 1964 Civil Rights Acts, confusing as they may have been, have driven how many organizations approached, and continue to approach, the topic of diversity.

Commitment as an Organizational Asset

The story of the Caucasian family taking food to their Japanese friends is a demonstration of interpersonal commitment. Although stirred to do so by anger, what they did came from their feelings of friendship

---

Personal

My personal commitment to begin the process of valuing diversity:

Monday

Tuesday

Wednesday

Thursday

Friday

Saturday

Sunday

To keep my commitments, I need the following support:

Interpersonal

The person I will contact to honor this commitment is:

The support I need to honor this commitment is:

Organizational

The person who can help me fulfill my organizational commitment is:

The skills I have to make a contribution in this area are:

(If you feel unable to make any impact on the organization, then state that, and then think of another person who could have such an impact and contact that individual.)

Figure 3-2. Worksheet.

and compassion. In whatever context, *commitment* is defined as taking a stand for who we are and what we do. It means that we are willing to go public with our beliefs and intentions and allow someone else to hold us accountable.

Commitments must be made on the basis of an articulated set of values and not feelings. As individuals and as members of a team or workforce, we do not always feel like doing what we commit to. Resistance to dealing with diversity issues comes about for most of us because we do not want to take a look at ourselves, to reexamine our values and behaviors, and to change old ways. If we make a commitment to diversity, we know that it will mean embracing change, in terms of how we behave personally, with family, friends, and coworkers, and as a member of a larger group, whether our workplace or our community affiliations. Many times, we will be asked to revisit some of the deepest things about our heritage, recalling and recounting how we were raised and what we were taught. Eventually, we will need to let go of old ways of thinking so we can move on to new possibilities—to a future in which everyone contributes, everyone has a voice, and diversity is no longer met with resistance but, rather, is seen as the asset it is.

4

Diversity Issues in the Workplace

Frances E. Kendall

Introduction: Valuing Diversity in the Nineties

As referred to in Chapter 2, according to *Workforce 2000*, a demographic report published by the Hudson Institute in 1985, by the year 2000, 85 percent of the people entering the workforce will be white women, indigenous people of color, and immigrants. Only 15 percent will be white men born in this country, the group that has for generations been the major group from which employees came. While some parts of the country—California and New York, for example—are changing more rapidly than others, workplace diversity is at everyone's doorstep. The motivation for communicating about differences is clear. All organizations are changing; employees and clients are more diverse than ever before.

We are also in a time of increasing awareness of the issues related to difference. We can hardly pick up a daily paper or listen to the news without hearing stories about race or gender. Frequently, they are stories of hiring discrimination or of organizations that are unable to manage the diversity they already have. More and more, we read about organizations that are working to recruit and retain diverse employee groups because they are clear that well-managed diversity is one of the keys to their success now and in the future.

Things are different now than they were 30 years ago in terms of managing differences at work. In the late 1960s and in the 1970s the equal employment opportunity laws sent a clear message to America: "It doesn't matter what color a person is, she or he has a legal right to equal access to employment." The underlying message was: "Differences are only skin deep. Race doesn't matter." Now we know more. We know that, in fact, differences matter a great deal. For example, using a wheelchair to get around gives a person a very different perspective on workplace facilities than a temporarily able-bodied person has; being a gay man or a lesbian provides a different experience in organizations than being heterosexual does; having been born in the 1940s rather than the 1960s affects a person's approach to managing. Differences matter. And, in order for people to feel genuinely welcomed in the workplace, their differences should not only be recognized but *valued*. Thus, we get to *valuing diversity*—creating a work environment in which people are appreciated for who they are as members of their race, their gender, their age, their physical ability status, their culture—for their differences as well as their similarities.

The differences that individuals carry with them that most affect the workplace are race, gender, sexual orientation, age, physical ability, religion, class, ethnicity, culture, and body size (most frequently of consequence for women). While there are certainly other elements of difference that we bring to work with us (for example, shoe size, regional accent, athletic ability), this chapter will focus on those elements that have most impact on an employee's success in an organization.

Successful organizations are reframing their definition of professional workplace communication. No longer are comments, jokes, or negative behaviors based on someone's race or ethnicity, gender, religion, sexual orientation, or physical ability acceptable in the workplace. Smart organizations are not only making that clear but they are also providing opportunities to gain new skills in dealing with employees' diversity.

Issues of Difference

Historically, there have been organizations that considered valuing employees and providing a hospitable work environment part of their mission. They emphasized the well-being of their employees not only because they saw it as "the right thing to do" but also because it made good business sense: Employees who are happy work harder and are more loyal. Increasingly, as organizations become more diverse and globalization becomes a reality, issues of diversity are squarely on the plate of organizations that want to thrive in the future.

In "Managing Cultural Diversity: Implications for Organizational Competitiveness" (*Academy of Management Executives,* 1991, vol. 5, no. 3), Taylor Cox discusses six ways that managing and valuing diversity create a competitive advantage for organizations: "(1) cost, (2) resource acquisition, (3) marketing, (4) creativity, (5) problem-solving, (6) organizational flexibility." In each of these areas, organizations stand to benefit from diversity if it is managed well. Lower turnover rates and low absenteeism as well as satisfaction with career development and the feeling of acceptance of cultural differences save organizations money. Satisfied employees stay where they are appreciated. The ability to attract and retain a diverse workforce brings the "brightest and best" to an organization. Further, because clients choose organizations with a strong employee base, they too are drawn to such organizations. With globalization, the marketplace demands that organizations be able to manage cultural differences inherent in doing business with other countries. Studies show that the most innovative and creative teams are heterogeneous ones, and that the most effective groups in terms of making decisions and solving problems are diverse ones in which the issues of difference are managed well. Finally, Cox reports that "managing diversity enhances organizational flexibility." And the more flexible an organization is, the greater its chances of being able to respond to a changeable marketplace. We are no longer asking whether we should become diverse but rather how well can we manage it.

Each of us brings all of who we are to every interaction—our racial identity, our gender, our sexual orientation, our class, our religious and spiritual beliefs, our age, our ethnic and cultural history, our physical abilities. And, while we are all unique individuals, we are also affected by the ways in which the world sees each of us as a member of a race and gender group, an age and sexual orientation group, and so on. For example, we live in a society that views men as strong, brave, aggressive people and women as nurturing caregivers. Women who are not stereotypically nurturing are often seen as "not feminine enough"; men who are caring individuals are frequently considered "too nice to get the job done." When women walk into a meeting, they carry with them their experiences of being female in a male-dominated environment, and they come face to face with men's stereotypical expectations of the role women should play in the workplace. For men the same thing is true, although the expectations are different. Often, these expectations are subtle, sometimes even unconscious, but gender is always a major player in interactions between individuals.

For white people, for people of color, and for people of mixed racial heritage, race affects an individual's daily experiences at work. We only have to look at a few minutes of the segment of a *20/20* episode titled "True Colors" to recognize the role that race plays in so many of our interactions. In the program two men, one white and the other African-American, are filmed shopping at a department store, a record store, and at an automobile dealership. In the shoe section of the department store, the white man is helped immediately; the African-American, the only customer in the area, waits for eight minutes (the production crew at ABC timed it). The salesperson watches him, but he never offers to help. At the car dealership the white man is quoted a price that is $1500 *less* than the one given the black man for the same car. They each apply for the same job and try to rent an apartment. The manager of the apartment complex, an older white man, talks enthusiastically with the white man about his renting the apartment. The manager offers him the keys to look around. When he arrives two minutes after the white man leaves, the African-American is told that the apartment is no longer available—that it was rented by a woman early that morning. Their experiences are entirely different, and those differences are clearly based on race. Each of us carries such experiences with us into every meeting, every job interview, every interaction. The task of managers is to recognize that differences play a role in everyone's interactions and experiences rather than acting as if everyone is treated the same.

Managing People Who Are Different from Us

There are four steps to meeting the challenge of managing people who are different from ourselves:

1. Acknowledge the differences.
2. Educate yourself about differences by reading, listening, and putting yourself in situations where the other group is dominant.
3. Figure out how the person you are working with is like what you have discovered about the group of which he or she is a member and how she or he is not.
4. Work to value those differences.

To put it another way, we must gather as much cultural information as we can, and then we must hold it to one side as we look to see in what ways it may be relevant to the individual with whom we are dealing.

Let's apply these steps to a scenario.

First, assume that Ed, the African-American man in the *20/20* segment, is your employee. You are a Filipino-American woman; your experience with African-Americans is limited. After participating in ABC's study, Ed returns to work and begins to tell you about it. Your first task is to listen to his story and to acknowledge that your experiences are very different. His recounting is painful to hear; it's hard to believe that these things can happen in the United States in this day and time. Because you are not African-American, your next step is to find out as much as you can about the culture. You go to the library and to bookstores, particularly those in African-American neighborhoods or those focusing on black literature. You might attend a church service at the African-American Episcopal church in your community or go to an exhibit of black artists currently displayed in a museum near you. The third step is to observe how Ed is like the culture you have read about or met. How do the things you learned apply to him? This is best done by observing, not by asking Ed a million questions about himself. It's not that you shouldn't ask Ed any questions, but it is important that he not be your main source of information. It is not Ed's job to educate you; as the manager, it is your job to learn about your employees as you interact with them and listen to them talk about their experiences. Finally, remember that Ed brings all of his life experiences with him to work, just as each of us does; his perspectives are different from yours and from those of most of the other people in your office. By creating a *shared* reality—a combination of experiences, understandings, and ways of doing things—your employees will not only feel more valued but will work harder to see that goals for the whole organization are achieved.

We can never know everything about each of the cultures from which our employees come. In truth, that isn't even the goal. The focus is to become knowledgeable about those areas most affected by differences. We can learn to ask the right questions—become curious about what motivates an employee and become as sensitive as possible to differences in experiences, beliefs, principles, and customs. To be able to manage people effectively, we must acknowledge their experiences in the world. To create an environment that is hospitable for all who work in it, individuals must feel valued for all the experiences they bring to the table.

Exploring Cultural Information

Culture is our way of knowing and doing. The culture (or cultures) we come from greatly affects the lens through which we see the world. For every group there is real cultural information, and there are norms. For example, in many Asian cultures harmony is paramount, while Western European cultures are more competitive. In female culture (as we are told in Deborah Tannen's book, *You Just Don't Understand*, Ballantine Books, New York, 1990), the purpose of communication is making connections, while in male culture the purpose of communication is putting oneself in a position of power. Latino/Hispanic cultures place great value on extended family; those of Native American people put considerable store in the wisdom of the old people.

Each of us grew up with a set of cultural messages—values, attitudes, beliefs, and ways of doing things—basic truths, if you will. We got them from the people who raised us, from our environment, from the books that were read to us or the stories that we were told. We absorbed them from observing how others around us were treated and from direct teaching. Because we were so young when we learned this body of information, we rarely stopped to question its value or veracity. The cultural information we received ranged from the superstitious ("Don't walk under a ladder," "Breaking a mirror will bring you seven years' bad luck," "The third time is the charm") to rules of behavior ("Children should be seen but not heard," "Children are always welcomed—they are the heart of the family," "Eat all your food—remember the starving Armenians") to attitudes about work ("An honest day's work for an honest day's pay," "A woman's work is never done," "Never send a woman to do a man's job") to information about people different from you ("Never turn a stranger away from your door," "Never trust a stranger," "Asians are inscrutable," "Jews are clannish," "Men only want one thing"). Unconsciously we took on attitudes, prejudices, and stereotypes about men and women, about sex, about people who were culturally and racially different from us, about age, about work, about what is and is not normal. These too were part of our cultural messages.

Often, we miss cultural differences because our own cultural way of doing things is so deeply embedded that we can't imagine anyone really thinking of doing something another way. Added to that, of course, is that voice from our mother (or whoever was the carrier of cultural information for us) telling us, "A good person would do it this way," or "This is the right [read "only"] way to do it." A seemingly unimportant, but interesting, example: Think for a moment about how you learned to fold towels. Was it in twos? Was it in threes? And what messages did you get about people who folded them differently? "Didn't her mother teach her the right way to fold towels?" "Don't they know how to fold towels?" (The towel example is about socioeconomic class. Upper-middle and upper-class people learned to fold their towels in threes so that the monogram on the towel would show. We get many class messages, but because we pretend that America is a classless society, they are sometimes analyzed as ethnic or regional messages.) How we fold towels, like so many other tiny details in our lives, is often affected by the bundle of cultural information we got as children, too early in our development to question the adults who "knew." We bought it whole cloth, if you will, because it was the "normal" that was presented to us—simply the way things are done.

Cultural Differences in the Workplace

As far as the workplace goes, it probably doesn't matter how an employee folds her or his towels, unless, of course, you are in the laundry business. Let's look at another seemingly unimportant example: greeting people at work. Every culture has its rules and conventions about how people greet one another. In some cultures it is done by bowing, in some by nodding, in some by hugging and kissing, and in some by shaking hands. In some cultures it is appropriate to look the person you are greeting right in the eye. In others, one never looks an authority figure in the eye—it would be an act of arrogance. For each of the dominant ways of greeting, there are, of course, many variations and rules that apply in different situations—whom you kiss, how you kiss him or her, when, and so on. Each of us learned the "appropriate" ways to greet different people—aunts, grandmothers, friends, brothers, sisters, mothers, fathers, people we know and people we don't, strangers who are men and strangers who are women. We got lots of small pieces of information (based on our own culture's way of doing things) about how we "should" connect with people when we first meet them and when we meet them again after a period of time.

In the global business world, which is basically governed by white-male Western European cultural ways, the most commonly used greeting is that of looking a person in the eye and shaking hands. Most men and some women in the United States were raised to shake hands firmly while looking the other person "squarely in the eye." People who shook hands differently had a "cold fish" or a "dead fish" handshake. "You shake hands like a woman": Nothing could be worse. There were also lots of negative messages about people who didn't look you in the eye as they spoke to you: They were "shifty" or lying or sick or didn't have any manners. Remembering that we take all of who we are and what we've learned with us everywhere we go, we enter the world of work. People who were raised to greet people in ways other than looking them in the eye are at a disadvantage. What their cultural norms call "rude" is considered essential in European-American cultures. How many Asian-Americans, Native Americans, or African-Americans have not been hired because their downcast eyes were read as dishonest, shifty, or uninterested? How many white American women have been judged as too aggressive because their handshakes were particularly firm? Very often what we deem the "right" way to do something is so much part of our being that we are not conscious of the power of our judgments. We don't hire the person who might have brought a new perspective to a job because our cultural biases get in the way.

We have dealt with the challenges of cultural differences for centuries, but we still don't seem proficient. How many books do you still see on the shelves, for example, that talk about men and women communicating? And now we have some new challenges. We are coming in contact with lots and lots of people who are very different from us—people who grew up in different parts of the world and who are coming to America to make their homes. We are faced with incredible complexities of clashing cultures, that is, ways of doing things, and our job is to figure out how to live and work successfully with one another. Often we believe that if we just follow the Golden Rule everything will be fine. The problem with that solution is that each culture has its own Golden Rule, and how I want to be treated might be quite different from how someone of another culture wants to be treated. Further, we can't rely on old patterns or on our old intuitions to keep us on the right track when we are talking to someone who is different from us because our intuitions are culture based.

Examining Our Cultural Biases

When we think of culture narrowly, as affecting only the ways we celebrate or what we eat, we miss a great deal of information that affects the way we do our jobs. *How* we do things—greet someone, conduct a work conversation, interact physically, determine what is private and what is public information, how we view time, how we spend money—is often affected by the cultural rules by which we were raised. Take a moment to do the *cultural bias checklist* in Fig. 4-1. As you do it, note how many of the qualities you would have thought of as personality traits rather than cultural ones before doing this exercise. Our task is to understand that none of the words has universal meaning and that all of us bring our own culture's values to the definitions. When you choose your words in each category, be sure to think about what those words mean to you. For example, if you select "fun-loving," does it mean "enjoys life and works to the fullest" or "doesn't

Circle five adjectives/terms describing people you like, and underline five adjectives describing people you do not like to be around. You may add adjectives of your own.

adventurous	neat
affectionate	needs much praise
ambitious	obedient
anxious for approval	optimistic
appreciative	orderly
argumentative	rebellious
big-hearted	resentful
candid	responsible
competitive	sarcastic
complaining	self-centered
critical of others	self-respecting
demanding	self-satisfied
discourteous	sentimental
distant	shows love
dogmatic	shrewd, devious
dominating	shy
easily angered	sociable
easily discouraged	stern
easily influenced	submissive
efficient	successful
encouraging	sympathetic
enthusiastic	tactful
false	talkative
forgiving	teasing
fun-loving	thorough
gives praise readily	thoughtful
good listener	touchy, cannot be kidded
helpful	trusting
indifferent to others	uncommunicative
impulsive	understanding
independent	varied interests
intolerant	very dependent on others
jealous	warm
kind	well mannered
loud	willing worker

Discussion   How might each of the descriptions you have selected be related to your *cultural* perspective. How might each affect your work style? What strategies might you use in working with someone who has one of the five qualities you like? What strategies might you use in working with someone who has one of the five qualities you don't like?

Figure 4-1. Cultural bias checklist. (©1994 Griggs Productions, San Francisco, Cal.)

take work seriously and is really interested in having a good time?" If one of your criteria for a good team member is that the person enjoys his or her job but is not so "fun-loving" that she or he never comes to work, you might misunderstand an employee who had received the cultural message that work should be fun and that, if you can't have a good time doing a job, you have chosen the wrong occupation.

Each of the words listed in the exercise is value laden and has the potential of being open to cultural definition. It is very important to note in this connection that there is not one right way to do almost anything. There is no "right" and "wrong," there is "different." That doesn't mean we put aside standards or requirements. (It also doesn't mean that there is no moral right or wrong and that we have given up all morals and ethics to create a work environment that is generally hospitable.) The expectation is that the job will be done; the standard is that it will be done well. The *way* it gets done might differ depending on the person who is doing it or the procedure that the group has agreed on.

Let's look at the concept of "team." In a group that is racially and culturally diverse, all of the employees might agree that being a team player is essential. What is meant by *team player* might mean entirely different, if not contradictory, things based on how each member's culture sees the concept. For one cultural group, it might mean doing the very best you can on your segment of a task so that no one has to leave his or her work to help you complete it. For another group, being a team player might mean dropping everything you are doing to help someone else with her or his portion of a job. The expectation of other team players in the first scenario is that they will do their jobs as well as they can and that they will not interrupt you as you work on your part. In the second, the belief embedded in the definition of *team player* is that no ones task is for him or her to do alone; you expect that others will come to your aid if you run out of time because you had stopped doing your task to help another person or if you had gotten stuck on some part of it. Because the definition of *team player* is, at least in part, culturally determined, chances are good that it didn't occur to any of the employees that they were working from very different starting places. Each might well believe that the team was not functioning and that the other individuals were simply not doing their jobs. The manager who knows that cultural messages affect the ways we see much of the world could easily get at the root of the conflict by asking what each group means by *team*. "When I tell you that I want you to be a *team player*, what does that mean to you?" And then, "How can we work together to create a *shared* definition of *team player* so that we all know what is meant here?" The conflict doesn't magically disappear, but there is now a shared basis from which to talk about what is going on.

Distinguishing between Cultural
Information and Stereotypes

One of the greatest challenges in dealing with cultural differences is educating ourselves about genuine cultural information and then using that information as advisory only. Let's look at the issue of time. Every culture sees time differently. (In his book *The Silent Language* [Doubleday, N.Y. 1980], Edward T. Hall reports that the Sioux culture, for example, has no words for "time" or "late" or "waiting.") Even in cultures that have been interacting with European Americans for hundreds of years, like the Latino/Hispanic culture or the Native American cultures, there are specific cultural norms about time that are very different from white Western European ones. We know that in most European American cultures a 9:00 meeting is a 9:00 meeting. (Each business has its own cultural norms so that a 9:00 meeting may really be a 9:07 meeting in your organization.) In other cultures, a 9:00 meeting is a meeting that begins as close to that time as you can get and still do all of the things that need to be finished before the meeting starts. Look at how this might play out in the office.

You, an African-American, hire two new employees, one white German person and one Latino/Hispanic. Because you want to be a sensitive manager and because you have never really known any Latinos, you read about Latino culture. One of the things you learn is that time is seen differently in some Hispanic cultures than it is in Irish or English or French cultures. You schedule an orientation meeting for 10:00 one morning. Both new employees are late. Here is the sticky place: Using the cultural norm as one possibility but not thinking stereotypically and *assuming* that that is the determining factor, and given that you know time is viewed differently in some Hispanic cultures, you think, "Juan is late because people in his culture are always late. Sigrid must have hit bad traffic because German people are never late." That's stereotyping. The truth is you don't know anything about why either of them is late. To use cultural information effectively, you think to yourself, "Juan may be late because he is trying to get everything done before he comes to the meeting; or he may have had a car accident; or he may be sick. I don't really know." And, while the stereotype of Germans is that they are never late, Sigrid as an individual may have a real problem with being on time. Often, responding to a situation stereotypically, the manager disregards Juan because he is late ("Oh those Hispanics, they are always late, I probably shouldn't have hired him") and excuses Sigrid ("Sigrid must really be having a hard time with child care, but I know I can count on her because Germans are rarely late.")

For managers to be effective in a diverse workplace, they must

- Know as much as possible about the various cultures to which their employees belong

- Be very aware of his or her own culture to know the basis from which each assesses situations

- Rather than just applying the information they have to each individual they meet from a specific culture, using that information as one possible explanation for a situation and asking questions to find out what is really going on

The hazard of having a little cultural information—Asian women are taught to be passive, for example—and then thinking stereotypically is that you expect Asian women to be passive: "We can't send an Asian woman in to see those clients. They'll chew her up." It is true that the cultural norm for Asian women is to be more reserved; the challenge is to see if Kim is quiet because she is following the cultural standard, if she is not feeling well, is simply a shy individual, or is remaining quiet because the environment doesn't seem to her to be safe or supportive.

Working on the Three Levels

As you have read in the preceding chapters, each of us functions on three levels at all times: the *personal*, the *interpersonal*, and the *organizational*, or *systemic*. The *personal level* is the one in which we hold all of our attitudes, biases, and prejudices about everything—work, play, sex, manners, food, school, race, gender, age and aging, religion, and so on. These are the thoughts we have in the shower or commuting to work or walking down the street. Our fantasy is that no one else knows these thoughts, that they are private. We erroneously believe that when we walk into our workplace, for example, we hang our attitudes and prejudices on the coat rack and our thoughts never enter into the work that we do.

The *interpersonal level* is the behavioral level. It is the level on which we interact with people. This level overlaps the personal level and is strongly affected by the attitudes carried at the personal level. A prototypical story: A president of a large university in the West was introducing a young Latino man who was being given an award in engineering. During his speech, the president commented on the fact that he was sure that the man had gotten interested in engineering when he had been young and was driving big cars really fast on the highways of Los Angeles, running away from the border police. The truth was that the man was not from Los Angeles, and, in fact, was fourth-generation American. When the president was confronted about his biased assumptions, he made the situation even worse by saying that he should never have said in public what he believed in private. The first two levels, the personal and the interpersonal, so affect one another that there is no way one won't be reflected in the other even if we would rather that it didn't happen.

The *organizational,* or *systemic, level* is the one on which we function in the organization. It's the environment in which we work: the people, the formal and informal rules, the levels and functions, the way decisions are made, the ways people are hired and fired. It is the "big picture"—the organizational context into which everything goes.

In order to make changes in an organization, we need to be clear about the interactions between the three levels and how they work together. Let's look at an example.

In a medium-sized organization, there are very clear procedures about the ways that people should be hired and promoted. They were designed by the human resources department and are known to all supervisors and managers. At this specific organization, as in most others, these procedures are frequently not followed. Managers hire people they have known for years without doing a real search; people are promoted without the job being posted. This is an organization that is working hard to learn to value the diversity it has and to become more diverse. But because failure to follow procedures is business-as-usual in this organization, there is a perception throughout the organization, and in some instances it is an accurate one, that "it's not what you know but who you know." At the *personal level* there is a sense of lack of fairness in promotions and the feeling that it doesn't matter how well you do your job. That perception is reflected at the *interpersonal level* in that often employees don't back one another up or support their supervisors. And, of course, at the *organizational level,* there are feelings of mistrust, the never-say-anything-because-you-never-know-who-your-next-boss-might-be phenomenon. This is an example of the interactions among the three levels at which we all function all the time. What happens at one level greatly affects each of the other levels. To change this feeling of it-doesn't-matter-what-you-do, modifications have to be made at each level. At the personal level, managers need to look at the fact that, if they individually begin to change the ways they hire, fire, and promote and if they talk about it with their peers, they might be able to change the organization from the inside. At the interpersonal level, all employees, but particularly supervisors and managers, must begin to follow strictly the hiring and promotion procedures set up by human resources. And again, they need to communicate and demonstrate their commitment to these procedures. Over time, as employees begin to see these changes, the organizational level should begin to change as well.

Seeing the Organization as a System

To be successful, we need to understand how our organizational system works; we also need to see the ramifications of our actions in a systemic context. For example, our actions communicate information to those around us; sometimes the messages we send by our behaviors are intentional; in other instances they are not. In a single action, because we work in a system, we send messages at each of the three levels. Consider the following scenario:

A team of people was going on a business trip together. As usual, the manager assigned people roommates for their hotel stay. One member of the team, a self-identified lesbian, had worked with the group for a couple of years and seemed to be well liked. When the rooming list was published, the roommate of the lesbian, a heterosexual, came to the manager and requested that she be given a separate room because she didn't want to room with a lesbian. (The company's policy about sharing rooms was clear: Because of tight economic times, employees must share rooms on business trips. The managers work to put friends together and to assign smokers to the same room. If individuals want a single room, they must pay for it themselves.) In this case, the manager agreed to have the company pay for separate rooms for the heterosexual and the lesbian. The manager never talked to the lesbian or any other members of the team, but everyone heard through the grapevine what had happened. What were the messages sent by the manager's behavior? At the personal level, by acting as if no one knew what had happened, she communicated to her employees that difficult issues regarding differences are not to be openly discussed. At the interpersonal level, by not asking the heterosexual to examine her prejudices and assumptions and by changing her rooming assignment, she told the team that they didn't have to take the lesbian seriously as a person or as a team member—that she was dispensable. At the organizational level, her actions suggested that the company's personnel policies don't apply to everyone; that it is permissible to discriminate against some people but not others.

The issue of sexual orientation is a complicated one. We all come to this subject with lots of unresolved emotions and questions that frequently cloud our professional judgment. If you, also, struggled with this scenario, think about how you would respond if a white employee had refused to room with an Asian-American, or an able-bodied person with a person in a wheelchair. Would you have given the white person a separate room and charged it to the company? Would you have addressed the issue more openly if the situation had been about a person with disabilities? None of this is easy. But regardless of your personal thoughts about these scenarios, the central point is this: All of our behaviors in the workplace send messages to those around us, and the messages sent are at the personal, interpersonal, and organizational levels, whether or not we mean them to be.

Recognizing the Messages We Send by Our Behaviors

To be clear about the ramifications of your behaviors, fill out the chart in Fig. 4-2. As you complete the task, think about the messages you would *like* to send and how you might alter your behavior to accomplish that.

How Issues of Power Weave through the Process of Valuing Diversity

One of the least-discussed aspects of creating an organization in which diversity is genuinely valued is the issue of *power*. We ignore it because we are so uncomfortable with it, and we fool ourselves into believing that, if we just act as if the playing field is a level one, everything will be fine. We are all human beings, the thinking goes, and even though she is a different color or he has a more prestigious title after his name, we can still interact as individuals. That notion, as far as it goes, is absolutely accurate. We can, do, and should work with one another as unique individuals, each bringing a history and a set of stories to the workplace. But it is naive and unfair, not to mention unwise, to ignore the systemic differences in our experiences based on race, gender, sexual orientation, age, religion, class, and so on or to act as if they don't matter. We all take those experiences with us everywhere we go; they greatly affect our lives and our interactions.

There are two separate but connected aspects of power that we need to be aware of in the context of this chapter: the power inherent in being a member of the mainstream group and the privileges attached, and the power connected to one's job. In each case, it is foolish to behave in ways that ignore the role that power plays.

In the present-day American workplace, we do not all enter with the same possibilities for success. In the United States in 1988, according to the Equal Employment Opportunity Commission, women got paid $0.59 to $0.61 for every $1.00 than men were paid for comparable jobs. Only 2 percent of all of the managers in companies with more that 100 employees were black women, and only 3 percent were black men.

Describe the behavior:

_____
_____

Consider the messages sent by this behavior:

_____
_____

At the personal level:

_____
_____

At the interpersonal level:

_____
_____

At the organizational level:

_____
_____

Determine the message you would like to send:

_____
_____

Describe the behaviors that are more likely to send that message:

_____
_____
_____

Figure 4-2. Ramifications of our actions: Determining underlying messages.

White women represented 23 percent of the managers. Unless we believe that black men and women, for example, aren't able to manage, then we have to acknowledge that institutional discrimination exists.

What is the practical day-to-day meaning of the statistic that in companies with more than 100 employees only 2 percent of the managers are black women? For Wanda, an African-American woman in middle management, it means that she is usually the only person who looks like her in a managers' meeting. It means that, when she makes a comment, she often feels she is speaking for herself as an individual but is being heard as a representative of her race. It usually means that she feels the need to be extremely careful about allying herself with other people of color who may not be doing well in the organization for fear that either she will be perceived as less qualified or as a trouble-maker. It means that, if someone tells a racist joke and she objects, the perception is likely to be that she is too sensitive or that "she is looking for race behind every tree." (Johnnetta B. Cole, *Conversations: Straight Talk with America's Sister President,* Doubleday Books, New York, 1994). If she is promoted, many of her non-African-American peers will believe, regardless of concrete data to the contrary, that she was promoted only because she is black. It means that the outside work experiences she brings to the workplace are different from those of her white colleagues. It means, simply, that if she is working in a predominantly white organization, she doesn't have the *systemic* power, support, or assumed qualifications behind her that her white colleagues do.

This is not to say that all white people, as individuals, feel powerful or have power. They don't. As usual, the reality is far more complex than that. Layoffs, downsizing, and the growth of technology affect everyone. And the issues of class, gender, sexual orientation, religion, physical ability, and position in the organization are all intertwined. In every interaction, however, as the title of Cornel West's book makes clear, *Race Matters.* And how it matters is frequently connected to the issue of institutional racism as it affects people of color at the personal, interpersonal, and organizational levels.

It is also vital that the role one's job function (and the power connected to that position) plays in the workforce not be dismissed. It would be absurd, for example, to act as if objecting to a comment made by a person you manage carried the same element of risk as confronting your boss about a joke he or she told. Yes, we are all human beings, but for a variety of reasons we do not have the same amount of power in an organization. As George Orwell said in his allegorical *Animal Farm,* "All animals are equal, but some animals are more equal than others."

We could certainly spend a great deal of time analyzing the issue of power as connected to roles in an organization, but for the purposes of this discussion, it is important to acknowledge that to be successful in an organization one must be able to assess the formal *and informal* ways in which power is played out. By really understanding your organization, you are better able to calculate the possible ramifications of any risks you take and to strategize about how best to make the changes you want to make with as little fallout as possible.

Communicating with People
about Issues of Difference

Few of us are particularly comfortable with communicating about the
sensitive subjects of gender, sex, race, religion, culture, and sexual orientation. As children, we got very clear messages about what was
polite to talk about and what was not. And, while we weren't all
taught the same rules, we were all issued both verbal and nonverbal
guidelines. For example, a white mother and her 4-year-old daughter
were in a suburban shopping mall. The little girl saw an African-
American mother and daughter and said in a very loud voice, "Look,
Mom, there's a little black girl." The white mother, caught off guard,
loudly shushed the child, told her not to mention such things, and
hurriedly left the mall, all the while praying that the sidewalk would
open up and swallow them both. Developmentally, the child's behavior was totally appropriate; it is the job of 4-year-olds to identify who's
who and what's what. She was probably simply noticing and stating a
fact, but the mother's behavior clearly signaled that race is not something we acknowledge noticing. Similarly, when a child comments on
a person in a wheelchair, he is likely to be told, "It's not nice to stare,"
or "Be quiet, you don't want to make him feel uncomfortable."

Just as the mother at the shopping mall was uncomfortable about
acknowledging differences, that same lack of ease exists in the workplace today. A colleague calls to tell you she has just hired a new manager. If you ask "What color is that person?" it is quite likely that your
friend will stumble with her answer. She might tell you she didn't
notice and ask you why you are asking. On the other hand, if you ask
her what *gender* the new hire is, chances are good that she won't think
anything of telling you. She certainly won't tell you she didn't notice!
In American organizational culture, it is all right to see gender, but
there is discomfort in acknowledging seeing race or physical ability.
There is a sense that if you notice race or physical ability, you are
"racist" or "prejudiced," or at least rude. The challenge for the manager is to become comfortable with acknowledging the immediately
apparent physical differences associated with everyone's race, gender,
culture, class, and physical ability *without* attaching value judgments
to that information. No skin color is good or bad; it just is. We are not
better or smarter if we are one gender rather than another; we simply
are who we are. So, just as you would say, "I've just hired a Latina to
work for me," you would also say, "I'm interviewing a white woman
for a position this afternoon." Is the Latina (or Hispanic) inherently
any better than the white woman or vice versa? No, each one's race is
simply a part of who she is, an important part in terms of the woman's
experience in the world.

Thinking about Why Differences Matter

"But why do I need to notice these things? Aren't we all human beings?" "I grew up in the sixties being told that differences don't matter. Now you tell me they do!" "My religion teaches me that we are all God's children—it doesn't matter what color we are." "If we notice differences, aren't we just labeling and stereotyping people?" "If we notice differences, are we prejudiced?" "Can we have prejudices and still be good people?" "I never notice color." As indicated, more resistance is attached to identifying differences in race rather than in gender. Probably the most frequently asked question when we hear someone has had a baby is, "Is it a boy or a girl?" Sometimes that's connected to a value judgment. ("Oh good, that's what they wanted," or "Too bad, they already have six boys.") But most frequently it is a question that directs us to the stereotypically appropriate gift—a pink blanket or a blue one, a truck or a doll.

As young children, we spent much of our school life in lines that were gender specific. "OK, all the girls line up behind Ms. Brown, all the boys behind Ms. Smith." And we were marched into school or into the cafeteria or to the library. When we say "A new man has joined our team," we don't perceive that we are stereotyping or labeling; we are simply giving information. Why is it then that when we say, "I just hired an Asian man to manage the Pittsburgh office," we feel like we are boxing someone in?

Another interesting piece of this puzzle is that the greatest reticence about identifying race seems to come from those of us who are white. For people of color, race is a conscious aspect of everyday life. That is not to say that people of color have no racial prejudices or that they don't attribute greater value to one race or another; it is simply to say that being a member of a race doesn't come as a surprise to them as it does to many white people. For those of us who are white, it is almost as if we believe that if we don't mention race, we won't have to deal with its ramifications—with the reality, both past and present, of personal and institutional discrimination against some racial groups—or deal with our own ambivalence toward our behavior as it pertains to race. So we act as if race doesn't matter: "We're all the same under the skin." If we don't notice race, people of color won't be victimized by racism. If we don't notice race, we won't have to deal with the experiences of our colleagues of color.

Communicating More Effectively about Issues of Difference

Given that we want to communicate better with people who are different from us, or about sensitive issues of difference with people who are like us, what do we need to do? First, each of us needs to know about ourselves and how we communicate, and, second, we need to think about the reality of the person or people with whom we are working.

Knowing Ourselves.   The first step on the journey toward valuing diversity is knowing ourselves. While this is only a part of our task, it is essential. If we are not clear about what our biases and prejudices are, what roles gender, race, regional background, and so on play in our lives, what our values and assumptions are, and how we communicate, we will be unable to forge whole relationships. Our goal is to be conscious and intentional about our communication. The following questions are a guide to that process.

What Style Do I Use Most Frequently?   Do I interact with people formally or informally? Do I ask questions and listen to the answers, or do I basically give people information? Does my style change when I interact with women as opposed to men? With people of color as opposed to white people? With the people I manage versus those who manage me? If I am dissatisfied with the way I communicate, what changes would I like to make?

What Are My Values about Communicating?   Do I see it merely as a way to get things done? In other words, am I interested primarily in the *product* of a conversation, or do I see the conversation itself, the *process* of the communication, as the more important, or am I somewhere in between? What we are comfortable with in our communication is often determined by values we don't even know we have, or we mistakenly assume everyone has the same ones. So we need to know what cultural and personal messages we carry around with us.

Below is another exercise in knowing yourself.

What Are My Cultural Biases about Openness, Honesty, Voice Level, Conflict, and Language?

Openness. What does being "open" mean to you? Does it mean welcoming input from others? Sharing aspects of your personal life with people at work? Pushing yourself to try something new? Challenging yourself to examine your attitudes and values even though it might be hard? Welcoming everyone, even though they might be very different from you and hold different values?

Honesty. Does being honest mean you say everything you're thinking? Does it mean going against social conventions, like really telling someone how you are when they inquire casually in the morning? How does "honesty" get played out in the culture to which you are most connected and/or in your family of origin? Do you honestly say what you think, or do you say what you think the person wants to hear?

Voice level. In the family in which you grew up, what was the accepted voice level in conversations? Did a louder voice signify hostility or depth of feeling? Did a softer voice represent withdrawing or politeness, or was it just the normal conversation tone?

Conflict. What did you learn as child about conflict? Were you "allowed" to be angry, or was anger seen as an unacceptable emotion in your household? Does *conflict* mean disagreeing with someone, or is the tone of voice an essential element in determining what is conflict and what is not? For you, is it conflict if you raise your voice or only if you yell at someone in public? What about the aftermath of conflict? Were you supposed to feel guilty about entering into conflict, or were you taught to act as if the incident had never happened?

Language. What constitutes "appropriate" language for you? What words upset you? Four-letter words? Using religious figures' names casually? How are manners and language linked? What does "proper English" mean to you? What is your response to people who don't use "proper English"? Do you feel differently about a person who speaks English as a second language than about a person for whom English is a first language? What judgments do you make about people who speak English differently from the way you speak it?

Continuing our exploration, let's look at possible *biases and/or stereotypes* about persons with whom you communicate to discover how they might affect your interactions with them.

How Do My Biases Affect My Interactions? Biases and stereotypes often take the following forms:

- "He or she is not as smart as I am (where the assessment is based on regional accents, less formal education, or education at less prestigious schools, a lower socioeconomic class, or a different race)." Remember, expecting someone to be smarter than you are for one or more of these reasons is as much a barrier to communicating as believing he or she is not as smart.

- "She or he doesn't speak English as a first language and so can't possibly understand my perspective, hold the same values, have similar goals and ambitions, and so on."

- "He or she speaks a different language even though we both speak English." The other person talks in sports-speak, perhaps, and you don't care about sports. Or she speaks computerese, and your highest level of technological skill is knowing how to work an electric pencil sharpener.

- "We have a totally different life experience and reality." He's a baby-boomer, and you were born in 1928. He hears a symphony through his ears, and you hear it through the hands of an American Sign Language interpreter.

- "I know we are not really going to be able to communicate because...he calls women 'girls'...she's constantly telling Polish jokes...they live in the South....she has a chip on her shoulder..."

- "They aren't going to listen to me because...I am white (or black or young or gay or a born-again Christian, or I am fat)."

- "I'm not going to listen to them for the same reasons...."

Recognizing Differences in Personal Realities. To make communication work effectively, we have to be conscious of the fact that we have different life realities depending on who we are in terms of race, gender, class, age, and sexual orientation. How we see the world and how the world treats us is affected by these aspects of us, and we, in turn, carry those experiences into the workplace. For example:

You are a white woman who manages a group of 15 account managers. One of them is an African-American woman named Terry. During lunch one day you and Terry decide to go shopping. After browsing at several stores, each of you ends up in the rug section of a department store buying exactly the same throw rug. Terry gets in line a couple of people ahead of you. She charges her rug and waits for it to be wrapped. The saleswoman carefully covers the rug with paper and then ties it with string. She staples the sales slip to the outside of the bundle and tells Terry to show the receipt to the guard, "so that he won't think you stole it." Terry leaves the department, saying she'll see you at the office. Moments later, you are waited on. The same salesperson takes your charge card and wraps your rug. You notice a curious difference: She tucks your sales slip inside the package so that it isn't visible. She never mentions the guard to you or suggests that anyone might think you were a thief. As you walk back to work, you think about the interactions—so similar and yet so very different. You have heard Terry and the other women of color talk about the phenomenon of constantly being followed around the store by guards expecting them to steal; part of you thought they were either paranoid or too sensitive. Now you have witnessed it for yourself. You hear yourself thinking, "What does Terry do with all of the anger she must be carrying around? How can she be pleasant to clients after that experience at lunch?"

Here is another example:

You are planning a holiday party for the company. You have looked at all of the possible sites to find the one that has just the right atmosphere—warm and inviting. You have selected the caterer and the musicians, and the invitations have been mailed. One morning, Jorge, one of your direct reports, comes to talk to you. He is upset because he drove by the place where the party is being held and realized that it is not wheelchair-accessible. Because he uses a wheelchair to get around, he won't be able to attend the party. As an able-bodied person, you sometimes forget about Jorge's reality. Even though the company had the bathroom door widened when Jorge was hired, you spend so much time with him you just think of him as another one of your employees. In fact, you remember saying to him a couple of months ago, after you had asked him if he wanted to run in the company's 10K race, that he's so capable you never think of him as disabled. When he laughed and said he might be willing to roll in the race, you realized that by not paying attention to the fact that he is in a chair, you are ignoring a big part of his daily life. You had meant it as a compliment, but suddenly it didn't seem like a very sensitive thing to say. It is confusing for you. Now Jorge is embarrassed to talk to you about the holiday party, but, since this is the second experience like this in two months, he feels he had to say something about your continuing inability to see him for all of who he is. He's angry, and you are embarrassed and feel dumb. Your communication is strained, and your working relationship is affected, at least for a while.

Neither of the managers in these stories had done enough thinking about the realities of their employees. While their intentions were probably good, their lack of consciousness about issues of race and physical ability had caused them to ignore the ways that Terry's and Jorge's life experiences might impact their work. Managers who are striving to create diverse work environments that are supportive can't afford that lack of consciousness. Their job is to examine themselves and the ways in which who they are shapes their world, to acknowledge the differences that exist within their teams, and to develop an ease about discussing sensitive topics with all of their employees.

Establishing Guidelines for Discussing Differences

Some of the following guidelines for discussions about differences (developed by Dr. Price M. Cobbs, Pacific Management Systems, San Francisco, Cal.) apply to any conversation you have in which you want to communicate successfully. They are basic to good communication and are part of *active listening*—listening in which you participate fully in the interaction by being receptive instead of by talking.

Other guidelines are specific to interactions about differences. While there are no guarantees that any conversation will bring about the results you are looking for, if you are *intentional* about what you want to say and about how you say it, chances are greater that the conversation will achieve your goals. As you enter into a conversation about differences, remember that none of this is easy to talk about, but the opportunities to learn from one another, and to create an environment in which everyone is genuinely comfortable, make the risks worth it.

- The success of these sorts of conversations is the responsibility of both persons.
- Don't assume you know what the other person is going to say.
- Don't finish the person's sentences.
- Don't hedge with phrases like, "Don't you think…" or "Wouldn't you say…"
- Really listen; try hard not to be defensive.
- Acknowledge the risks of conversations about race, sex, sexual orientation, culture, etc., and then *have the conversation.*
- Remember that a person's difference is not the problem.
- Recognize that good intentions are not enough and are sometimes beside the point.
- Remember that you might do a really good job and the conversation might still be a hard one.
- Share your goal of the conversation with the person/people with whom you are speaking.
- Remember, this conversation is not to be a one-shot experience; it is about building relationships.
- Bear in mind that the issue of institutional power is often involved in a conversation about differences.

Let's look at each in turn.

The Success of These Sorts of Conversations Is the Responsibility of Both Persons. At the beginning of a conversation with someone who is different from you, or just a conversation about differences, it is helpful to talk about what each of you would like to gain from the conversation. The point here is not to begin a conversation just because you want to but because both of you are interested in or committed to opening doors, learning from one another, and moving forward. Success in this context is clearly a shared responsibility.

Don't Assume You Know What the Other Person Is Going to Say.
It is difficult for many of us to suspend our assumptions that we know what the other person thinks or is going to say, based either on prior knowledge of or on our stereotype of what someone *like* him or her would say. What we lose if we do make those assumptions are: the clues to what's actually being said, the chance to hear a perspective or a shared reality of a situation, and the opportunity to learn something new about the person.

Don't Finish the Person's Sentences.   It is often hard to quiet our minds long enough to listen to someone genuinely and all the way through. We are tempted to jump in, interrupt, and take the conversation off on an entirely different tack. If we really want to connect with someone, we have to know what *they* think, not what we think they think.

Give the Person with Whom You Are Talking Your Total Attention.
Listening to someone with your whole mind engaged is quite a challenge. We think on many tracks at once: "This person is saying some pretty interesting things...." "That reminds me of a comment I heard someone else make...." "I am so excited it is Friday afternoon. Two whole days without work!" And, of course, when we do that, we have stopped listening to the person who is speaking. Our focus has shifted from what the speaker is saying back to our own thoughts. Many people are composing their response instead of listening to what the person is saying. When we are talking with people whose thoughts and experiences are different from ours, it is particularly important to give them our total attention.

Don't Say, "Don't You Think..." or "Wouldn't You Say..."   Very often in conversations, when one of the participants is uncomfortable, or is hearing something new or being challenged, or wanting to gain control of the conversation, she or he will say, "But don't you think...?" or "Wouldn't you say....?" While it sounds like a genuine, open question, it is not; it is a closed question. The answer to either is yes or no. These questions often mask the sentiment: "I have the right answer; Don't you agree?" Authentic questions, those truly aimed at getting more information, might be, "What do you think about...?" or "These are my thoughts; what do you think?" or "How would you respond to...?" These questions are open-ended ones that allow the person being questioned to give her or his thoughts rather than confine the respondent to boundaries set by the questioner.

Really Listen, Trying Hard Not to Be Defensive. The essential part of this ground rule is "try hard not to be defensive." Whenever we are faced with new information or information we're not really sure we want, one of our first reactions is to stop listening and shut down emotionally. Obviously, when one of the participants is closed, the conversation can't be successful. "This all sounds great," you may be thinking, "but how do I stay open when I am feeling uncomfortable or, even worse, attacked?" A few suggestions: First, take some deep breaths to slow down the conversation and refocus on the interaction instead of on your feelings. Then you might say, "I'm having a little trouble understanding you. Tell me again what you just said." Or you could tell the person what you think you heard: "I want to be sure I understand your thinking. This is what I heard." Or you could say, "This is really a hard conversation for me, and I'm feeling a little [or a lot] defensive. Could you slow down so I can hear you better?" Each of these options changes the movement of the interaction, allows time for refocusing, and gives the other person an idea of what is happening to you. Because you are using *I* messages and talking about your own experiences, the other person is likely to move toward you rather than becoming defensive in return.

Acknowledge the Risks of Conversations about Race, Sex, Sexual Orientation, Culture, and so on, and Then Have the Conversation. Conversations about sensitive topics are, by definition, risky. We all walk into them with loads of thoughts, feelings, and unresolved emotions that make us feel vulnerable. Most of us are embarrassed that we have biases and prejudices; many of us *assume* we should have worked out all of these issues long ago. If we are members of the group being discussed, that only adds to the discomfort. And if our group is the numerical minority in the organization or if people who look like us don't hold powerful positions, our feeling of being at greater risk and thus needing to be more careful is probably accurate. Those are the givens. The reassuring fact is that none of us has done all the thinking we need to do on these issues, and all of us feel uncomfortable about revealing that to someone else.

That said, there are some ways to make these conversations flow more easily. Begin by talking about how risky the conversation feels.

- "You know, race is not something I talk about very often. It's not that I don't want to, but I know I don't have all the answers, and I'm afraid my prejudices will leap out."

- "As one of the only two people of color in this organization, it feels risky to talk about race with one of my white peers."

- "My wife always tells me I'm a sexist, and so it feels risky to talk about gender issues with a woman."

- "Often, when women raise the issue of sexism in this office, the men get defensive and shut down. But conversation is risky for both of us—you might be nervous about being called 'sexist,' and I am worried that I'll be discounted because of my concerns."

- "There are so few gay men or lesbians who are 'out' in our organization that I am nervous about even raising this issue."

- "I want to be supportive of the lesbians and gay men in our organization, but I'm afraid I'll say the wrong thing."

Even if you feel unable to let yourself be vulnerable enough to say these things, practicing talking about the risk will help you move into actual conversations. As in everything we do, the more we talk about these issues, the easier it becomes. And the more they are talked about as part of the normal course of events in an organization, the better able the organization will be to genuinely embrace diversity.

Remember That a Person's Difference Is Not the Problem; It Is Other People's Response to the Difference That Is Most Frequently Problematic.   "George, I don't know why you hired a woman. We have never had any women working here before, and it's bound to cause trouble. I mean, we'll have to change our language, take down our calendars—everything will be different."

Often, as we begin the process of talking about differences, it feels like a chore. "I never had to have a conversation about women until Julie arrived," might be running through this manager's head. While there is always an adjustment period when an organization undergoes change, it is important to be clear that the new person is not the problem and that the new persons difference is not the issue. The issues are people's reluctance to change and the possibility of losing some element of comfortableness. Even when long-time employees are well intentioned, most people struggle with change. Change is hard. In response to the employee's comment in the vignette above, George might talk to him about what a great background Julie brings to the team and remind him that some men in the organization had already complained about the calendars and the language. George might also get some ideas from employees about what they can do to make the whole group feel more like a team. The manager should also have a conversation with Julie alerting her to the fact that there might be some discomfort initially and being very clear that the problem is not with Julie but with the men who have been for so long in an all-male organization. He should go on to say that he is behind her all the way and that if she has any feeling of discomfort, he hopes she'll come and talk with him. (And he needs to mean it!)

Recognize That Good Intentions Are Not Enough and Are Sometimes beside the Point. The issue of good intentions is a hard one. Many of us were brought up to believe that if we mean well—if our intentions are good—that is all that matters. Though not added in so many words, the underlying assumption was that we weren't responsible for any pain we caused. (Or, as long as we apologized, we assumed the matter was over.) The fact is that what counts is our *behavior* and the *impact* of that behavior on individuals and on the organization. Let's look at an example.

In a meeting, the manager invites staff to participate in an AIDS bike-a-thon. One of the employees, Nancy, comments that only gay people will be there and that she doesn't feel comfortable with gays. Ned, a gay man with whom she has worked for years, asks her what she means. She responds, "Oh, Ned, you're so normal I never think of you as gay." Her intentions were most likely good. She was including him in the "normal" category with her and paying him what she thought was a compliment. But, in fact, what she is really saying is, "Let me strip that part of you that makes me uncomfortable and see you as I want to see you." The manager's job is to help Nancy and the other employees recognize that good intentions are not sufficient—that the challenge is to be responsible for the impact of our behaviors.

The issue of good intentions also comes into play in individual conversations about differences. Because working on our issues about differences is an ongoing task for all of us, we periodically say things that hurt and offend others, even when we have no intention of doing so. As in the example above, our task is to recognize the impact of our words and take responsibility for changing our behaviors, knowing, that at some point, all of us make mistakes.

Remember That You Might Do a Really Good Job but the Conversation Might Still Be a Hard One. There is nothing simple about talking about differences. We all have work to do on these issues, and each of us feels insecure about these discussions, which are laden with thoughts, feelings, and imaginings. Our fantasy is that if we are willing to broach the subject, the person with whom we are speaking should thank us for our generosity and willingness to take risks. Sometimes the person addressed doesn't feel like doing that because the pain the situation has caused is still too fresh. Remembering that this is a process, not an event, helps. With the expectation that the conversation will simply *begin*, it is easier not to be upset if that is all that happens. The assumption that one conversation will solve everything can lead only to disappointment.

It Is Sometimes Helpful to Share Your Goal of the Conversation with the Person or People with Whom You Are Speaking.   "Rachel, I need some help. You and I have worked together for a long time, and I know you feel strongly that we shouldn't play Christmas music on our telephone hold system in December. I have heard other Jewish people talk about this, but I don't know them as well as I know you. I wonder if you would be willing to spend some time with me helping me to understand." The speaker has made his goal very clear. He wants help understanding the feelings of some of the Jewish people with whom he works about holiday music that doesn't reflect their belief system. He is not demanding that Rachel explain it to him; he is issuing an invitation and letting her know the goal he would like to accomplish by talking.

Remember, This Shouldn't Be a One-Time Experience; This Is a Process about Building Relationships.   One of the goals of learning to value differences is to build relationships between individuals. Another is to create an organizational system in which all employees are treated fairly and equitably. Building relationships is a *process*. It takes time and commitment. When we enter into a conversation with someone who is different, or with someone who is like us but the conversation is about an issue of difference, it is important to remember that this is not a one-time event; it is a part of an ongoing series of interactions.

Bear in Mind That the Issue of Institutional Power Is Often Involved in a Conversation about Differences.   As was noted in the introduction to this chapter, differences matter. Each of us has a different amount of institutional backup and support based on who we are. In a conversation with someone who is different or a conversation about differences with someone who is like us, it is essential that we not act as if both have the same level of risk in the interaction. Most obviously, in a discussion between a manager and her or his boss, the manager is at far greater risk in expressing opinions than the boss is. One of the ways to deal with this discrepancy in power is to acknowledge that risk at the outset of the interaction. While that doesn't alleviate the risk, it makes the reality of the situation clear to both (or all) of the people involved.

How to Intervene in a Difficult Situation

We often do nothing when someone makes a racial comment, tells a "dumb blonde" joke or a gay joke, uses sayings that reflect stereotypic thought ("Indian-giver," "Jew him down," "Mexican standoff,"

"Chinese fire drill") or stereotypes a person because of what part of the country she or he comes from. Sometimes we don't say anything because we don't want to make a scene, but most frequently we don't respond because we don't have a clue about what to do. Unfortunately, there is no book of recipes entitled, *How to Tell Somebody You Are Offended by What She or He Said, Get Your Point Across, and Still Be Friends.* So here are some guidelines for dealing with such situations.

- Identify the *goal* of the interaction.
- Weigh the costs and benefits of *when* to say something.
- Examine the options of *what* to say, that is, what message you want to deliver.
- Think about *how* you want to deliver your thoughts.
- Use *I* messages.

In all of our communications we have many options in terms of *why* we speak, *when* we speak, *what* we say, and *how* we say it. To communicate most effectively, we must make our first step identifying the **goal** of our interaction. What do we want the outcome of our interaction to be? Do we simply want the person to know how we feel about a specific topic or do we want him or her to be quiet immediately? Do we want the person to take some action based on our recommendations and/or do we want to begin an ongoing conversation about an issue of difference prompted by the person's original comment? If we never want to speak to this person again, for example, we don't have to be nearly as careful with our words as we do if we want to maintain and/or strengthen our relationship. By taking the time to identify what we want from the communication, we enhance the chances of communicating clearly and reaching our desired outcome.

When we say something is a crucial yet complex decision with important ramifications. People often put off responding immediately and/or in public for fear of making the situation worse, getting in "big trouble," or looking "like a fool." Let's look at a couple of examples.

You are at an awards and motivational dinner for the manufacturing division of your company. The company has hired a speaker to kick off the event. During her or his presentation, the speaker adopts a stereotypically Jewish persona and begins to speak very loudly about how much money he or she can save by shopping at this company's outlet. "So, dollink, I'm telling you, such *bargains* awready! Only 2 cents more than wholesale." Many of the 300 people in the audience are laughing, though some of your colleagues are rolling their eyes and shaking their heads. You are not only embarrassed but also offended. You have some choices. You could, of course, stand up in the middle of the speech and tell the speaker how embarrassed you are by her or his comments. Realistically, while this *is* an option, it is not one that most people would choose because standing up in front of 300 people is a very big deal. What you would gain is to make a point and, perhaps, get the person to stop making the stereotypic remarks. If the remarks are serious enough, that may be exactly what you want to do. If the speaker has a question-and-answer period, another choice is to make some indirect comment to her or him in front of everyone: "It's good that our customers are not so stereotypic as the one you portrayed." Or "While our customers are not as stereotypic as the one you portrayed, they obviously come to the outlet in search of bargains." If you are the master of ceremony for this event, you also have the opportunity to say something as you are thanking the speaker. A third possibility is to wait until the event is over and talk to the speaker, telling her or him how you felt. If this is your choice, it is important to understand that by not speaking publicly, you have tacitly told the group that anti-Semitism is acceptable. It would also be a good idea to take your concerns to the committee planning the event. A fourth option is to talk with the committee and write a letter to the speaker, bypassing any personal interaction with the presenter. Obviously, a fifth choice is to do nothing but complain to your colleagues about the bigotry of the speaker and the stupidity of the committee for choosing her or him. If this is the option you choose, it is important to remember that you have then participated in the offensive act because you recognized it and did nothing to communicate your concern to the people who would be able to address the situation.

Let's look at another example.

You are in a meeting with about 10 people, and your boss makes the same comments that the speaker made in the previous example. In this scenario, the risks and the ramifications are very different. Speaking up in front of 10 people is not as hard nor is it as big a deal as doing so in front of 300. However, any time you address a person publicly, particularly your boss, you should know the benefits of doing so as well as the costs of *not* doing it. Again, there is no way to express yourself that is guaranteed to be effective. Some possibilities are: "You know, Gene, I understand your point, but I'm not comfortable with your presenting Jewish people in such a stereotypic light. Everyone likes bargains." "Gene, what's with stereotyping Jewish people? I haven't turned down a bargain in a long time, and I am a lifelong Quaker." "Gene, I don't want to make a big deal about this, but I really don't feel comfortable with your stereotypic comments."

The risk of public comment is that you might embarrass your boss. (On the other, if your organization is really a healthy one in these matters, you will be viewed positively for speaking up even though it creates an uncomfortable moment. Organizations that genuinely value diversity reward people for calling such things to attention, as long as it is done in a caring and constructive manner.) The costs of not saying something on the spot are clear: By your silence, you have condoned your manager's behavior. It is also possible that you have signaled to your colleagues that you wouldn't support *them* if they decided to say something. The question is whether the risks of interrupting, at an interpersonal level are outweighed by the drive to get to a healthier communication process at the organizational level.

Another option is to speak privately to your boss. You have several options here. You might do so in his or her office with the door closed, you could invite your boss out to lunch to talk, or you could talk in a secluded area during a coffee break. The obvious benefits of addressing the issue privately are that you allow the manager to feel less painted into a corner. It also gives the boss the time and opportunity to respond gracefully, deciding whether or not to apologize to the whole group at the next meeting or in a written memo.

When to Interrupt an Inappropriate Comment

In making your decision about when to interrupt a comment, it is helpful to ask yourself the following questions:

- What are the informal rules about who says what to whom, and how it is couched?

- What do you think good communication would sound like in your organization?

- How can you help shift communication styles from what they are today toward more functional ones?

- How do you "manage your manager"?

The last question involves thinking about what is safe to say to your manager, remembering the differing amounts of power held in the organization. How do you say "unsafe" things in the wisest manner? What are the best ways to approach your boss? Openly and honestly? Or is it smarter to work with one or more of your peers to present loaded issues through group discussion? What are the other possibilities? What are the costs and benefits of each of your options? And, finally, what approach feels most comfortable to you? There are some people who are quite comfortable speaking up in public, there are some who are able to do it if the situation is right, and there are others who cannot conceive of ever raising an issue publicly.

What you say is directly related to the underlying message you want to send. While that may sound obvious, let's look at an example to see why it's important to keep the desired message in mind.

An employee brings a flier to work titled "Application Form for Niggers." It was going around his wife's company, and he thought it was funny enough to share, but only with white people. You, a new manager in this company, arrive at work to find him standing in a group of people laughing, and you ask what they're laughing at. The employees hand you the flier, laughing all the while. You read it and are horrified and outraged. While you collect yourself, you think about all of the possible things you could say—everything from "How could I have such a group of stupid racist pigs working for me? You're all fired!" to "I'm all for fun, but this goes beyond the limit."

Remembering the guidelines for what to do when you're offended by something someone has done or said, focus on the messages you want to send. First, you want all of the involved employees to know immediately that this is a very grave matter and that this kind of humor is *not* acceptable at work, ever. As a new manager, you are beginning to let your employees know who you are by setting boundaries for behavior. Second, you want the original bearer of the flier to understand the seriousness of his actions, but you aren't interested in stooping to his level of behavior in responding to him. Given those two desired messages, you have narrowed the range of best responses. The "I'm all for fun, but..." comment doesn't communicate how serious you are, even though it is a soft way to make your point. The following approach is clear but not so emotional that the group is able to dismiss you as being "too sensitive": "It may be that this was seen as appropriate behavior before I came, but it is not something I am willing to tolerate. My expectation is that all of us in this office will be respectful of one another."

You then turn your attention to what to say to the employee who brought in the flier. "You are a racist dog," really doesn't meet your message criteria. While straightforward, it is not particularly professional. Obviously, there are choices about whether to have the conversation in public or private. Though it is true that the way you treat this employee will send a message to all of the others, the fact that you responded immediately and publicly gives you latitude in dealing with the bearer of the flier, something you might not otherwise have had. You also have decisions to make about whether to put a note in his file or simply to give him a verbal warning about future behavior. Something like "I want it clear that I am taking this extremely seriously. Even if it was not your intention to hurt anyone, such behavior could jeopardize the trust in our team as well as putting possible relationships with clients at risk, should they hear about it." Again, while not berating the employee, you have made your point. If you are clear about the message you want to deliver, you are most likely to respond in a way that achieves the appropriate balance of professionalism and humanity.

How you say things should, again, be connected both to your goal and the message you want to send. Particularly when a situation takes you off guard, it is important to remember that you have options about how you respond. Consider this scenario:

You are a blonde-haired white woman. One of your peers constantly tells jokes about blonde women and, at the end of each joke looks at you and says, "Present company excepted, of course." So far you have said nothing; it hasn't seemed worth the trouble. You imagine his intentions are good, and he is pretty nice, all in all. But you are beginning to notice that the other men in the company aren't taking you and the other women in the office seriously and that the number of sexist jokes and off-color comments are rising. You have lots of choices about how to let this person know what you're feeling. You could be straightforward and clear: "Jim, I've listened to your jokes about women for a long time. You might not mean them, but I am really tired of them. I would like you to stop telling them, at least around me." Or you could approach the jokes as the problem (as opposed to Jim being the problem): "Jim, I need your help. It seems to me that the number of jokes and comments about women has really increased recently. I know that they are getting on my nerves. What do you think we might do?" Another option is to tell him how you feel: "Jim, your jokes are making me feel crummy. It is hard enough to work in a situation where I am only 1 of 3 women in an office with 12 men. Your jokes make it worse." Obviously, the last example makes you most emotionally vulnerable; that is a choice you may or may not want to make.

When you are working on *how* you want to say something, think about what *your* typical style is in talking about sensitive issues. What is useful about your style? How would you like to change it? None of the processes of communications should be set in stone for any of us. Each of us is constantly growing, learning, reassessing the ways we interact with others. Communication is by nature a dynamic, ever-changing process. Our job is to accept the challenge of ongoing reexamination of what we say and how we say it.

A common feature in each of the preceding scenarios is the use of *I* **messages.** Presenting a thought, a feeling, or an idea from your perspective is an extremely effective communication tool. Often, when we

To determine how best to respond to a difficult situation, follow these steps:

1. Describe the situation.

2. Identify your options for responding.

3. Identify the goal of your action.

4. Determine which action will best achieve your goal, given the costs and benefits of each option.

5. Outline strategies by thinking about why, when, what, and how.

6. Describe what happened when you applied your strategy.

7. Evaluation

   What were the strong points of this approach in this situation?

   What were the weak points of this approach in this situation?

8. Additional notes

Figure 4-3. A model for intervening in difficult situations.

are angered by something someone has said, we go on the offensive. Remarks such as "If you hadn't made such a stupid comment..." or "You have really offended me..." or "You make me really mad..." or "I want to talk to you about your behavior..." all focus attention on the other person. *I* messages allow the other person to remain in the conversation without getting defensive because the person you are talking about is *you* and not her or him. "Joan, I would like to talk to you about my response to what you said in the meeting..." or "Lou, I am really having a hard time with something you said yesterday..." or "May, I was really hurt by your joke about fat people yesterday." If you put your thoughts in the context of your personal experience and speak for yourself, the resulting conversation is more likely to send the message you want to send.

Interrupting a behavior that is offensive to you is never totally easy or comfortable. Regardless of how hard we try to communicate clearly and from our perspective, we are in fact giving someone feedback she or he might not expect or want. Typical defensive responses are "You're just too sensitive..." or "I didn't mean anything by it..." or "What's the matter? Don't you have a sense of humor? It was just a joke!" or "I didn't know you were one of those women's libbers... or a similar comment designed to make *you* look like the problem. If you are able to remain focused on your goal for the interaction and the message you want to send and how you are saying it, the discussion has a far greater chance of being effective.

Remembering that no tool works for every situation, the model in Fig. 4-3 outlines the steps for identifying the best interventions for difficult situations. It is designed to allow you to adjust it to your own specific situations.

It is not hard to recognize that we are living in a rapidly changing world. The signs are everywhere—the safety announcement at the beginning of an airplane flight is given in two languages even though the flight is a domestic one; elevator instructions are in English and Arabic numerals and in Braille; signs for public restrooms are depicted by international symbols. The work environment we are in is different from the one for which most of us were prepared. To work well with our clients, our colleagues, and our employees, we need new (different, additional) skills as well as a broader lens through which to look at the world. Our long-standing belief that the people we deal with in our daily business life speak our same language or, even speaking the same language, will attach the same meanings to the words they use, are assumptions we can't afford to make if we are to work well together in the future.

5

Teamwork and Diversity

Rafael Gonzalez and Tamara Payne

Why Diversity Teams Are Important

Organizations all over the world are discovering that in order to maintain a competitive edge, they need to use their resources more creatively. "Your *human* resources are your most valuable resources" was a popular saying in the eighties. In the nineties, a critical challenge for companies is to find ways to effectively motivate and fully take advantage of the incredible creativity, energy, and skills of all their employees. A General Electric (GE) employee captured the essence of the challenge during a diversity training session when he said a company must "talk it and act it."

Organizations nationwide are examining how they use their workforces and are searching for new ways to reduce costs and increase productivity. Multinational organizations in the United States are also realizing that to be successful and maintain their U.S.-based operations, they must shift their approach to dealing with their workers.

The fact that the workforce is and will continue to be increasingly more diverse is having a ripple effect on the way people form teams and the way these teams operate. The diverse needs, skills, perspectives, and approaches beg for some attention to these areas if workers are to successfully deliver the objectives of any business.

Such familiar strategies as total quality management, customer service, employee involvement, and diversity are all pointing at the *inclusion* of people—often in teams—to problem-solve, innovate, and deliver on stated objectives.

A team that values diversity is more than a collection of bodies put together to solve a problem, develop a strategy, or share information. Rather, a *diversity* team brings diverse people together to create an environment that will allow them to learn from each other and to care about each other as they consider the task, the process needed to complete it, and the impact of the actions they take. A diversity team is conscious of the contributions of mind and heart as they work to contribute to the excitement, success, and spirit of an organization.

Diversity teams don't waste time. They capitalize on their moments together to learn and to share. But not everyone realizes the value in that. Many people deem anything not focused on specific tasks and priorities as "touchy-feely" exercises and wasteful efforts. But to work well as a unit, for themselves and ultimately for the organization, teams need to deal with issues of credibility, trust, and partnership and pay attention to any lack of understanding that can impact information sharing and, ultimately, productivity.

There are definite benefits to diversity teams. For example, you eventually have workers in the organization who

- Know how to create a learning environment
- Have discovered how to work with and embrace diversity
- Possess the skills to work in other multicultural environments
- Feel more invested in the organization because of their experience on a diversity team

Creating Teams in a Diverse Community

We can't necessarily assume that just because people work together, they're working *together*. That's why team building is "in." It's popular with many trainers, whether they're in human resources, training organizations, or organizational development. It's also popular with the organizations these trainers and consultants work for. Organizations are reengineering the entire structure of their workforce. They are becoming self-directed and moving toward "flatter" organizational structures (meaning fewer "head honchos," fewer levels of command—fewer steps up the proverbial corporate ladder).

Like most good things, effective work teams don't just materialize out of thin air. Organizations have found that they have to make conscious efforts to build teams out of groups of people who work together. Why go through all this work? Because, in work, as in life, working together can make you stronger—and quality performance and quality products or services are only two of the results.

Yet despite the popularity of the activity itself, we have to be careful about the term *team building*. It can be somewhat of a misnomer. In a diverse workforce, the term can be met with suspicion, misunderstanding, and rejection. That's because, for many people, the word *team* connotes sports. Understandably, people approach the idea of a "team" depending on their personal experiences with being on, wanting to be on but being left out of, or just watching teams in action.

Some people's experiences with team sports are empowering and fun. They have fond memories of victories and camaraderie. But for others, team sport experiences are either nonexistent or felt like boot camp. For those people, team building is met with a shudder and often with memories of humiliation. One executive, for instance, remembers being hollered at by his high school football coach. "You call this playing football? You're a bunch of sissies!! Shape up or you'll all be on the bench!" Fortunately many people today realize that name-calling, sarcasm, and threats are not good motivational techniques. Most people cringe at the term *sissy*.

Women traditionally get the credit for objecting to the prevalence of sports and military references used by too many men. They've often been the ones to say that it's a "good-old-boy" mentality since, until recently, women weren't given many opportunities in sports or the military. However, there are also many men who find that these sports and military analogies don't exactly fill them with the adrenalin of team spirit.

With the diversity of people in the workplace, the expression "as American as baseball and apple pie" no longer has currency in our broad-based culture. Some folks identify more easily with concepts like harmony and symphonies. Others may have a positive view of sports, but they may also enjoy Yoga or Tai Chi, for example, and those activities are more individualized and less team oriented. So, again, the terminology might fall short of being helpful.

One example of how the team concept can sometimes result in a culture clash is with the "workout" concept:

Designed to be less hierarchical and more self-directed, the workout concept was initiated by a large organization to offer an opportunity for teams to lay out on the table any issues or concerns they had. These open and honest forums had been extremely effective at the organization's American plants. When the company did business in Asia, they decided to continue with the practice, believing they had a good thing going—why reinvent the wheel?

But the workout didn't go as expected. Americans and Taiwanese, it seems, have different cultural norms when it comes to direct feedback and what is regarded as appropriate behavior toward management.

We're not saying that feedback and team building aren't important in other cultures, but vehicles for building a work team should be consistent with the culture and needs of the work group.

Historically, our approach to doing business with other countries was with the mind-set that we are American organizations—so people should fit into the way we do things. It was a sort of superiority complex. Why should we have to change the way we do business just because we're in a foreign land? We relocated most of our management staff from the states abroad, and nationals who worked for our organizations abroad had to fit into the American organizational culture. A few years ago a sales executive for a Fortune 500 computer company noted, after spending considerable time in Europe, "Unless you go outside the plant you'd never have known you weren't in the United States."

Now, we are shifting our strategies so that we can work with some important trends. For example:

- Our global economic structure is changing.
- New trade agreements are being negotiated.
- Our competitors are no longer just other U.S. companies.

In this regard, one development is that organizations are using more nationals to run operations abroad. After all, they understand the local culture and customs. We are also becoming more flexible in our culture and customs. We're trying to recognize, respect, and, most of all, build successful work relationships with organizations and firms in other countries and other cultures.

All of these factors have implications for how we make up our work teams—the individuals we choose for our team membership. Not only is the "face" of our teams being shaped by the changing demographics in the United States, it is being transformed by our struggle to be effective and successful in a fast-paced, complex, and changing global market. To be productive in cross-cultural work relationships, we need to reconsider our traditional interactions, dialogue, and training.

Doing business in a diverse community sometimes requires a little extra planning. For example, arranging a meeting or conference takes some extra thought, especially if your audience is unfamiliar to you. The following planning tips (reprinted with the permission of General

Electric Company's Nuclear Energy Diversity Council, San Jose, CA) will help make your gathering a successful one, wherever it is scheduled to take place:

- Identify your audience.

- Review calendar for potential scheduling conflicts with holidays, religious days, local festivities, etc.

- Make sure that your speakers, mediators, panel members, etc. reflect diversity.

- Gear presentations to your audience needs.

- Review menus and include a variety of selections (vegetarian, low-fat, kosher, ethnic foods, and so forth).

- Understand the cultural norms of the attendees:

  Is it appropriate to "get down to business" immediately or should you plan to build rapport first?

  What are "appropriate" topics for building rapport and establishing relationships?

  How is the normal workday structured? Start early or late? What are noon-hour habits? Close of business? Evening activities?

- Understand the group's normal decision-making protocol. Will they:

  Investigate/research individually or in groups?

  Understand information first and then make decisions or use a combined process?

  Receive and digest information beforehand or during discussions of meetings?

- Find out how decisions are usually made. Is it by group consensus or individually?

- Learn how typical meetings are structured:

  Who attends? (Implementors, evaluators, owners? Everyone together or in separate meetings?)

  How should people be seated? (Randomly or by organizational hierarchy?)

  What are the "speaking" norms? (Managers or individual contributors speak first?)

  Who should open the meeting? (Manager or individual contributor, or customer?)

The way we define the term *team* will also have an impact on how we measure team success. The traditional sports team definition of *success* focuses on *winning*. Competition and striving for excellence can

be a very positive aspect of team formation; on the other hand, sometimes using this traditional definition of *success* can, again, create frustration, alienation, and lack of cooperation. For example:

There was once a manufacturing company that had several production
teams. Management rewarded the team members who produced the
highest number of items. This was their way of providing incentives for
employees and building a sense of team. They gave the highest
producers a pizza or some other token "treat." For one contest, the
reward was team jackets. Not surprisingly, the team that consistently
won the pizza prizes also won the jackets. This outward show of
superiority was the last straw for the other teams. They were struggling
with personnel issues around diversity and supervision and became
so frustrated at what they saw as the lack of support from management
and their own inability to "win" that they began sabotaging the line
to create problems for the superstar team. Needless to say, overall
production suffered.

Many times, people's concept of team as a whole ignores some very
important relationships: those within the team and the interactions
between separate teams. In fact, sometimes people interpret antagonism between teams as team spirit. Often, people see winning only in
a win-lose perspective; that is, they don't normally define *winning* as
giving everyone on the team a chance to play or having everyone on
the team be healthy and happy with no injuries or collaborating with
another team so that both improve their game. People usually determine winning by who gets the bigger score.

Yet there are also many helpful concepts and terms surrounding the
word *team,* such as *strategy, coordinating roles and plays,* or *positive competition* and *striving for excellence.*

When asked about the specific qualities that describe the most effective
teams they've been a part of, people's responses often cover such areas as:

- *Structure.* Clarity of objectives, roles, and so on.
- *Relationships.* Everyone contributed.
- *Environment.* Open, risk-taking allowed, fun.
- *Results.* We surpassed our goals.

People versus Projects

Teams must always deal with two elements:

1. *Relationships on the team.* How will people work together?

2. *The task.* What is the group's goal?

Many teams in American organizations, however, skip over the first and focus on the task, paying little, if any, attention to the relationships of the people who will be working to accomplish that task.

To be successful, teams of diverse membership have to carefully consider relationships. It is a lack of interest or understanding of its individuals that often creates obstacles for any team. In sharing with each other, it is helpful to have people share both personal and professional information about themselves. This process of disclosure helps build relationships. It assesses a person's cultural and technical skills as a member of the work team, and it gives the group a better sense of how to best use members' life experiences to accomplish the task.

You can start the process by having people share something about their name—its history, literal meaning, cultural significance, and so on. This simple exercise allows people to share personal history in a fairly safe and open way.

You can also discuss how people prefer to work and team characteristics they find useful and not useful. One way to do this is through a "norming exercise." Ask group members to talk, individually, about groups they've been a part of. They should share the qualities and characteristics they felt were effective about the groups as well as those that were ineffective. Then, ask individuals to identify two or three key norms or behaviors that are important to them when working on a team. Discuss these norms, and then consolidate them into a set of working norms or team behaviors. Some key norms a diverse group might need to address are:

- How to address the leader
- Feedback
- Language issues
- Courtesy and expectations (timeliness, preparedness, and participation)
- Cultural values

Leadership in a Diverse Community

One of the first things that happens in team development is that leadership emerges. The initial leadership may not be the leadership structure ultimately decided on by the work community. However, someone—or a few people—will emerge as leaders early on to begin to focus the group and move it forward.

Leadership Qualities Valued by U.S. Organizations

Traditionally, team leadership has been hierarchical. We've allocated formal power based on title, seniority, or position. In keeping with tradition, U.S. organizational culture has recognized certain characteristics as "leadership" qualities:

- Rugged individualism (the maverick, doing it alone)
- "I did it my way" (popularized by Frank Sinatra and creative, high-powered, entrepreneurial business people)
- Played-down status (use of first name; we even refer to our presidents as "Bill" and "George")
- Initiative (a "self-starter," one who needs and wants little direction or supervision)
- Direct, honest statements
- No fear of speaking up (no shrinking violets)
- Persistence (don't take no for an answer)
- "A deal is a deal" mentality

These leadership qualities are very effective in an environment that values these principles. If you're in a leadership role with a diverse work community, however, not everyone may value these qualities. There may be miscommunication and misunderstanding due to people operating from different sets of assumptions.

Leadership Qualities Valued by Those Outside the United States

Compare what we assume to be "correct" in this country with some of the values held by organizations outside of the United States:

- Use of formal titles (as a show of respect)
- Respect for authority and social order
- Indirect language and thought patterns reflecting both respectful behavior and socialized cultural cognition and language patterns
- Group orientation, conformity

As we focus more on employee involvement and self-directed organizations and strive to make sure we're a viable entity in the global market, leadership requires new skills.

Leadership Values in a Diversity Context

We define successful team leadership in terms of creating and maintaining effective and productive teams. But a more diverse range of leadership styles is possible if we measure successful leadership based on a work community's output rather than on the leader's specific personality characteristics. Significantly, such a practice provides more opportunities for people of differing cultural backgrounds to be successful leaders.

Employee involvement and empowerment are two of the key thrusts we see in organizational strategies designed for the nineties. Both carry diversity implications. Given the cultural and associated style differences in today's work community, employees can be expected to behave in a wide variety of ways—and team leaders, therefore, need to be open and flexible. For instance, they need to understand that employees may see "involvement" differently if they are operating from a cultural model that expects a structured, authority-driven, leadership model. Similarly, employees might feel empowered in their work roles and still interact with leadership in a manner consistent with their conditioned respect for authority.

Once leadership emerges or is assigned, a team must have direction and structure. But exactly who defines that structure, sets the direction, or creates and facilitates the process for doing so, needs to be open and flexible. The group can determine what leadership works best for them. This doesn't mean that the leaders have less work than they would in the traditional hierarchical leadership model. Rather, it means that leading a diverse work community requires a new set of skills. Let's look at a few.

Leadership Skills

Know Thyself: Identify Your Team's Challenges and Strengths.
The leader must see that the group identifies both its strengths and challenges. That doesn't mean the leader has to be the one to facilitate this process. He or she just needs to make sure that the process occurs. In fact, the leader may want to be a participant and team member for this process because the leader's own strengths and challenges are a critical element in the group dynamics.

The facilitator can use a variety of different methods to help identify a work community's challenges and strengths. For instance, she or he can use testing instruments—personality, cognitive, or learning style indicators—as a way to identify and then discuss areas of differences, potential conflict, weak domains, and the group's strengths and opportunities.

A skillful team leader and/or facilitator doesn't use these tools to judge or devalue a person's preferences or the way a person does things. These tools, properly used, help to create structure, systems, and group norms that will make the most of what each member brings to the work group. Figure 5-1 is an example of a form that can be a quick and easy tool you can use to identify some of the diversity of values in a multicultural group.

Cross-Cultural Values Assessment: Work Styles. Each member of the work community should rate himself or herself on the continuum shown in Fig. 5-1, between the left and right columns, rating themselves on the likes, preferences, and orientations indicated. Each participant can

---

Indicate preferences between two where midpoint is neutral.

Want clear deadlines and expectations	Work better at own pace; renegotiate expectations as I go along
Change	Tradition; ritual
Focus on task	Focus on relationships
Succinct, content-driven communication	Process oriented, facilitative communication
Data-driven; analytical	Trust gut reaction to make decisions
Debate a variety of ideas	Avoid conflict, promote harmony
Assess self in relation to others	Success measured by effort and growth
Like structured, clearly defined tasks	Like open-ended questions, undefined process, and structure
Focus on individual	Focus on group

Figure 5-1. Cross-cultural work styles.

then compare ratings with others, using the similarities and differences of their value preferences as a vehicle for discussion of potential group dynamics around work style. The group should then begin to assess how these preferences will create challenges and opportunities for the work community as a whole.

Once the group identifies its challenges and strengths, it has the building blocks it needs to develop structures for how team members will work as a group, how they'll get their tasks done, and how they will achieve their goals.

Don't Get Lost: Defining Structure and Setting Direction

Discussing the group's challenges and strengths helps you to define the structure of the work team. This structure should be designed to make the most of your group's strengths.

General Electric Aircraft Engines used the cell concept for its team structure. Each workstation team was fully cross-trained, and each cell team decided for itself the best way for the group to structure its rotations and job assignments. The rewards have been flexible coverage of a variety of tasks, individual and team growth and learning, and good cross-access between jobs.

A group's structure can be defined in many different ways. For some, the structure may be so flexible it hardly seems like structure at all. Others may prefer to have clearly delineated roles and tasks. The important thing is that it be the most effective structure for the particular group.

Roles are an important aspect of structure. Again, in some cases, every team member will have clear lines of accountability, hierarchy, job description, and so on. In others, the roles can be more flexible, with overlapping responsibilities, sharing of power and leadership, and loosely defined tasks.

Most groups vacillate between structured and unstructured arrangements, depending on the particular roles in question or on larger issues such as reorganization. In a diverse environment, it's important to recognize that employees will have differing levels of comfort with structured and unstructured roles. Sometimes the group will be able to accommodate individual preference. Sometimes a group can establish roles based on each member's strengths and still leave room for development and growth. Clearly, it's to the team's benefit to allocate roles and responsibilities so that members will be most successful.

Regardless of a team's ability to accommodate individuals with structured or unstructured roles, each team member has to have a clear understanding of the group's expectations and how performance is being measured. If each member has this information, she or he can be successful regardless of whether roles are unstructured or changing or somewhat structured. And if each member of the work community is successful, the team will be successful.

Setting direction should also develop from the work group's structure, challenges, and strengths. If the group is newly formed or in transition, it may not have a clearly defined task, mission, or goals. It's worth spending time creating a mission statement, defining expectations and tasks, and setting goals—especially in a diverse community where individuals bring with them a wide variety of assumptions and expectations.

Creating a mission statement, among other things, helps avoid time-consuming and potentially costly misunderstandings. Also, in the course of developing it, the group has to wrestle with a lot of important questions:

1. How well do we understand our task and how it fits into the larger objectives of the organization?
2. What impact does our group activity have on other employees and on our customers?
3. What principles and values are we promoting personally and organizationally?
4. How does this group's mission relate to the organization's mission or vision statement?
5. What personal interests and needs, or group strengths and challenges, do we have that may influence how we approach our task?

To create a mission statement, define the group's task(s), and set goals, you should be sure to involve as many individuals as possible, if not everyone in the work community. The process should include opportunities for discussing personal and organizational needs, challenges, and strengths; from these exchanges, similar and diverse perspectives will emerge.

Ideally, the process of creating a mission statement should result in an easily referenced document that can be shared with other teams throughout the organization, when appropriate. That is, the mission statement can serve as a tool for making links and building partnerships with other teams, or as a basis for collaborations or coordination of tasks or initiatives, or as a check that the team's business strategies and goals are consistent with the mission of the work community.

As suggested above, just going through the process of devising a mission statement has its rewards. Community relationships are formed when people wrestle together with issues, listen to each other's points of view, and look for common ground.

Archaeology 101: Creating a Team Culture

When you create a work community by building a team environment, you're actually developing a culture. Within the boundaries of a work community, you are establishing roles, defining tasks and directions, and building structure and systems. The group's norms, values, and expectations of how they'll relate to one another is what cements the pieces together.

Team culture is a structure of experience that gives individuals

- A sense of who people are
- A sense of belonging
- A sense of behavior and an understanding of what they should be doing
- A set of problem-solving tools for daily coping in a particular environment
- The capacity and mechanisms for transmitting coping skills and knowledge

If a team environment values diversity, the group will mesh all of its members' experiences and values. If the group shapes its community culture collectively, then the environment will be inclusive and supportive for all members.

In most cultural groups, individuals often are unaware of how many aspects of their culture they have learned unconsciously. They have so absorbed informal norms of behavior associated with their culture that they don't even notice them or distinguish their behavior as coming from their culture. Outsiders to the culture, however, notice these characteristics right away.

An effective team culture cannot be rigid. As group members develop and personnel changes, the culture should also develop and change. A rich and exciting work community is one in constant flux, one in which dynamic and creative tension exists as new individuals are assimilated into the group.

Once developed, the community needs to be maintained. One way to do this is through formal or informal ritual. Rituals may include catching up on news at Friday staff meetings, throwing birthday parties on each team member's birthday, hanging out in the cafeteria together for morning coffee, or having family outings. Less formal ways of maintaining the work unit are meeting to chat over lunch, touching base in the hallways, or helping a group member rearrange his or her office. These behaviors and interactions connect and reconnect relationships within your community.

Uncovering Your Team Members' Cultural Norms

Some of the ways to start finding out about individuals' cultures and the norms they have incorporated into their behavior, whether or not they are fully aware of it, are demonstrated in their

- Greetings
- Dress and appearance
- Breaks, mealtimes, food
- Timeliness, time needs
- Relationships with coworkers
- Definition of family and roles of family members
- Primary values
- Beliefs
- Celebrations

The Middle Ages

The Middle Cycle (To Be Confused with Midlife Crisis!)

Once a group has determined its strengths and weaknesses, defined its structure, set direction, and established a community culture, it's in its "middle cycle." Just like people in "real life," if the group hasn't set a solid foundation, it will probably have trouble in the middle cycle.

Even if a work community has done a great job at establishing its foundation, though, members still need to be careful not to lose momentum or focus in the middle cycle. Like all growth and development processes, there are changing issues and challenges to face at each developmental phase.

Support and Maintenance of
Work Communities

Work communities are a microcosm of life. That's why we can guarantee that as group members go about their roles and tasks, they are bound to come across stumbling blocks, obstacles, and challenges. In specific terms, these can range from a shortage of important production material, a computer system crash, or a hardship or loss occurring in a team member's personal life.

As group members struggle with these challenges, the work community will struggle to determine and follow through on its support role. For some work communities, providing support will be easier than in others. The particular community culture, as well as the triggering event, generally determines how easy or difficult the job will be. If, for example, the community culture is one that focuses mainly on work activities, then providing resources or sharing work responsibilities when called on may come naturally. On the other hand, such a group may see personal issues as being outside their concern or capacity to address.

Here is an example of how a group might compartmentalize its responses to individual crisis within the group:

In a very family-oriented work community—the group held family picnics, had child care on the premises, and so on—one worker in the group had a son with health problems. The group rallied around her, delivering a computer and modem to her house so that she could work from home. Her coworkers covered much of her on-site responsibilities.

At the same time, there was a sales team member in the group who had good sales numbers but was struggling to master the new automated ordering and tracking system. It caused customer problems when the orders were incorrect, entered late, or tracked incorrectly, which happened as he was learning the system. Whereas the team had pulled together to support the woman whose family crisis had created performance issues for her, they felt the sales team member just couldn't keep up in a changing environment. They made no effort to provide extra training or to explore alternative ways he might process the sales forms to reduce errors.

The reality is that, whether home- or work-related challenges, all crises affect team members' productivity. How the work community deals with such issues will set a tone for the environment. Members will share or not share information, request or not request help, based on whether they feel they will be supported or rejected by the work community. The danger is that team members in a nonsupportive environment will be reluctant to ask questions, ask for help, or communicate openly. This may cost the team in mistakes, productivity, scheduling, and, ultimately, the erosion of the relationships that bind the community together.

Assessment and Feedback

For a team to be successful, it must figure out whether it is accomplishing its task or tasks effectively. It must also provide a feedback mechanism so that members have the opportunity to adjust behavior or performance to be more in line with goals. Performance assessment is especially valuable in a diverse community where there's a greater chance that people will have divergent expectations and perceptions about a task or project. The assessment process should reinforce the role and task expectations established in the beginning cycle.

Formal performance evaluation is one type of assessment. Organizations usually give performance evaluations annually or biannually. In many cases, they're connected to promotion and salary issues. If this is the only type of assessment an organization does, people are likely to approach them with trepidation and anxiety. It's not exactly relaxing to know your whole livelihood is connected to only one conversation on performance record. That's not conducive to creating a relaxing assessment environment. Performance evaluations of this kind are often not interactive and often do not include assessments of the employee's activities as a team member, for example, which require the ability to cooperate and collaborate and to communicate clearly.

Hand in hand with assessment should be a feedback mechanism. Without productive and effective feedback, assessments, whether of an individual worker or a team, have limited value. For example, it's not unusual, even in Fortune 500 companies, for an organization to conduct a survey or assessment, and then another a few years later, and not report back to employees about the results. For workers, these surveys seem like a waste of time and money. They're futile, they say, without any helpful feedback.

Feedback can be a delicate process in any circumstances, but in a diverse work community it can be fraught with complexity. Many things can affect how the team members receive and give feedback: culture, style, experiential differences with authority, roles, public personae, and so on. One person's constructive criticism can be another's nightmare.

Some members of a work community may prefer to get feedback in front of the team. They feel it allows for the input of a variety of perspectives and lets them get feedback as a situation occurs. For them, getting immediate and "real-time" feedback means that the feedback is clearer and tied directly to specific behaviors or situations.

Other members of the work community, however, taking feedback as chastisement or humiliation rather than a supportive and helpful discussion, may not be able to process it in a public setting. They need to hear it away from the group. These differences make it important to find out what form of feedback is most helpful to each team member.

Feedback also needs to be balanced between positive reinforcement of what is going well and notations of areas where growth or challenge is called for. The best way to sabotage morale is to provide only negative feedback. Not only can this kind of feedback be demoralizing, it can also be confusing. It only points out what the worker should *not* be doing, or what is *not* working. It doesn't point people in the right direction or supply building blocks for future progress.

Feedback is best when it is mutual. Even if a feedback discussion is between a manager and employee, the conversation should include areas of skill and growth for both of them, not only the employee. They should discuss what the manager is doing well to support the employee and what ways the manager is making it difficult for the employee to be successful. This exchange promotes mutual responsibility, support, and involvement and empowers both.

The More Things Change...

Development and Growth

No group remains static. The ideal work community supports and provides for the development of its members. Clearly, member development can enhance performance and skills that in turn may increase team productivity and profitability. Development also has an added bonus: It usually increases members' enthusiasm and commitment.

In a diverse community, not paying attention to development can create serious problems, as in the following example:

In one organization, lack of attention to employee development caused problems with employee morale and trust of management.
Employees saw, time and time again, people brought in from the outside to fill higher positions. The organization didn't try to train the employees they already had or to help them grow. Some employees had been in the same job for 20 years.

Compounding the problem was the fact that the industry overall was not traditionally a field that had lots of diversity. Because there was no team development, most diversity was found at the lower-level jobs in the organization. The traditional, dominant population filled the more senior positions.

Eventually, this dynamic became an equal employment opportunity concern, with all of the price tags—conflict and confusion, anger and frustration—that usually accompany such situations. Any sense of team community became a thing of the past. The overall productivity and efficiency of the team became a concern.

Realistically, of course, increasing a team's productivity and profitability may mean increasing the team membership. Some work communities do a wonderful job of creating a community environment in the beginning cycle but cannot seem to make the transition through to include new members. Successful teams will always experience some level of growing pains. But if the work communities haven't established a culture with an inclusion element to introduce new members, the team can begin to deteriorate.

One diversity council had existed for about a year. Their meetings were characterized by cheerful banter, enthusiasm, cooperation, and a sense of community. Then, a few new members were accepted onto the council in liaison positions with other groups. Suddenly, the tone of the meetings changed. Rather than the positive atmosphere demonstrated up to that point, there was bickering, resistance, absenteeism, and lack of direction. When the original group was finally pushed on what the real issue was and what had changed, they stated that they didn't trust the new people. They didn't know where they were coming from and why they were there. Most of all, they said the new folks just didn't understand what the council was about, so they were unable to add any value.

Of course, these comments said more about the preexisting team community than they said about the new members. The team clearly did not have a vehicle for including and incorporating new members into the group. There were no methods for information transfer, the natural shifting and flux of accommodating and assimilating new members, or flexible boundaries allowing for growth. The substance of the team's cohesion—the glue they felt they needed to stick together—became a pattern of excluding any other than the existing community members.

In such a case, even when the original team had a diverse membership, it was not, in essence, a diverse community. A diverse community, one in which diversity is recognized, valued, and used to best advantage, must be an *inclusive* environment. Otherwise, the group has just created a team culture that is as isolated, as resistant to change and growth, and as limited by its membership as any traditional environment.

Not Necessarily the End

The Closing

The "closing" is not necessarily the termination of the group or team. The closing may be the completion of any major project or task, the loss of a group member, or any other significant change in team structure, mission, or orientation.

Transition and Change

Transition and change are uncomfortable even when the change is desirable and beneficial. It's stressful to adjust to new frameworks, shift from the familiar, do things that aren't habitual.

People deal with transition and change very differently; in a diverse community, these differences may be even greater. Cultural perspectives on "endings" and change vary. Members will react according to their perspectives. If the closing or change includes risks, it will affect members' anxiety levels depending on their socioeconomic backgrounds and familial status.

The role of the work community in transition is to manage the process in a careful way. Members need to maintain the highest possible productivity throughout and minimize unnecessary anxiety and stress in the group. Information flow and communication are critically important at this time. Change generally spawns rumors and speculation. Ideally, the team can be a clearinghouse of available information and a vehicle for sifting through the reams of rumors to identify facts.

In addition to providing information and fact-finding, a team can provide support, balance and continuity. As individual team members, or the group itself, go through transition, other aspects of the work community will go on, and they provide structure and grounding. It is important, therefore, to continue to do the things that the group normally does. Many members will find it helpful if the rituals of break, celebrations, or work patterns remain the same as much as possible.

If the overall group is going through changes—of its task, mission, or even a relocation—the focus of the closing cycle should be on making a successful transition to the new. The team must acknowledge what it is leaving behind or letting go of before it can bridge to envisioning the new. The work community then explores what it is taking with it into the new setting—those things that will not change. For many, only then can they create a vision for the future and focus on it in a positive and productive manner.

Losses: Dealing with Change

It is important to identify what changes the transition will cause and to discuss together how these dimensions will affect both individual members and the work community as a whole. Some of the "losses" people will feel occur in their

- Work space or environment
- Systems and structures
- Vision of the future
- Relationships
- Identity

The Rumor Rap

It is important to deal with rumors. Some concerns employees might have can be brought out into the open by asking the following:

- What rumors have you heard about the transition? (List all no matter how ridiculous.)
- What do you know for a fact to be true about the change?
- What do you know for a fact *not* to be true about the change?

For the Record: Record Keeping and Evaluation

As part of the closing cycle, the team should evaluate what went well and what members should do differently if they perform the task or a similar task again. This not only ties up loose ends for the work community, it provides data for the next time this team or another team approaches the same task.

One fund-raising team held an annual fund-raising event. In the past this team had brought in almost all of the operating budget for the organization. Because the organization's financial stability would be threatened if the event failed financially, there was a certain amount of stress associated with being on the fund-raising team and coordinating the huge event. The team leadership tried to provide continuity, but the work was demanding on members, and turnover each year was high. Eventually, leadership had to struggle to find new members to join the team.

One year, leadership decided to hold an additional meeting after the actual fund-raising event. Its purpose was to catalog the structure used to coordinate the event, evaluate what worked well, and record suggestions for the following year. They followed this wrapup meeting with a small party to celebrate their hard work. The following year, they lost no members. And there was a waiting list to be on the team.

Closure was very important to this team. It served to acknowledge the hard work put in by members and provided an evaluation vehicle. That way, members felt the event wouldn't be "the same thing all over again." Instead, they felt they were starting ahead of the game, making progress, moving forward, and improving the process. This helped boost morale, but it also gave team members an opportunity to reflect on their learnings and experiences.

It just goes to show that there should always be closure within the team when members complete tasks or meet goals. As the fund-raising team discovered, celebrations and/or acknowledgments do wonders for morale. These rituals can also cement the relationships team members built and solidify the things they learned from their team experience.

Celebrating group accomplishments can also be a way to prepare for the next step in the process. A simple yet effective exercise is to schedule a potluck or meal or snack event with a diversity theme. The group can be asked to generate data about their successes as a team and/or as individuals. This information serves as a basis for discussing next steps for the team, the task, or the individuals involved.

Team's successes need to be made known to others outside the group. This reinforces team members' individual value in particular and the value of diversity in general. (But, as already mentioned, publicizing successes needs to be handled with sensitivity for diverse values and perspectives in the group.)

As we have made clear in this chapter, we need to think about *team* in a whole new way. We need a new vision, one that has an expanded understanding of winning and success, one that focuses on relationships and processes in the interpersonal and organizational worlds, as well as the larger environment, one that promotes cooperation and collaboration rather than antagonism—whether between individual workers, units, or teams within the organization, or between organizations here and abroad, trying to succeed in a competitive global market. We need a vision of a team that balances assimilation and accommodation, that recognizes that a place where people have fun, feel cared about and supported, know they're viewed as valuable and important, and feel trust and *are* trusted, is an environment in which everyone in the organization can be creative, innovative, committed, and productive.

In short, we need a vision of team building that includes the creation of community.

6

A Cultural Rapport Model

Fostering Harmony in the Workplace

Percy W. Thomas

Introduction

In discussing the cultural rapport model, I will concentrate on how the model relates to improving cross-cultural relationships within organizations. The model itself is a communications paradigm (see Fig. 6-1). Effective application of the model will allow individuals to transcend the complications of cross-cultural, intercultural, and intracultural communications; it will also set the stage for the development of productive relationships between culturally diverse employees.

Building effective relationships, or rapport, is at the heart of all diversity issues and is a bottom-line economic concern of business, government, industry, and academia. Twenty years of studying, teaching, and seeking to understand human reactions to differences of all sorts has led me to three conclusions: (1) People lack the communication skills, sensitivity, understanding, flexibility, and trust necessary to establish effective relationships; (2) many reactions to people who are culturally, racially, ethnically, and sexually different are based on irrational fears and nonsensical stereotypes; and (3) people do not know

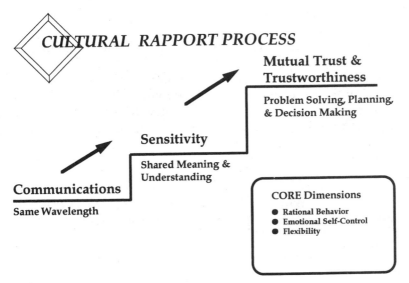

Figure 6-1 Cultural rapport model. © Percy W. Thomas, Sc. D.

how to deal with their irrational fears, attitudes, beliefs, and behavior as they relate to inappropriate and counterproductive responses to diversity.

The characteristics associated with the conclusions I have drawn operate in many organizations and prevent some managers from fully using all the talent available to them. As a result, companies lose millions of dollars "chasing the wind" by settling employee grievances, EEO complaints, and expensive class-action suits, and, furthermore, they lose their competitive edge in the marketplace. The costs that stem from maintaining a culturally insensitive environment can be staggering. Many studies show that employee dissatisfaction costs the company large sums of money. Increased use of sick leave, high absenteeism, and simple anomie among workers are often indicators of a culturally insensitive work environment.

Organizations striving to have more productive and rewarding work environments for all their employees must spend time creating an organizational culture that is conducive to these goals. Organizations should therefore encourage hiring people from different cultural orientations, races, experiences, and lifestyles and then work with the employees to establish effective working relationships. Management in forward-looking organizations must make clear that it expects people working in the organization to develop rapport by building trust, dignity, and respect for one another. Organizations send a strong message, internally and externally, by writing cultural diversity into their mission and vision statements. The cultural rapport model stresses building rapport as an organizational intervention strategy that can be used to improve multicultural interactions. It is intended to assist organizations and individuals to establish productive working relationships and to transform their organizations into cultures of diversity.

The model focuses on those aspects of communications that appear to transcend all cultures:

- Rational behavior (taking personal responsibility for managing all unwanted irrational behavior and fears associated with "loaded" situations)
- Circumstances and phenomena arising out of ethnic and cultural differences
- Emotional self-control when exposed to cultural differences
- Maintaining a degree of flexibility
- Being on the same wavelength
- Sensitivity
- Mutual trust and trustworthiness between employees.

The model has a core dimension and three levels. As indicated in Fig. 6-1, the core dimension has three components: rational behavior, emotional self-control, and flexibility. These levels are broken down to trust/trustworthiness, sensitivity, and same wavelength, each one having its corresponding subset: planning, problem solving, and decision making; understanding and shared meaning; and communications. It is hierarchical and must be implemented in ascending order to obtain maximum effectiveness. Once the third level (mutual trust) is reached, however, maintaining rapport involves all levels of the model—that is, the core dimensions become inextricably connected and interdependent. If there is a breach at any level due to a malfunction in any component of the core dimension, irrational behavior may occur and cause serious damage to the relationship. Let's discuss the core dimensions in turn.

Rational Behavior

The practice of treating people differently based on their culture or ethnicity is sometimes conscious, but often it is unconscious. The behavior we display in reaction to a person from another culture has been learned over time. We have been conditioned to believe that what we learned about them is the truth, whether objectively so or not. As a consequence, our responses are often automatic and irrational. No place in life are automatic responses more prevalent than in relation to individual differences in the workforce. Women, minorities, and others are often affected by these automatic, irrational responses to their presence in the workforce, their sometimes different work styles, and their patterns of behavior. Newcomers, with their own way of seeing and doing things, are coming in contact and sometimes colliding with members of well-established, hierarchical, and, until recently, closed, white-male-dominated organizations.

When cultures collide in the workplace, it is often emotions and irrational behavior that dictate the way people treat each other. Most people react to cultural collisions spontaneously, without thinking. Further, most people believe that the way they respond to life events is beyond their control. It is as though their responses to things with which they are not familiar or not comfortable have a life of their own.

For these reasons, learning to think and behave rationally is the first step that needs to be addressed. This part of the model stresses personal responsibility for the way in which a person responds to differences in general and cultural differences in particular. Countering automatic responses requires *emotional self-control*, the second core dimension.

Emotional Self-Control

Human emotion is inextricably connected to the way people perceive individuals from other cultures. Depending on how people perceive events or behaviors of another culture, they may judge it to be a subculture or a counterculture; further, they may ascribe some devaluing meaning to the people and their mores, customs, and folkways. In doing so, they often experience an irrational emotional response toward the whole culture and its people. Irrational emotional responses can be connected to any person or event perceived as unfamiliar or different.

Human emotions are one of the most talked about and misunderstood of all our behavioral expressions, and, when associated with cultural differences, the subject becomes even more complex. *Emotion* is defined as "a state of excitement or perturbation, marked by strong feeling," and usually gives impulse toward a definite behavior. If the emotion is intense, there is some disturbance of intellectual function, a measure of dissociation, and a tendency toward irrational action.

Many pay little or no attention to the notion that they can control their emotions. When it comes to responding to people from another culture, few even recognize that the emotions they feel are the result of their cultural conditioning. Their response is nothing more than learned behavior. A person might feel unable to control it—that the behavior is automatic and, as such, not subject to reflection or change. The notion that we can't control our emotions in confronting cultural situations makes it easy to blame our own behavior on the person who is culturally different. Not acknowledging that we can control our emotions also makes it easy to retain prejudicial, bigoted, and discriminatory attitudes and assign the source of our attitudes and beliefs to some unknown origin, as if our emotions are the result of magic.

It is difficult to establish effective relationships with people we hold negative attitudes and beliefs about. We relieve ourselves of the responsibility for our actions and negative responses toward other cultures and give ourselves rational justification for continuing our closed-minded thinking, comfortable ethnocentric behaviors, irrational thinking patterns, offensive communication styles, and inflexible ways of interacting. In short, we continue to demonstrate our cultural incompetence. To overcome cultural incompetence, everyone in the workplace will have to work at becoming *culturally competent.*

Closed-minded, emotionally charged, irrational thinking on the part of women, minorities, gays, lesbians, physically challenged, and others about the traditional, well-established, white-male power group constitutes a real barrier to harmony and productivity in the workplace, let alone to the possibility of developing cultural competence. On the other side, many white males, with their negative perceptions of these members of the workforce, also create barriers to developing an emotionally healthy work environment.

An emotionally healthy, multicultural work environment—where employees perceive that they can contribute to and benefit from the success of the organization—can come only from the experience of positive interactions in the workforce. To that end, it is critical that each person understand that managing diversity means understanding emotional reactions. Negative emotional responses to those who are different from us are at the heart of why diversity is creating such a stir in organizations across America.

Many of us have little knowledge about how our emotions trigger spontaneous reactions to differences. All we know is that we react to various situations positively, negatively, or neutrally. We know even less about how emotions positively or negatively affect our companies. In the past, creating a healthy emotional environment has not been considered important to the way most organizations conduct their work.

When our responses to cultural, ethnic, or gender differences are negative and emotionally charged, we run the risk of offending or, worse, not recognizing the potential growth and benefit that can emerge when diverse elements come together.

Peter Senge in *The Fifth Discipline* (Doubleday, New York, 1990) supports the notion that diverse elements come together to form positive results that may not have been possible standing in isolation. Senge states:

> In engineering, when an idea moves from an invention to an innovation, diverse "component technologies" come together. Emerging from isolated developments in separate fields of research, these components gradually form an "ensemble of technologies" that are critical to each other's success. Until this ensemble forms, the idea, though possible in the laboratory, does not achieve its potential in practice.

Negative responses to cultural differences work against the coming together of an "ensemble of diverse employees" and the establishing of cultural rapport.

The problem in the work environment is that many employees do not understand that they *choose* their emotional reactions to people and things. Their choices are based on behavioral conditioning stemming from their personal and interpersonal orientations. Thus, understanding how to control emotions and irrational behavior regarding cultural differences is an essential step to being effective in a multicultural workplace where all types of differences abound. This understanding is also essential to establishing cultural rapport and bringing into practice an effective multicultural ensemble of creative and productive workers.

Why is it necessary to emphasize emotions in relation to cultural diversity? It is important to understand that emotions are inextricably connected to our responses to what we see, hear, taste, smell, and physically feel regarding other cultures. The same holds true for our responses to individual differences and changes taking place within our own culture. And so it might be helpful here to take a few seconds to examine the makeup of an emotion.

Maxie Maultsby, Jr., psychiatrist, author, professor, and chairman of the Department of Psychiatry at Howard University School of Medicine, depicted an emotion as being made up of three components: (1) our perceptions (what we see, hear, and so on), (2) our thoughts (only the ones we believe), and (3) our feelings. When we have an emotion, we first perceive (that is, see, hear, physically feel, and so on) something. Next, we think and believe something about our perceptions. Finally, we have a gut feeling caused by our thoughts. All three combine in what he defines as emotion.

How does this work as it relates to exposure to people from other cultures?

First, Helen hears Maria's Spanish accent.
   Second, Helen thinks to herself (and believes): "There is no way that she can do this job; she can't speak English. My customers will stop calling for deliveries, and I will lose business."
   Third, these negative conclusions about Maria's accent make Helen feel skeptical about Maria's ability to do the job.
   Hence, Helen decides not to hire Maria.

The above example shows how Helen's thoughts and beliefs about an event give rise to her feelings. From a cultural perspective, it is important to note that Maria's accent (1) did not directly cause Helen to feel skeptical (3). It was her *thoughts* and beliefs about the accent as it related to her business that made her feel skeptical. If she had different thoughts about Maria's accent, she might have felt differently about Maria and thus behaved differently toward her.

If you were reared in America, you have probably been in Helen's shoes many times dealing with people who are different. Most of the time you were probably unaware of why you responded in the manner that you did. After a while, you might even have felt uncomfortable with your decision, or had afterthoughts like, "Maria was such a lovely person—too bad she didn't work out." But your beliefs would have prevented you from hiring her. Even with such second thoughts about Maria, Helen is helpless to do anything about her feelings—or so she thinks.

What Helen needs is a process to assist her in thinking about multicultural diversity in the workplace. Without a process for sorting through the millions of cultural habits and biases that she has developed over the course of her life as a result of her acculturation in a certain region of America, Helen responds in automatic ways. She lacks the information she needs, but that can be remedied. What she will also need is personal flexibility.

Flexibility

The final component of the core dimension is *flexibility*. Without the capacity to be flexible, it is unlikely that you will benefit from or avoid the unpleasantries associated with cultural conflict. *To be flexible* means to bend without breaking, to be easily persuaded to look at another view, to be adjustable to change; put negatively, it means not to be rigid or intractable.

To successfully apply the cultural rapport process model in your personal life and in your organizational environment, you will first need to determine whether you are flexible or inflexible. You will also want to determine whether your organization's culture is flexible or inflexible. Inflexible people and organizations will have great difficulty in using this model. Personal and institutional flexibility are necessary to make the model work. To deal with differences effectively, people must be flexible enough to allow themselves an opportunity to learn from the behavior of others. Being flexible within the context of the model means making every effort to see the world as others do.

If you determine that your organizational culture is inflexible, you should seek to change it by creating a culture that values and thrives on being flexible. Inflexible organizations are sluggish and slow to recognize opportunities, and managers who are culturally competent and have experience managing diverse work groups know the importance of being pliable.

At the same time, many otherwise competent managers have difficulty being flexible in a multicultural environment. The thought of having to adjust their management style to accommodate the myriad differences in people who report to them is emotionally disturbing. In the context of diversity, I define *flexible* as being open to and capable of making changes in your personal and professional behavior for the purpose of understanding the perspectives of others and seeing the world from their viewpoint. Further, being flexible has to do with one's willingness to suspend personal judgment about others and seek to identify them in the way *they* wish to be identified.

Let's turn now to the three levels of cultural rapport indicated in Fig. 6-1.

Same-Wavelength Communications

When an organization or community is made up of many people from different educational and cultural backgrounds, simple differences in terminology can create communication problems. Diverse groups of people in the workforce bring different lifestyle behavior to the workplace, behavior that is often in conflict with traditional values and norms of the organization. For some, it boggles the mind just to think of having to communicate with groups of single parents, gays and lesbians, the physically challenged, and the learning disabled, to name a few, all coming to the table with their own terminology, language, and communication patterns.

In organizations as in other settings, when cultural, racial, sexual, ethnic, and gender differences are introduced, emotions are heightened, and irrational fears proliferate. To uncover why so much negative emotion and fear is associated with coming into contact with cultural differences, we have to begin with an exploration of self. And the exploration of self begins with establishing where we are *mentally* in relationship to another human being. Are we on the same wavelength? For the first step in attempting to bridge the gap between two very different people is to first find areas where they are in synchronization—or on the same wavelength. Think about trying to listen to classical music while tuned into a hard rock radio station, for example.

The same wavelength from a cultural communications perspective refers to the perceptions, experiences, beliefs, attitudes, values, and expectations of both the sender and receiver in any communication exchange. Our perceptions, experiences, beliefs, attitudes, values, and expectations are shaped by our acculturation. To a degree, all of us are placed on "automatic pilot" by our culture. Although it is useful not to have to question every single act of daily living, being on automatic pilot with respect to the way we look at those different from ourselves makes it difficult for us to get on their wavelength.

We have learned a lot from our own culture that we cannot see—it is buried in our subconscious mind. And others cannot see it either. Yet, what we have learned and accepted as truth at a subconscious level is the power behind everything we say and do pertaining to our reactions to cultural differences. Assuming this to be true, it is easy to understand why it is so difficult for people to connect with each other. In a sense we all suffer from intercultural and intracultural blindness. It is difficult, for example, to get a clear picture of ourselves or others from an internal-personal, external-interpersonal, and environmental-organizational perspective.

When people are reared in the same culture, however, certain cues, customs, behaviors, communication styles, and ways of understanding their environment are shared. This commonality allows them to get on the same wavelength quickly and with minimal distraction and output of energy. Lacking those shared experiences obviously makes it difficult to get on the same level—a whole host of cultural cues we may not be consciously aware of are missed or misinterpreted.

This is particularly true in organizations where the newcomers bring their own behaviors and languages from their countries of origin. It is foolish to think that these newcomers can or should immediately adopt the "American way," even though it is the "American way" that has created this rich mix of people with high hopes of achieving the "American dream" regardless of their race, ethnicity, gender, national origin, or sexual orientation.

	Other	Self
Concept of organization		
Delegation of authority		
Patterns of superior and/or subordinate relationships		
Patterns of decision making and problem solving		
Attitudes toward dependence, independence, and interdependence		
Concept of time: past, present, and future		
Roles in relationship to status by age, sex, class, and occupation		
Patterns of handling emotions		
Preference for competition or cooperation		

Figure 6-2 Aspects of culture conditioning outside of our primary awareness.

To understand what is meant by the many characteristics about people that lie outside of our awareness, examine the list in Fig. 6-2 and place a checkmark next to an item you can safely say you know about people with whom you come in contact in the workplace, and then place another checkmark for the things you know about yourself.

How did you do on this exercise? If you are like many people who interact in the workplace, you probably never considered these things when initiating communications with your colleagues, nor did you think it important to do so. Most of us are not conscious of how our attitudes, beliefs, and values about the behavior patterns, management techniques, and other concepts that appear on the list affect our interactions and relationships. Yet these are the very things that get in the way of establishing effective relationships, block communications, result in cultural collisions, and pose serious barriers to our getting on the same wavelength.

Wavelength Barriers

It is important that we get on the same wavelength to begin the process of establishing rapport and to participate in an effective communication exchange. Let's look more closely at the barriers to getting on the same wavelength with others who appear to be different from ourselves:

Personal barriers:

- Language
- Dress
- Appearance
- Identity
- Age
- Sexual orientation
- Time orientation
- Personal style

Organizational barriers:

- Mission statement
- Vision statement
- Rules and regulations
- Company policies
- Informal communication networks
- Socialization protocol
- How employees get promoted
- How employees get rewarded
- How employees get fired

Ask yourself this question: Do I have strong negative reactions to people who speak a different language, dress differently, look different, are of a different age, different sexual orientation, different time orientation, and/or different personal style? Do I have a similar reaction to people who are out of step with me on the items that appear on the organizational list above? If your response is yes to both, then you have made the point to yourself. You know that these items are important barriers to overcome if you expect to engage in successful cross-cultural interactions. If some of you still have doubts as to whether these items reflect true barriers to getting on the same wavelength, check your reactions to the following examples:

- An African-American female fired from her job as desk clerk at a major hotel chain for wearing her hair in corn-row braiding

- Negative references made about people working in government and corporations across the nation because they speak in dialects or with accents ("I can't understand a thing she said"; "They can't even speak English—how could they possibly get a job here?"; "She obviously comes from a culturally deprived background.")

These examples are just the tip of the iceberg regarding wavelength barriers. Moreover, they reflect serious personal inadequacies that prevent us from being effective in our human interactions with individuals who are culturally different.

The Relationship of Sensitivity to Shared Meaning and Mutual Understanding

Sensitivity is central to our developing understanding and shared meaning of events, situations, communications, and daily interactions involving cross-cultural relationships. It is absolutely a prerequisite to establishing effective relationships with people who use words or symbols and who exhibit behaviors that are not universally understood and shared. For example, do you understand the language and meanings conveyed in Langston Hughes's poem "Motto" (*The Langston Hughes Reader*, New York: George Braziller, 1958)? Read the poem in the left column and then my translation in the right column.

"I play it cool	I am calm
"and dig all jive	and understand all languages
"That's the reason	That's the reason
"I stay alive.	I am still living.
"My motto,	My motto,
"As I live and learn,	As I live and learn,
is:	is:
"Dig and be dug	Seek first to understand and be
"In return.	understood in return.

Those of you who are familiar with Langston Hughes's work, and particularly the language he uses, will have no problem getting on the same wavelength. Those of you who have sensitivity and openness may see his style of communication as different from what you are accustomed to and will actively seek to understand it and the messages it conveys. Others will be frustrated by its foreign quality and will endeavor to discredit it. Spend a few minutes analyzing the poem and your thoughts and feelings about it. Afterward, ask yourself the question: Am I sensitive to poetry that characterizes aspects of the lives of black Americans?

Sensitivity means "being susceptible to stimulation." In a more particular sense, it is "the ability to be affected by and respond to stimuli of low intensity, or to slight stimulus differences." With reference to diversity in general and cultural diversity in particular, to be sensitive means to have a low threshold for various types of cultural encounters. Another way of looking at sensitivity is to examine your level of tolerance for things and people different from you. If you have a high degree of intolerance for differences in general, you will more often than not be intolerant of cultural differences as well.

A lack of sensitivity toward the behavior, linguistic patterns, and cultural style of people from other cultures may cause you to be blind to your own behavior as it is directed toward, even offensive to, others. Insensitive people tend to see only that behavior in others that is markedly different from their own. This point emerged clearly in the analysis of data gathered in the "reverse stereotype" exercise (Fig. 6-3) that I use in my workshop on cultural diversity. The exercise is designed to elicit what you think you do that annoys individuals from different ethnic or lifestyle groups.

Although all groups had difficulty completing this exercise in the studies I have conducted, Caucasian males and females had the greatest difficulty and African-American and Hispanic participants appeared to have the least trouble—which points to the fact that with certain groups of people we pay very little attention to what we say and do that may be offensive to them. Thus, we are more likely to reduce the chance of establishing the rapport needed if we are to have effective communication.

Some of the responses from participants after completing this exercise were: "I don't know what I do to annoy others." "If I knew what I did to annoy somebody, I wouldn't do it" is a common comment from those who experience great difficulty with the exercise.

What did you experience in doing the exercise? What did you learn about yourself in relationship to the other groups on the list? What groups did you find that you have absolutely no actual experience with or in fact have never ever had any personal contact with? How difficult was this exercise for you to complete? What thoughts came to your mind? Did you have any angry feelings? Were you able to come up with comments under each category on the list?

The majority of people attending my workshops learn that they are quite ignorant of the cultural characteristics of groups other than their own. They also come to the realization that they have been relatively insensitive and closed to individuals and groups who either don't look like them or who don't reflect the behaviors with which they are most comfortable. Most minority group members who have taken my workshop have little or no difficulty completing the exercise. By contrast, white males and to a lesser degree white females,

List under each group designation below the things you occasionally do that you think annoy them.

Asian
_____
_____

African-American/black
_____
_____

Hispanic/Latino
_____
_____

Native American
_____
_____

Physically challenged
_____
_____

Gay/lesbian
_____
_____

Elderly
_____
_____

Women
_____
_____

White males
_____
_____

Figure 6-3 Reverse stereotype.

both of whom find the exercise difficult, have from time to time expressed anger and hostility at my including the exercise in the workshop. The point of the exercise is to demonstrate how little we know about our own behavior that offends and annoys other people. And if we don't know what we are doing to annoy others, how will we ever know what behaviors we need to change to establish rapport? The other point the exercise demonstrates is that groups in power rarely receive consequences for their behavior toward others; therefore, they don't receive the feedback necessary for them to become sensitive. Minorities, for years, have gotten instant feedback on their behavior, and in many cases it has been negative, frequently resulting in some form of personal trauma. Given their experiences, it is understandable that some groups have more data to report than others, and that some of us, because of our conditioning, are more sensitive and open than others. For everyone, the exercise generates a great deal of emotion.

The Culture Iceberg

Another way of understanding how important sensitivity is to establishing rapport is to acquire knowledge of how the levels of culture apply to human interactions. Sharon Ruhly, who modified the concepts presented by E. T. Hall in his now-famous book, *The Silent Language* (Doubleday, New York, 1991), provides a system for analyzing different levels of culture: technical, formal, and informal.

The "culture iceberg" is a system for analyzing different levels of a culture. Following Ruhly's model, the tip of the iceberg, that which is easily seen, represents the technical level of a culture. Communication is generally straightforward and little emotion is attached. Partially above sea level and partially below the tip of the iceberg is what she refers to as the "formal level of culture," which contains society's wide-ranging rules, many of which are learned through observation and/or trial and error. This level is associated with high emotion. At the informal level, the proportionately greater portion that is fully below sea level, behavior is automatic and learned largely through modeling and socialization. Here, emotional content is intense. Violations, for example, such as making inappropriate hand gestures, touching, initiating business conversation too soon after meeting, and so on, cause personal offense and engender strong reactions.

The iceberg analogy of a culture is particularly useful in that it accurately depicts the apparent and hidden aspects of a culture as people experience it in their daily interactions. Let's take a closer look at an iceberg: The human eye sees only that part of the ice that is out of the water. The larger part of the iceberg that is submerged below sea level remains out of our line of vision. The part that can be seen is what Ruhly calls the "technical level." Things we learn to master at the technical level of a culture (the alphabet, the numeric system, perhaps the fundamentals of jazz or various food-handling and sanitation practices, for example) are those that can be readily grasped or easily taught through a pedagogical process. They seldom are cause for cultural misunderstanding and, therefore, seldom trigger emotional responses that need to be dealt with. In other words, disagreements, misunderstandings, or differences in meaning can be resolved simply by providing additional technical information, relying on precepts that both parties are aware of and have a common understanding about. Employees in the high-tech industry, for example, are communicating at the technical level of culture when discussing data, software packages, information systems, or technological innovations in the workplace. As long as they can keep the communication strictly at the technical level, their interactions with others will be relatively smooth.

In transactions between two people from different cultural backgrounds and lifestyle experiences, however, it is difficult to hold communications to a technical level. Take the following situations:

Two people engage in a conversation at the technical level of culture (where they are on the same wavelength), and during the conversation one person begins to praise the other for his insight and abilities and then adds that he has already told several people in the company how outstanding that person is. Depending on that person's cultural values, this well-intentioned comment might be regarded as a breach of privacy, at the least, or a breach of deeply felt cultural norms against any form of boastfulness in public.

A man arrives at your office wearing a loin cloth, kilt, or some other garment not acceptable in the workplace. Both parties find themselves a bit uncomfortable with each other's attire. Beliefs and attitudes about the appropriateness of each one's appearance surfaces in their minds. Inevitably, emotions come into play. At this point they can no longer interact at the technical level of culture.

Learning to be sensitive to the values and norms of other cultures is key to workplace harmony.

Personal Characteristics of Sensitivity

- Ability to be open
- Ability to be tolerant
- Ability to suspend judgment

Let's discuss each.

Openness

Because of the strong impact of cultural conditioning, most of us develop a closed view of the world, a view that is reflected in our beliefs, attitudes, and values. These beliefs, attitudes, and values have been firmly established over time and have solidified into cultural *habits,* habits so strong that they put us on automatic pilot in the way we behave toward those culturally different from us. Furthermore, most of us believe that our cultural habits are the only *right* ones and that they cannot be changed. All of these factors militate against our being open to differences we find in those from other cultures.

To even begin the process of getting on the same wavelength with another, we must replace the habit of being closed to aspects of other cultures to being open to differences. In essence, we must become more flexible at the personal level.

Tolerance

The ability to tolerate differences is a key component of developing sensitivity and establishing effective cross-cultural relationships. Many Americans, having been acculturated in an *action* ("just do it") *mode,* lack tolerance for those who do not operate from that orientation. Many the new entrants into the workforce obviously bring with them the skills and behaviors that have worked effectively for them in their own cultures. It requires tolerance to allow them an opportunity to demonstrate how they do things and to observe whether, in fact, the way they do things is acceptable, unacceptable, or an improvement.

All too often we are so blinded by our cultural conditioning that we cannot see the merits of doing things differently. Being blind to the positive results that may occur from applying different ways, we quickly become intolerant and critical of newcomers and their behavior. If we develop the habit of tolerance for differences, we stand to find that out of differences may come positive economic and human gains in our society.

Tolerance has to do with the need to change our behavior at the interpersonal level of functioning. Since *interpersonal* implies the way individuals interact with each other, tolerance is critical to our getting on the same wavelength and developing sensitivity.

Judgment

Another critical interpersonal skill that must be developed if we are to be effective across cultures is the ability to suspend our judgments about the world around us. Cultural conditioning plays a huge role in our judgments about the things we observe and come in contact with. Our culture teaches us the meaning of the things we say and do. People from other cultures may assign different meanings and judgments to the things that our cultural experiences have led us to regard as "truth." Learning to suspend judgment is essential if we are to become sensitive to the many nuances involved in cross-cultural communications.

Issues in Sensitivity Training

Let's now look at some key issues that go into sensitivity training, starting with *beliefs and attitudes.*

Beliefs and attitudes as they relate to cultural sensitivity and cultural rapport issues are largely responsible for the negative emotions and irrational fears directed at those culturally different from ourselves.

Personal Beliefs

What are beliefs, and why do they exert so much power over us? Beliefs are "semipermanent mental units" we hold as a result of thinking about situations or events to the extent that it causes feelings, emotions, and behavior to surface even without the event's ever taking place (Maxie Maultsby, *Help Yourself to Happiness*, Institute for Rational Living, New York, 1975). Let's examine how beliefs operate in relation to culture.

A worker believes that an Asian manager will be appointed as her new supervisor. In her mind, she believes that Asians don't make good

managers and that she will therefore do poorly under this
manager. Despite all the information that has been disseminated to say
that the new manager is competent and skilled and the best person
for this job, the worker persists in her negative beliefs about the Asian
manager.

Is it surprising, then, to see this employee submit her resignation
before the new manager comes on board or, alternatively, to begin to
look for ways to undermine the authority of her new boss?

Beliefs in Relation to Culture

In every culture, beliefs are necessary to make life understandable for
its people. It is through the beliefs embedded in the culture that people
come to know the nature of their society and the meaning of most
things that occur within it. Because beliefs affect all relationships, they
necessarily become an issue among coworkers in the workplace. Beliefs
fuel our thinking, and, as stated earlier, our thoughts direct our behavior and our emotions. Given that throughout our nation and throughout the places where we work, we are becoming more ethnically,
racially, and culturally diverse, we are bound to come into contact with
those who hold divergent beliefs. It is the negative reaction to these
divergent beliefs that creates conflict and hampers organizational communication and effectiveness. Irrational behavior that stems from irrational beliefs about another person's culture, lifestyle, or customs
impairs our ability to be sensitive and open. Clearly, negative beliefs
block us from reaching the sensitivity, understanding, and shared
meanings we need to form productive relationships in the workplace.
The beliefs that individuals hold from their cultural conditioning often
determine whether they will or will not seek to establish rapport with
people from a different background or origin. Think about ideologies
we grow up with—such as Christianity, capitalism, communism,
racism, socialism, and democracy; each one constitutes a major force
that controls human behavior. No one will argue the importance of the
role that beliefs have played in the development of civilization. The
power of beliefs is that most people behave in accordance with them,
whether their beliefs have a positive or negative impact.

Negative Beliefs about Cultures

Negative beliefs about cultures abound. They range anywhere from
beliefs about food, dress, and child-rearing practices to age, sexual orientation, religion, and business practices. Holding onto negative

beliefs about another culture prevents us from ever getting on the same wavelength because it locks us into a way of responding before we evaluate the facts. As stated before, strongly held beliefs become so fixed and real in our mind that often there is no need for an external event to validate them.

Interestingly, everything said about negative beliefs holds true for strongly held positive beliefs. All strongly held beliefs result in strong behavioral responses. Positive beliefs about other cultures result in positive behavior toward that culture. We now have some idea about the power of our beliefs; what about *attitudes* in relation to our culture?

Attitude and Culture

First, let's get on the same wavelength regarding our understanding of the relationship between an attitude and a belief. Beliefs and attitudes are kissing cousins. An *attitude* is a constellation of beliefs that predisposes one to act. Therefore, when we look at an attitude, what we are really doing is observing behavior or analyzing an individual's belief system. According to Maultsby, an attitude, like a belief, is a "semipermanent mental unit" that is the result of our pairing valuative thoughts about an event such that behavior, feelings, or emotions usually follow.

An attitude about a cultural encounter, if it is negative or positive, generally triggers automatic behavior. Yes! our attitudes cause us to respond to cultural events or situations without even thinking about them. Thus, holding negative attitudes about people from different cultures because of their customs and their way of doing things—without any rational basis for our attitudes—is a major barrier to effective communication that demands we get on the same wavelength and work toward developing shared meanings, greater understanding, and sensitivity. Continuing in ascending order from the cultural rapport model, let's take a closer look at what sensitivity entails with respect to cultural diversity.

In other words, sensitivity is the heart and soul of the rapport process and is vital to arriving at understanding and shared meaning. Further, sensitivity is necessary to deepen our ability to be open and receptive to differences, a step we must accomplish to get to the next level: trust/trustworthiness. From a practical, organizational standpoint, here is a list of things that require mutual understanding and shared meaning:

- Corporate, organizational, and institutional jargon
- Dress and appearance codes (written and unwritten)

- Policies, rules, and regulations
- Time sense (promptness, when assignments are to be turned in)
- Process for promotions
- Attendance at meetings and social functions

Unless you are sensitive, open, and willing to share with others the meaning of things germane to your culture, it will be difficult for people to get to a level of mutual understanding. Managers who strive to share the meanings of their language and the signs and symbols germane to their organizational cultures are modeling effective relationship-building skills. These skills are important when the workplace is made up of diverse employees who have not yet proven their value in accordance with organizational expectations and norms.

All of us tread on thin ice when it comes to dealing with issues of cultural diversity. While we are sure of our own microscopic place in the world, there is much that we do not understand about the world of others. We don't realize that when we are functioning in a diverse environment, we are, figuratively speaking, the "bull in the china shop." With the slightest gesture, we may offend a nation, group, or an individual. This kind of insensitivity in the workplace may result in products not being delivered on time, absenteeism increasing, the work environment being hostile, workers being dissatisfied, and the loss of employees who could have contributed to the organization's success.

Let's explore how sensitivity and mutual understanding sets the stage for developing mutual trust and trustworthiness, the third level of the cultural rapport process.

Trust and Trustworthiness between People

Without trust and trustworthiness between people, there will be little opportunity to develop meaningful productive relationships. More often than not, it is a lack of trust or trustworthiness that leads to a lack of cooperation and misinterpretation and miscommunication. When there is no trust or trustworthiness between coworkers or between management and staff, a climate of suspicion, hostility, and resentment sets in. The environment will be characterized by low productivity and high absenteeism.

Trust and trustworthiness are two conditions that have to be present in order to establish effective cross-cultural relationships. In the rapport model, employee involvement is essential. Employees want to be involved in the decision-making, planning, and problem-solving processes that affect their work. To that purpose, the establishment of trust between the employee and manager is critical. If a manager trusts the employee, she or he will involve the employee in decision and planning processes commensurate with the employee's ability to perform the job. This gesture on the part of the manager sends a signal to the employee that she or he is trusted. The process of establishing trust is a two-way street. It is not just the concern of the manager. Employees have a responsibility to be *trustworthy*. If the employee is not perceived as trustworthy by his or her employer, she or he will probably be left out of the decision-making, planning, and problem-solving process.

Trust must be built on the concept that every employee will be treated fairly and with respect and dignity. When there is mutual trust and trustworthiness, coupled with respect and dignity for both employees and managers, cultural differences will be minimized, and each person will be able to focus on how to work effectively with others.

The benefits that come from operating out of a position of trust and trustworthiness, regardless of our particular cultural background, is that we can explore the strengths each person brings to the workplace rather than spending valuable time concentrating on what we perceive as weaknesses. By continuing in this way, we gradually develop a mind-set of valuing diversity. In other words, we begin to look at our differences as strengths. To behave in this way of course requires that we recognize and capitalize on behavior and information that may be out of our comfort zone. And here, the key is to be flexible.

Flexibility, the third "core dimension" of the cultural rapport model, is the glue that makes the model hang together. Flexibility is not only the ingredient that allows us to step outside of our comfort zone to experience the culture of others. It is also something that fosters a sense of openness—and it is openness that ultimately allows us to reexamine the attitudes and beliefs that have been driving our stereotypes about groups and individuals.

7
Ubuntu

Applying African Philosophy to Diversity Training

Lente-Louise Louw

*You might have much of the world's riches,
and you might hold a portion of authority, but
if you have no ubuntu, you do not amount to
much.*
ARCHBISHOP DESMOND TUTU

Ubuntu is a subtle and not easily translated concept. As a white Afrikaner whose family fought alongside black farmworkers in the Boer War, I grew up as *Puleng* (Rain) in a rural province with black children as my constant playmates. And so, it was my good fortune to *experience ubuntu* long before I knew the word. Certainly, it was decades before, as a change strategist, clinical psychologist, and counselor, I sought to define it for others so that its richness could be understood, its precepts learned and valued, and its practice extended beyond black Africa.

The Philosophy of *Ubuntu*

A Nguni word, *ubuntu* simply means "the quality of being human." *Ubuntu* manifests itself through various human acts, clearly visible in social, political, and economic situations as well as among family.

According to sociolinguist Buntu Mfenyana, it "runs through the veins of all Africans." Elaborated, the quality of being human, for Africans, is embodied in the oft-repeated: *"Umuntu ngumtu ngabanye abantu"* ("A person is a person through other people"). While this African proverb reveals a world view—that we owe our selfhood to others, that we are first and foremost social beings, that, if you will, "no man is an island," or, as the African would have it, "One finger cannot pick up a grain"—*ubuntu* is, at the same time, a deeply personal philosophy that calls on us to mirror our humanity for each other. To the observer, *ubuntu* can be seen and felt in the spirit of willing participation, unquestioning cooperation, warmth, openness, and personal dignity demonstrated by the indigenous black population. From the cradle, every black child inculcates these qualities so that by the time adulthood is reached, the *ubuntu* philosophy has become a way of being.

The word used to capture this elusive concept varies from one regional dialect to another. In Shangaan, we say *munhu*; in Zulu, *umuntu*; in Xhoza, *umntu*; in Se-Sotho, *motho*; in Venda, *muthu*, and in Tswana, *motho*. Whatever the term used, the philosophy embodied in *ubuntu* is one that honors a trusting, interdependent, reciprocal relationship delicately balanced with individual needs for autonomy and self-expression.

The Consequences of *Ubuntu*

It is understandable that when we act upon a deeply felt sense of being connected to others by our common humanity, when we truly regard self and other as one, when we cherish human dignity, all of our relationships and the level of our behaviors and actions are raised to a higher plane. By contrast, it should be evident that, without such a binding ethos—and scores of societies, particularly in the West, are notably lacking in such shared values—human relationships deteriorate, remain instrumental, or are thwarted at superficial ritualistic behavior.

Willis Harman, founder of the Institute of Noetic Sciences and author of *Global Mind Change* (Knowledge Systems, Inc., Indianapolis, Inc., 1988) is not alone in expressing the need for a coming together of three prevailing views if the world is to survive and prosper: the manipulation of the external world that is characteristic of Western traditions, the focus on inner experience and reflection that is important in Eastern thinking, and connectedness to nature valued by indigenous peoples the world over. Each has a vital role to play, but they must be held in balance, no one dominating the other.

The Practicality of *Ubuntu*

If the spirit of *ubuntu* needs to be awakened for South Africa to thrive (and it does), think of the enormity of the problem in cultures with a "collective unconscious," as Jung would describe it, that provide no such philosophical road map. Providing a road map and making it useful to a diverse group of people is a key task for those of us who work as change agents—whether as managers, consultants, or trainers in multicultural work environments. (An instructor training psychologists to interpret Myers-Briggs personality tests once pointed out that individual diversity shows up immediately in the way each "personality type" delivers geographical directions: One will talk in miles or meters or blocks, another will highlight freeway exits and bridges, and another will cite key landmarks along the way.)

Given the profound place this richly layered concept holds in African culture, it is not surprising that contemporary observers and journalists believe that the problems facing South Africa must and can be resolved if the people strive to "create a viable and operative *ubuntu* culture." And it is not surprising that elsewhere, where few precedents exist to encourage people to the challenges of abandoning an either-or exclusionary world for a both-and participatory one, the call is even more urgent.

As for South Africa, where the exploitation and abuse of the black population is notorious and well reported, these deeply spiritual people, perhaps *because of* as much as *despite* efforts to strip them of their humanity, take comfort and find strength in each other to stand with dignity in the midst of outrageous circumstances that would fell a person who had not grown up with such strong guiding principles. There is also a vitality and warmth in the black population in South Africa that can be felt in its church groups, its educational organizations, and even in the grassroots organizations, especially the burial societies, that flourish on street corners.

It is the *connectedness* each individual feels with family, community, and nature (far more than Westerners, the black population in South Africa holds itself to be one with the earth) that is the reward of an "I am because you are because we are" belief system; the force of these binding relationships, experienced from infancy and reinforced throughout childhood, is what gives *ubuntu* its ultimate power. As an aside, it is worth noting here the central place that singing holds in African society, among both whites and blacks. Mothers sing to their children, and children grow up singing. But what is striking about the blacks' uses of singing (which has its counterpart in gospel singing that takes place in many black churches in the United States and, to some extent, in the rap of young black artists) is that much of the singing is a dialog, an exchange in which one person starts with a commentary on a day's events (often political), and the others pick up the theme, chanting in harmony until someone calls out a new verse elaborating on the first. It is a powerful spiritual and political force that effectively creates a strong human chain linking one to another, and all to a cause.

Yet, if *ubuntu* philosophy were capable only of instilling a population with a sense of joy and well-being or of enabling a people to survive in the face of threatening and divisive forces, such as have been well publicized in reports on South Africa but that prevail in every country and continent of the world, it would not be enough to seize upon as a model; it would not move beyond the boundaries of its culture of origin nor be capable of being learned by others. What the practice of *ubuntu* allows—that is, its promise for all of us in what is commonly described as the new global community—is far greater fulfillment of human potential than has yet been realized, far more creativity than has been thought possible, and far more participation and productivity than most organizations have forecast.

Relationship in *Ubuntu* Philosophy

Before discussing how others can apply the practical steps that, in my personal and professional experience, permit an indigenous African philosophy to be transformed into a viable and operative system, particularly useful to those who do business in today's global marketplace, we need first to understand the primacy of *relationship* in *ubuntu* philosophy. If the centrality of relationship, whether parent to child, wife to husband, employer to worker, or any other of the myriad relationships we form in our lifetimes, has long been eminently clear to psychotherapists, psychiatrists, and social workers, its vital place in the world of commerce is really only now being fully grasped. Just as our personal growth and development are strengthened by nurturing relationships that ultimately manifest themselves in our capacity to respect self and others and contribute more fully to society, so do groups, organizations, and corporations stand to gain by paying attention to the complexity of relationships within the workplace. After all, few will dispute that our places of work constitute a second home, a second family, with all of its pains and joys.

In South Africa, in fact, there is growing attention to what is called a "community concept" of doing business, which regards the organization as a community to which its workers (members) belong as a matter of choice more than any legal contract. Some large corporations in

Japan also try to create a family culture in the workplace, offering their employees many elaborate "perks" unheard of in the United States, where some would denounce the practice as paternalistic at worst and intrusive at best. It is true that the concept of creating a family community in the workplace must be done with integrity or it will be regarded simply by the employees as one more manipulation among a host of abuses that have made workers everywhere suspicious and justifiably mistrusting.

Although they omit the relationship of the individual to the community, the words of psychologist and author Abraham Maslow do have something to say about our personal and professional selves, and even organizational entities: "The self goes out and expands only in the presence of a respect and acceptance it can feel" (*Toward a Psychology of Being*, Van Nostrand, Princeton, N.J., 1968).

Most small and large businesses and organizations, nonprofits as well as profits, now know that we cannot continue to live and work in a competitive, exclusionary, mechanistic climate that imposes its "language" (in the broadest sense of the word) on others. Multicultural, multiracial, multiethnic workforces are not phenomena of tomorrow; they are here today. Integrating a diverse workforce, encouraging creative collaboration, building teams that cooperate rather than compete, and shifting to nonhierarchical organizational structures are no longer for a limited number of progressive, risk-taking firms or visionary CEOs. Fritjof Capra, the eclectic Viennese physicist-author who has become so popular in the United States, echoes a growing recognition of many serious social observers when he says, "The old is no longer working and we are not quite sure of the new" (*The Turning Point*, Simon & Schuster, N.Y., 1982). (Certainly, in the former Soviet Union, the truth of these words is being felt with great frustration and fear. Perhaps we all need to recall the best of socialist rhetoric that reminds us "you can't make an omelet without breaking eggs.")

In South Africa, evidence that the "old is not working" has become clear to many businesses as they struggle to remain competitive and profit making in the face of today's increasing demands that they give back to, *invest* in, the community. Like many other companies in many other countries, South Africa's stagnant economy must find a way to redress the problems of low productivity, absenteeism, and apathy among workers.

During the course of a survey I was conducting in a large South African corporation based in Johannesburg and well regarded for its progressive management, equitable salaries, and good health care and other benefits but steeped in long-standing prejudices about the capabilities of its unskilled ("lazy") workers, there was great resistance to the questions I was putting to the workers. Despite the aid of a translator, my words fell on deaf, unresponsive, and hostile ears. Finally, an older worker spoke up. Looking directly into my eyes, connecting with me so deeply and powerfully that I shall never forget the experience, he said: "We leave our *ubuntu* at home."

In the easy discussion that flowed thereafter, it became clear that management's denial of the workers' "personhood"—its lack of respect, lack of acknowledgment, and lack of recognition of workers as fellow human beings—effectively shut down the process by which "a person is a person through another person." The tyrannizing effect of these failures, as we certainly know in Western psychology, is the tendency of a person to *become* that which he or she is labeled, particularly when the labeling is persistently driven home for a long period of time. (And the labeling need not be verbalized to be felt and absorbed into one's identity.) Maslow's words could as easily be reversed to say: The self shrivels up and disappears in the absence of a respect and acceptance it can feel.

Increasingly, corporations and other organizations and agencies, here and abroad, are beginning to recognize that old-style hierarchical relationships within the firm are no longer working in their self-interest. The more enlightened are moving away from reactive and defensive postures to the realization that bottom-line profits are more likely to go up than down when the workforce is invited in and asked to play a more participatory role.

The loss of energy among workers in South Africa, the denigration of who they are and what they, in connected relationship to others, can achieve, is not confined to the African continent. Since Marx used the expression *alienation,* the forces at work in the world of work have been the subject for countless social scientists and entrepreneurs turned authors. And the alienation felt by all those who have had their personhood systematically denied by an exploitive ruling class is not confined to the workplace. In Allister Sparks' *The Mind of South Africa* (Knopf, N. Y., 1990), Adam Small, a black South African poet, is quoted on his growing struggle regarding the Afrikaans language in which he wrote—the language, he notes, through which he had achieved his fame. Although it was the language his mother had taught him from infancy, it was also the language of the oppressor. In deep, personal pain, he concluded that in the future he would probably write in English. Unlike Small, whose experience was connected to written language, my experience as an Afrikaner has been with spoken language: As a child, I was denigrated by some English-speaking South Africans for speaking in Afrikaans, but when I turned to speak my less fluent English, I was denigrated again for my accent.

Our experiences are not isolated, idiosyncratic events; they are shared the world over.

The essential task, then, for those of us who move into organizations as consultants and trainers today is to see to it that no worker "leaves his (her) *ubuntu* at home"—and, more important, that no potential is lost. Where do we begin?

Building and Fostering Relationship

In a multicultural context, we need to leave behind cultural dictates for what constitutes relationship:...codes of appropriate behavior...sex roles...codes of diplomacy and the strictly delineated institutional forms that we have used to define what is and what is not relationship.
    CHARLES JOHNSON, THE CREATIVE IMPERATIVE
    (CELESTIAL ARTS, BERKELEY, 1984/1986)

Relationship—that which connects one person to another, bridges differences, and, in some real way, creates the future—is vital to our personal, professional, and organizational lives. As individuals, we enjoy a network of relationships with family and friends; as members of our community, we form relationships with teachers, civic leaders, and a host of other public servants and commercial enterprises; as workers, we are the managers and the managed who spend significant portions of our daily lives in close interaction with coworkers, colleagues, customers, clients, partners, and those to whom we report.

When it comes to institutional life, the reaches of relationship are even greater. For example, just as hospitals rely on a continuing influx of patients, banks rely on adequate numbers of depositors and loan seekers, service organizations and commercial establishments demand our patronage if they are to stay in business—the list goes on—all institutions, by their very existence, are in relationship with us. Beyond that primary relationship of provider to consumer, every organization is obliged to manage relationships within their walls, setting forth institutional goals and seeking accountability from all who work for the organization. It is not difficult to agree, then, that relationships, whether personal, civic, or organizational, serve as the basis of our growth and development, our expression of warmth and creativity, our support and strength, in everything we do. Indeed, for renowned philosopher-theologian Martin Buber, "In the beginning is relationship" (*I and Thou*, Charles Scribner's & Sons, N.Y., 1970).

Consultants who look at dynamics in small and large organizations continue to note that *synergistic relationships*, those in which all workers feel that their contribution to the whole is vital to an organization's success, not only boost worker participation and productivity but constitute the difference between organizations that falter and fail and those that flourish. Much of the advice such consultants offer to CEOs, consequently, is aimed at fostering the kinds of relationships necessary, within the context of a given organization, to assure policies and procedures that do more than ask workers to come into alignment with organizational goals and, rather, makes it possible for them to have a real say in defining those goals. One of the common occurrences in organizations that invite this level of participation and trust is that workers, on their own, begin to set increasingly higher stakes for themselves, individually and as members of a group or team. Asa Joe Ndlela, a black human resources manager, remarked to me, "Trust is one-ness. It is being you, watching yourself in a mirror; that's what trust is."

The pioneering collaboration in the eighties between Toyota and GM was as demanding as it was daring; for American automotive workers, the Japanese way of working was counter to everything they knew. For whatever it did and did not accomplish (the outcomes went well beyond the production of the Chevy Nova), the experiment calls up the admonition of Charles Johnson (page 164) that we must walk away from all that we have known and felt safe with in working relationships where diversity, when it did exist, was confined to simple differences in gender, or age, or skill level. As he suggests, in a multicultural workforce, the demands on relationship are far greater than in relatively homogeneous settings, for the "space" between the managers and the managed, and between and among coworkers in such an environment sometimes looms as an unbridgeable chasm. Norms of behavior specific to each cultural, ethnic, or racial group—largely invisible in groupings where few are perceived as "outsiders"—are suddenly up for grabs in work environments with an ethnically or racially diverse staff. (We have discovered already, and continue to discover, the disruption that occurs when women are brought into professions or trades or power positions traditionally regarded as the exclusive provinces of men.)

On finding themselves a part of a diverse working team, the natural tendency on the part of most workers is to establish camaraderie with those who are *like* rather than unlike them, whether in race, class, gender, age, or country of origin. Among managers faced with a diverse workforce, the temptation for some is to gloss over "people" differences and focus on the *task,* hoping to avoid potential clashes of individual style, temperament, and relationship patterns that they feel ill-equipped to resolve and that they fear will have repercussions on productivity, and, of course, undermine them as managers.

Much the same situation is occurring now in our public school system, especially in populated urban areas where immigrant children are changing the face of the classroom. Not having a ready solution, teachers, administrators, and educational researchers find themselves to be part of the problem. Teachers, most of whom already feel underpaid, unacknowledged, and overburdened, are becoming increasingly frustrated, angry, and defensive about their inability to teach ever larger classes filled with children at wildly different levels of competence and language proficiency.

In the case of businesses and corporations, calling in outside experts and consultants is an accepted response when internal resources are strained and inadequate to the task. With the kind of coaching those trained and experienced in valuing and managing diversity can provide, CEOs and middle management are gradually made aware of the heightened potential their company has *because of* the diversity in their workforce. With this recognition, they begin to shed their reactive and defensive stance (how am I going to make do?) and adopt—even take pleasure in—striving to assure that, in their firm, *no potential is lost.* ("No Potential Lost" is the name of a core strategy I have implemented in my work with large corporations in South Africa, and it has been very successful.) From my perspective, and from the vantage point of all those working with multicultural organizations, the opportunity provided by the burgeoning global economy of the nineties is one of unprecedented breakthrough, creativity, and bottom-line profit that will be translated into but go beyond dollars.

As psychotherapists know very well from their clinical practices, and sociologists from years of field studies, most of us—regardless of our cultural, racial, or ethnic group or our gender, age, or occupation—are trapped by our belief systems, our unexamined values, our past experiences, and all of the associated emotions—fear, anger, and mistrust—that have been frozen along with them over a lifetime. This "baggage" from the past, combined with often unrealistic expectations of the future, is astonishingly effective in keeping us from being fully present to what is happening here and now. What does that mean? It means, for one thing, that a terrible deception is going on: We are allowing our preconceptions, past associations, and judgments made rigid over time to color and distort most if not all of our present interactions—without our recognizing it. The inconsequential judgments we all make in the presence of another ("She reminds me of my sister."

"He smiles a lot.") reside quietly next to far more insidious judgments we make (indeed, that we made long ago) about entire races or ethnic groups or people from a certain part of the world or a different socioeconomic class—and all of this on top of the more consciously held assumptions women hold about men and men about women, and both about dress, appearance, mannerisms, age, disabilities, and other differences we encounter every day.

Until we can see our unexamined biases as opportunities lost—opportunities for friendship, for learning, for broadening our perspectives, for reenergizing our creative impulses—we will remain locked into decisions we signed and sealed in childhood. Many, by the time they reach high school, are already unable to hear what those different from them are saying. They have settled into a pattern of evaluating rather than listening for understanding and are becoming well versed in the energy-wasting, Western practice of polarizing and labeling: right-wrong, black-white, good-bad.

Expanding the Concept of Relationship

While opportunities for expanding our network of friends, our awareness of other cultures, our knowledge of different languages, and our appreciation for multicultural art forms has been available for decades to an educated elite with disposable income to travel, to send their children to the best schools at home and abroad, and to fill their homes with art and artifacts from other lands, only now, with the shrinking of our world, is there the urgency for all of us to wake up and embrace the rich diversity of people and ideas at our doorstep. The oft-referred-to character in the Chinese language for *crisis,* made up of the symbols for *opportunity* and *danger,* has direct application here, as indeed it does in many arenas of contemporary society. I believe Charles Johnson speaks wisely when he says, "We will either come to relate within these new, more challenging roles or we will not relate at all. Meaningful existence in times ahead will be predicated on our ability to bring more to the experience of relatedness...."

Let's talk about some of the factors involved in expanding our notions of relationship. Some assume, for example, that the fewer the differences between them and others, the better the relationship will work. On the contrary, too much sameness creates little movement and, surprisingly, can cause a relationship to stagnate and eventually die. (The same general phenomenon has its counterpart in the educational arena where what seemed like a good idea—tracking students into classes where they were all at the same level of competence—turned out to have negative if not disastrous effects on both the gifted and the slow learner.) In the context of the work environment, this stratification also has damaging effects; without the spark, the provocation, the ideas that come from a diverse working group encouraged to challenge each other continually, an organization can lose its lead.

Conversely, when individuals from very different cultures come together, in work or play, the differences may be so great that they create polarization and end in hardened posturings on both sides. When the differences in culture, expectations, language, and the many other variables that enter into the relationship dynamic are extreme, remedies that rely on simple goodwill, high intention, or intuitive problem-solving skills are not likely to be effective. When this situation occurs between individuals where nothing is at stake, one can, and usually does, part company to avoid conflict. In a work setting, however, it is not as easy to walk away, for numerous reasons. What else do we need to know to agree that relationship dynamics are the life-blood of any organization and a rich source of innovation?

What is required to turn these situations around is a conscious strategy that focuses on *redefining* relationships. In my own work with small and large organizations, I suggest to people that relationship is a unique kind of ecological system, one in which all of the parts are in dynamic relationship, and, while each has its own unique contribution to make, no one part is as important as the whole. But learning to value diversity, to become conscious, as it were, of our ways of relating to others and their way of relating to us, is not something easily imposed from outside and certainly not a system that can be expected to take root immediately. Once the process is started, all participants need to be prepared for turbulence.

So how do we proceed? How do we tap people's common humanity and assist them to suspend judgments, shed past assumptions, and enter into relationships with unfamiliar "others" whose world view may seem to be in uncomfortable opposition to ours? How do we assist people to become more fully aware of what they bring to the "space" that exists between them and another human being? How do we encourage others to look at themselves, openly and honestly, without punitive judgments, recalling that sense of wonder and discovery we all had as children? For these are the first steps we need to take—before we look at the larger environment, the physical and mental space in which our workforce functions on a day-to-day basis; before we examine the policies, practices, and precedents that make up the organizational culture of our places of work; and before we assess the relational dynamics of the organization as a whole.

Remember that, just as individuals often mask their authenticity, or their "genuineness," the same applies to the organizations, many of whom spend millions to create an image that is often at odds with who and what they "really are." Indeed, some whose rhetoric convinces us of their commitment to whatever it may be—its "people," "the environment,"—often, under scrutiny, are found to have surprisingly archaic personnel policies and practices and other regulations.

In the eyes of this native South African woman, raised in black traditions for years before receiving her degrees in Western psychology, management, and organizational dynamics, *ubuntu* is a perfect vehicle for effecting the multiple transformations that need to take place in the way we relate to each other in all arenas of our lives. All of the necessary ingredients for these transformations are embodied in *ubuntu*; furthermore, its expression in the people of black Africa, who have endured and endured, and endured, is testimony enough to its sustaining power. For them as for others to whom the concept of *ubuntu* may be taught, the challenge, now, is to go beyond survival and to consciously and deliberately begin to create a new relationship dynamic which, through a process of guided self-exploration and self-confrontation will allow us to embrace the differences that, ultimately, will serve as our greatest source of strength and creative energy in everything we do in life. When we move out of a survival modality, then we can start to bring together the three dispositions described earlier as characterizing the thinking of Western, Eastern, and indigenous peoples. Certainly, a three-legged stool offers more stability than one on two legs. Regardless of whether we come from Western or Eastern traditions, self-knowledge is the wellspring of all actions we take in life. Self-knowledge is not static, of course; it is fluid and changing just as the process of self-exploration, if it is to have any meaning, must be ongoing throughout one's life. The means, or pathways, to self-knowledge certainly differ from one culture to another; as noted already, in the Eastern world, meditation is a significant way to journey within and set foot on a path to enlightenment whereas in Western traditions we tend to look outward—to books, to psychotherapy, to religion—as the way to know ourselves. For indigenous peoples the world over, meaning comes from a rich ancestral past where each person is connected to another and all to the land.

When working with a specific multicultural workforce, the background questions that drive the work are basic ones: How do present on-the-job relationships work? What can be done, by managers and workers, to make working relationships more effective, less destructive? What are or appear to be the main disruptive issues that need to be looked at? How much participation can we assure? How much time will be allocated for the process to be thoroughly learned? Before one can work on his or her relationships with one or more others, across gender lines, racial lines, ethnic lines, class lines, and hierarchical divisions between workers and management, each person needs to focus on a process of self-discovery. It is a critical first step that will be discussed in more practical detail later.

As participants learn to identify, define, explore, and understand their own beliefs, values, feelings, motives, and actions, it becomes possible for them to proceed to the next step: becoming aware of the various ways these feelings, beliefs, values, and past experiences influence their *perceptions* of reality (which many confuse reality itself) and result in stereotyping, racist thinking, exclusionary practices, and so forth.

As quickly and easily as these processes can be described in words, remember that the learning and practice of them are slow and gradual, punctuated by peaks, valleys, and plateaus that are on different timetables for each participant. Over time, however, by becoming familiar with the source of their beliefs, values, and thinking styles, they become more proficient in distinguishing those perceptions that are simply false from those that are true and relevant—and from those that are true and *irrelevant*.

Recently, in a call-in television program on attitudes about the surge of Spanish-speaking immigrants into the state of California, someone complained bitterly that when she called businesses in California, she simply could not understand the persons answering the telephone, "and why don't those people learn to speak English?" At first blush, it is easy for a liberal-minded person to denounce the caller's prejudicial attitude. On the other hand, what is equally to the point in this instance is a company's lack of judgment in placing someone whose English language skills may be inadequate in a customer service position, at least one that is not exclusively for the benefit of Spanish-speaking people.

Without question, it is difficult to motivate people, especially those raised in Western philosophy, to do serious, in-depth self-exploration. Some outside facilitation is almost always necessary. (An early work by Karen Horney, *Self-Analysis,* thoroughly explores both the possibilities and the pitfalls of going it alone, and, surprisingly, given how much the psychological literature has mushroomed in past decades, her words are as relevant today as in the forties when the book was published.) In working with groups for whom multiracial, multicultural work situations are new and without precedent, facilitation is always needed. Knowing that we are all most influenced by significant others in our lives, one strategy of the facilitator in these workplaces is to ask participants to identify those who serve as significant others for them. They may be family members, buddies, mentors, or even one's manager or supervisor; however, in this connection, it is important that participants understand that to be accorded the honor of being "significant" means that the individuals named are people with whom one feels respected, valued, and trusted. In many instances, those others will be family, but in some cases a person may feel the qualities of nonpossessive warmth, empathy, and trust in a colleague or boss are more genuine than they are among family members. That a significant relationship is powerful and empowering does not mean that it is with those in "power" positions.

As indicated earlier, most organizations recognize that it is in their self-interest to take whatever steps are necessary to build harmonious (what managers translate as "productive") relationships on the job. In the world of business, the payoff that comes from a sound initial investment is generally understood. In other words, after a period of waiting for things to straighten out on their own, most CEOs know that it is penny-wise and pound-foolish not to go to outside experts.

Those who do come into these settings as facilitators must, of course, be well trained and deeply aware of the issues that commonly divide one ethnic, racial, cultural group's norms and behaviors from those of another. The job is not for the novice nor for the timid. The only advantage such a facilitator has over the psychotherapist who deals one on one with the familiar obstacles of resistance, denial, and "fuzzy logic" the client unwittingly places in his or her own pathway is that the facilitator called in to the workplace has a captive audience. (And that, itself, can be an obstacle the facilitator will need to deal with at the outset.) It goes without saying that the facilitator must establish a safe, trusting, secure atmosphere for all participants—and that means knowing what constitutes "safety" for the different participants represented. Without such an atmosphere in which to proceed, the facilitator will hardly be ready to deal with the cross-cultural dynamics that occur, silently and overtly, from moment to moment.

The Qualities of *Ubuntu*

Before looking at some of the practical steps that can be taken to facilitate the creation of what I call an "*ubuntu* relationship space," I would like to talk about intrinsic qualities of *ubuntu*: what I consistently refer to as *warmth, empathy,* and *trust* but which also embody respect, understanding, and the capacity to be genuine, or what British psychoanalyst D. W. Winnicott would refer to as "authenticity." Obviously, these human qualities are not the exclusive province of *ubuntu*. They "have their roots in the antiquity of man," as someone once said, and stand as universal observations of the healthy, strong, supportive, loving relationships. The *ubuntu* relationship is what Carl Rogers would describe as a "helping" relationship. For Charles Truax and Robert Carkhuff (*Toward Effective Counseling and Psychotherapy*, Aldine, N.Y., 1967) applauded by Jerome Frank in 1967 for their breakthrough work in psychotherapeutic research, effective relationships are those in which the individuals involved

- Are reasonably well integrated, nondefensive, and authentic in their relationship encounters

- Provide a nonthreatening, safe, trusting, or secure atmosphere by reason of their mutual and unconditional positive regard, love, or nonpossessive warmth for each other

- Are able to grasp the meaning of or accurately understand each other and the relationship on a moment-to-moment basis

Those who have devoted themselves to training generally and cross-cultural training in particular have come to a similar conclusion, namely, that the people who adapt best cross-culturally are those who feel relatively secure with themselves and who have reasonably well-developed philosophies and approaches to life that are inclusive rather than exclusive of others.

When I compare *ubuntu* philosophy with Western psychology, I am also struck by the congruity between Carl Rogers's assertion (*On Becoming a Person*, Houghton Mifflin, Boston, Mass., 1961), "the degree to which I can create relationships which facilitate the growth of others as separate persons [is] a measure of the growth I have achieved in myself" and "Umuntu ngumtu ngabanye abantu"—a person is a person through other people. In other words, while I have gained significant insights through accessing the work of highly regarded learning specialists, social scientists from many parts of the globe, and a variety of eclectic thinkers of our time, I find the hallmarks of effective relationship as sketched by psychologists to be fully embodied by my black African models. As a people, they possess the requisite security of personhood, the trusting and supportive nature, the authenticity of expression, and the flexibility that are the cornerstones of success in moving through change. Not mentioned by others but of comparable importance in my mind is their joy and their mental, physical, emotional and spiritual stamina; it is, I believe, what has allowed them to endure, to bend where others break.

Needless to say, it is seldom that a facilitator walks into an organization, regardless of whether the workforce is homogeneous or culturally and racially diverse, and finds people to be as "highly evolved" as these statements from psychologists and training specialists suggest. On the other hand, it is useful information for trainers as a way of knowing where, ideally, the group should be directed. For practical purposes, when introducing these concepts to a Western audience, I have developed a chart (see Fig. 7-1) that indicates the multiplicity of expressions and behaviors involved in efforts to enhance cross-cultural relationships.

Having clarified that the basic components embedded in *ubuntu* are essentially those singled out by Western psychologists as being primary to all healthy relationships, it is interesting, also, to note that even in the relationship between therapist and client, the space must be one of warmth, trust, and empathy that the patient or client can *feel.*

Effecting Change

The process of change should not be a thunderstorm on barren land but a gentle rain over time.

As is readily apparent to those who have read this far, the kind of transformations required to bridge the distance from where most people are to where they need to be if they are to work in harmony together cannot be effected overnight. And, it might be asked, given how very simple and basic are the components of *ubuntu* philosophy that I have singled out as critical to the change process—primarily warmth, empathy, and trust—why am I suggesting they be introduced slowly and carefully, as "a gentle rain over time"?

If we start by looking at the concept of *warmth,* we can see that, desirable as it is for people to regard each other warmly and with understanding and acceptance, the expression of warmth is highly variable among people—beginning with what they have learned from the family environment in which they were raised, the geographical region from which they come, their country of origin and its cultural dictates, social norms they have absorbed in relation to others, and a host of other variables. For one person, and almost without regard to culture and race, the slightest nod of the head may be equivalent to another person's bear hug. In the *ubuntu* change process, as we shall see, the purpose is not to force anyone to abandon customary expres-

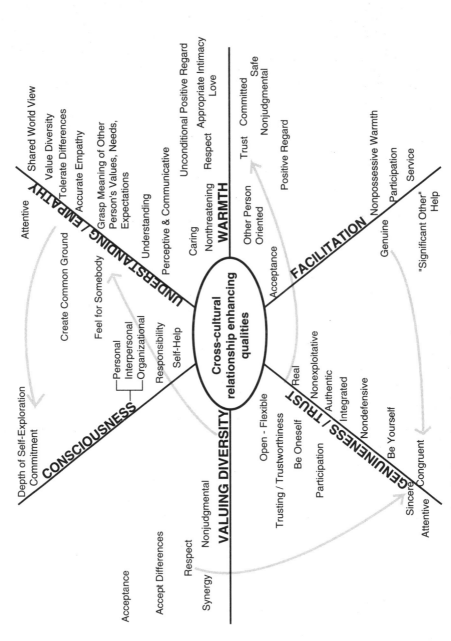

Figure 7-1 Cross-cultural relationship enhancing qualities.

sions of warmth, only to suggest that there is a neutral space, a space of possibility, in which each party to an interaction can construct a new, third way, of being together comfortably.

Empathy, again a familiar concept to most, is actually more difficult than it first appears, even among relatively sophisticated people. Often confused with sympathy, it is, rather, an ability to see from another person's vantage point, regardless of how you feel about a viewpoint or whether you agree with it or whether you "sympathize" with it. In popular vernacular, empathy is described as making the effort to "walk a mile in my shoes." Sounds good. Sounds easy. But it takes only a few examples to suggest that it isn't. Picture an urban white male trying to walk a mile in the shoes of a rural black woman, or an ebullient young Italian and a Pacific Heights matron. Life experiences and temperaments that are so removed from each other make questionable the extent to which either of these "players" can grasp, even fleetingly, the perspectives of the other, let alone walk a mile in their shoes.

The psychotherapist, of course, has first a strong disposition for empathy and then refines the delicate balancing act called for in any therapeutic relationship. The therapist learns how to maintain a non-judgmental stance, to "hear" what the client is saying, and to display, by manner, facial expression, and carefully chosen words, a kind of emotional knowing that does not pretend to agree or disagree, regardless of how fiercely some clients struggle to get agreement, unaware that acceptance means far more. Another skill exercised by a good therapist is the ability to slip in and out of the inner state the client both describes and relates. The therapist must make a strong effort to feel, albeit vicariously, what the client is feeling and then to step outside and make whatever observations will assist the client, and also, to step outside of his or her turmoil, frustration, distorted perceptions, and begin to assess their behaviors and actions more dispassionately and, eventually, more analytically. In this way, the therapist also models for the client the possibility of standing back and observing self. To a great extent, the facilitator, trainer, or organizational consultant working to improve employee working relationships in a multicultural environment must do the same.

As for *trust,* although most people know rather clearly where they stand on this issue, shifting from a place of mistrust to trust is probably one of the most difficult transitions a person can make. As a character trait, again, we see enormous variability among individuals as well as differences that are culture or race specific. Americans, as a people, for example, have a reputation of being open and trusting—at least in comparison with other cultures—despite the fact that on a person-to-person basis, some Americans are far more trusting than others.

Some trust nature and not people; others have no problems trusting other people but fear the dark, unpredictable, and ominous power they perceive in nature. Some trust family and friends but not strangers; some trust in certain situations but not in others; and some, of course, trust no one.

All of these differences are "in the room" when the trainer or manager or CEO enters. Indeed, in introducing *ubuntu* concepts to a group, one of the very first tests for those who serve as facilitators will be establishing trust between themselves and the participants with whom they will embark on this journey. While the trainer may slowly establish trust by revealing personal warmth and empathy, for most and at first, the facilitator is an intruder, an "other," an "outsider" and, if brought in by management, which in most instances will be the case, the space is likely to be abuzz with mistrust.

The *Ubuntu* Change Process

Having said that, let me reiterate the basic premise of this chapter: that *ubuntu* philosophy is a powerful instrument for change, that for nearly a decade I have used it as a methodology for effecting change even in the most difficult situations and circumstances, and that it can be taught, learned, and practiced in a wide range of settings and toward various end purposes. With specific reference to the workplace, the strategies I have developed and regard as the *ubuntu* change process empower individuals, workers, and management alike, to communicate better, work effectively in teams, increase participation and satisfaction, manage diversity, negotiate change, develop leadership qualities, provide better customer relations, manage crises, construct on-the-job training programs, and—of course—increase productivity.

I single these out because they are the hard-nosed demands of most businesses whose CEOs fix their gaze relentlessly on bottom-line profits and who know, from experience, that conflict and dissatisfaction among workers and managers is interruptive, distracting, and ultimately costly. One CEO of a Fortune 500 company aware of the importance of team efforts reportedly said: "If you really believe in quality, when you cut through everything, it's *empowering people* that leads to teams" (emphasis added).

The rewards that accrue to the individuals who participate in the process, however, go far beyond making the workplace a more satisfying place to be and coincidentally raising the organization's profit margin. The self-knowledge and awareness of others that they learn through participation in the *ubuntu* change process cannot help but spill over into their personal, familial, and social lives and provide them with skills for living fuller lives.

Although I am suggesting that this spillover is an inevitable, almost accidental, carryover that the process gives to those involved in it, the fact is that organizations competing in today's global market are really obliged to create a working environment that is conducive to both personal and organizational growth. The most effective organizations are and will continue to be those able to match the personal, individual needs of their staff and labor force with the larger goals of the organization. It is interesting to see that the shift in terminology made many years ago from "personnel" to "human resources" has yet to be translated into a system that truly values workers as either *human* or valuable, and valued, *resources*. Sooner or later, companies—small or large, profit or nonprofit, service or product oriented—must shift from a top-down, authoritarian, hierarchical way of structuring their business to a more humane (and powerful) system in which each person serves as a resource for everyone else and, in turn, receives support and assistance from others. And they must do so with integrity—not with an eye to finding better ways to manipulate a resistant workforce to increase profits. (Indeed, overcoming deep and justifiable suspicions may be a major obstacle any facilitator will face.)

That aside, without direct experience and measurable success in proving the *ubuntu* change process to be transmissible across culture, gender, race, and age, I would not be so quick to suggest that these largely intuitive precepts can be presented to widely divergent populations in widely divergent situations. And that does not mean that it is easy. Given the propensity toward inertia that exists in people as well as in matter, the going can be rough. However, the laws of inertia also mean that once in motion, things tend to stay in motion—and that is the aspect of the phenomenon I would emphasize here. I have used the *ubuntu* change process with children from disadvantaged communities, trapped in ghetto environments, often using second- or third-language skills; it has worked in dealing with a black trade union negotiating employee benefits with white management; and it has been an effective intervention in resolving relationship problems between white conservative foremen and black radical workers.

As we move to the implementation of the *ubuntu* change process, be aware that this process is, first of all, a process. Although I have singled out six seemingly linear steps for triggering this process, using the word *ubuntu* as an acronym, the reader should regard this merely as a device. (In my native country, I would ask—and have asked—for forgiveness for doing something that in any way trivializes a philosophy I deeply respect.) It should be obvious that in practice, the process is a dynamic one. Just as in the human body various processes—blood flow, hormonal changes, metabolic shifts—are in constant, dynamic interplay but, for teaching purposes, must be isolated and discussed in linear fashion, so it is with *ubuntu*, or any concept whose very nature does not lend itself to the kind of deconstruction system of analysis that is a cornerstone of Western thinking. Communicating the steps that will lead to expanding and expansive relationships without pummeling them into inflexible and unusable form is a delicate task. It is folly, for example, to think we can teach *intuition*, but we can teach people to *listen*, first to voices within themselves that many have simply silenced and then to similar "subtext" available in what others say and do.

There is no rigid order in which the steps are to be taken. As you discover in working with the *ubuntu* change process, each group has its own integrity, its own demands and needs, its own pace. Once the group is in motion, the role of the facilitator will often be simply to "ride the horse in the direction it's going."

A Workable System for Establishing *Ubuntu* Philosophy in the Workplace

The ultimate chant of the human race on earth is not to be conceived of as a monotone chanted on one note by one form of humanity alone, but rather a choral symphony chanted by all races and all nations in diverse tones, on different notes in one, grand, complex harmony.
OLIVE SCHREINER, THOUGHTS ON SOUTH AFRICA
(P. FISHER, UNWIN, LONDON, ENG., 1923)

With these words written decades ago, Olive Schreiner, a famous South African author, could have been spearheading a contemporary worldwide movement. Certainly, a major challenge facing South Africa today, where valuing diversity is no longer a moral issue or a "soft" option, creating a "grand complex harmony" is an imperative for all organizations. Without it, no South African organization will survive the years ahead. The same might well be said of countries outside of South Africa.

In this section, through a combination of Western and African constructs and premises, I present six practical steps for translating the concept of *ubuntu*, literally and figuratively, into a workable system for effecting change. Although in some ways the situation in South Africa is more critical than elsewhere, in other ways, the deeply rooted philosophy of *ubuntu* places the black population in an advantageous position. Allister Sparks, a journalist and correspondent for the *Economist* for more than 20 years, wrote in *The Mind of South Africa* (1990) "When the time comes, South Africa has, within itself, the ability to transform both its image and its role [and to become] the dynamo that energizes and drives languishing countries to become economically viable." For my part, that ability has everything to do with *ubuntu*. For example, the black African population does not have to learn what it means to place community and communal concerns first and foremost; their lives have been predicated on such assumptions. Certainly, in some European, Asian, and Latin American countries, as well as among Native Americans and other indigenous people, children are also raised from infancy to have deep respect for and attachment to family, community, and land. In Mexico, for example, part of the belief system is that illness is always associated with a transgression against family, church, or community, and, consequently, the illness cannot be treated without identifying and dealing with the triggering act. Similarly, medical practices in the East encompass the entire family.

But elsewhere, and especially in the United States, those who attain the esteem of their community are still, in nineteenth-century tradition, those who have excelled on their own (or presumably on their own). Regardless of how many other individuals and institutions made their achievement possible, and regardless of the fact that many accomplished individuals are aware enough and honorable enough to credit those contributions when they pick up their awards and prizes, the dominant cultural view is a strongly individualistic one.

If we are to succeed in the shrinking, highly technological global marketplace of the twenty-first century, what must be put into place, in the private and public sector and in nonprofit as well as profit-driven industries, is a whole new organizational culture, one in which management is eminently approachable, where each person's perspective is valued, where efforts are made to share at an emotional as well as an intellectual level, where there is a free flow of information, and, all in all, a harmonizing balance among the three philosophical dispositions referred to earlier. These are tall orders. Their implementation, the how of it as well as the timetable assigned, will vary with each organization and what its people bring to the table.

Although highly motivated "self-starters"—the term in currency in the United States today—can embark on a personal *ubuntu* change process relying on a network of relationships with family and friends, for my purposes here, let's assume a multicultural work environment where the organization has agreed to call in a facilitator and invest the time required to establish or renew good working relationships. As mentioned already, the first step, an ongoing process for each individual and for the group as a whole, is to know oneself and to come to know oneself through others and in relation to others. As we enter the first step of the six-step *ubuntu* change process, we will be dealing with all of these questions and more.

In the pages to follow, I will present the *ubuntu* process in the form of an acronym where each letter serves as a trigger for each of the six steps involved. As you read on, do remember, as indicated earlier, that the *ubuntu* process, in actual use, is a fluid, dynamic, and continuing one that is not nor should be quite so easily boxed. (Please note that a manual articulating, in detail, various strategies facilitators can use in working through the *ubuntu* change process with multicultural organizations is available from Griggs Productions. The material included in this chapter is intended to provide an overview only.)

The *Ubuntu* Change Steps

U = Uncover

B = Build and bridge

U = Understand

N = Neutral space, new input, and negotiation

T = Transformation

U = Utilization

Note: Each step will include a what-why-how-when and where-who chart that provides triggering questions to initiate and continue the task.

Step 1: Uncover

In "uncovering" (or unmasking), the intent is for participants to look inward, to their experiences in the past, to identify a lifetime of accumulated beliefs, attitudes, values, and "ways of looking" at one's self and others (Fig. 7-2). From there, they will start to examine where they stand in present time in relation to what they have just revealed. And finally, they will move into a future place of new possibility.

The most important aspect of the "uncover" step is to clarify our

Figure 7-2 Activator sheet: Uncover, unearth, unravel, unmask. (*Continued*)

What	Uncover *what* you know about yourself: existing ideas and attitudes, perceptions or values. Examine past memories, present realities, and future expectations of yourself. Uncover and discover as much as you can about others (those who are different as well as coworkers, friends, family). Make sure you have a firm foundation to build on. Find out what your values and perceptions are and where they came from.
	Ask as many "what" questions as possible: for example, "What do I value?" "What are my values?" "In what manner do I express different relationship qualities?"
Why	Think about *why* an individual should activate this step of the process. This uncovering or orientation will help you organize new ideas and values when you hear them later. Change and development do not take place in isolation. Perceptions and memory will be strengthened if a foundation exists on which to build. It is surprising what you already know. Often your existing reality must be triggered, remembered, and uncovered.
	Ask yourself as many "why" questions as possible: for example, "Why are these my values?"
How	Think about *how* you can uncover things about yourself and others. Turn cues into questions. Colleagues, teachers, or individuals should make lists of questions on the topic and discuss/think. Use the tools provided by the facilitator, or answer questions such as what, why, how, when, where, and who.
	Ask yourself "how" questions: for example, "How did I acquire these values?"
When and where	Think about *when and where* this step of the process is most applicable to your situation. Use this step before any in-depth interpersonal activities, especially across difference.
	Ask yourself "when" and "where" questions: for example, "When and where did I acquire these values?"

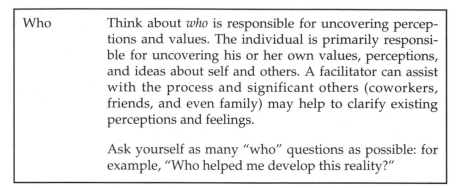

| Who | Think about *who* is responsible for uncovering perceptions and values. The individual is primarily responsible for uncovering his or her own values, perceptions, and ideas about self and others. A facilitator can assist with the process and significant others (coworkers, friends, and even family) may help to clarify existing perceptions and feelings.

Ask yourself as many "who" questions as possible: for example, "Who helped me develop this reality?" |
|---|---|

Figure 7-2 (*Continued*)

own identity and purpose, as well as to find ways of carefully observing others so we can find it easier to be sensitive to their differences.

The willingness to engage in this process may not always be there, at first. Individuals and groups come into this arena at different stages of readiness and ability, of course, and each person brings different expectations, preconceptions, styles of behavior, values, open and hidden agendas, and so forth. For those who have never engaged in deliberate self-inquiry, and for those who might have examined their values and beliefs but never in the context of the workplace and in the presence of strangers representing other cultures, races, or ethnic groups, taking the first steps in this direction might be difficult. It also demands each participant to be a keen observer and, at some point, willing to reveal the discoveries made.

It is up to the facilitator to create a safe space, to gain the trust of the group, and to lead it through this deeply personal process until the group participants begin to see what is demanded of them. A good facilitator will anticipate an atmosphere of hesitation and resistance and will be ready to deal with it until some breakthrough occurs—someone speaks up, for example, whether to ask a question or make a comment. Participants, also, often need to be reminded of their own responsibilities—primarily, that really no one can take this journey for them. They will be guided, but then it is up to them to do the rest. In providing the road map, the facilitator will, in effect, be *conveying* the warmth, empathy, and trust that the group, individually and collectively, is to gradually absorb and eventually mirror back. I think of the facilitator as akin to the African elder who, for each act of caring, forgiveness, bravery, or communal responsibility the young child exhibits, rewards with the words: *ke bothe bono ngoan'aka*—"that is *ubuntu*, my child.")

In the *ubuntu* system, the person who facilitates is not "the expert" who comes in from outside and imposes a system of beliefs on others. The term *facilitator* has been somewhat abused in the past decade; in many cases, it has lost its root meaning of "facilitate." In the work described here, that word needs to be taken seriously and at face value as the act of *making it easier for others* to accomplish their aims, whatever they may be.

The first and most crucial question each participant must wrestle with is *Who am I?* What are my values? What roles do I play in life? What key figures have influenced me? How do I perceive others? What feeling responses do I have in interactions with others? What feedback do I get about myself from others? What past influences and "self-talk" have imprinted my present attitudes, beliefs, and behavior? In what ways am I the same as and different from others? And, finally, what are my expectations for the future (lest I am condemned to repeat my past)?

An integral part of the uncovering process, while focused on the individual, will be a growing recognition of who one is in relation to others. For in the *ubuntu* approach, self-confrontation and self-exploration is a task that a person accomplishes by himself or herself but not alone. In practical terms, the facilitator will invite participants to call upon significant others in their lives to assist in the mirroring integral to the change process. Most likely, those selected will be people regarded as being *like* us; in a personal context, of course, they will be represented by close family, friends, or ministers. In the workplace, they may constitute a coworker, a colleague, a buddy, and even, for some, a respected supervisor or self-selected mentor. What is critical is that those persons identified by the participant be persons with whom he or she feels comfortable and can risk revealing vulnerabilities. In exchanges between individuals (and in small groups the facilitator might designate at some point), there will be an opportunity to focus specifically on what it means to relate to others who are unlike us, to note what labels we have openly or tacitly attached to those unlike us, and to observe and discuss how the qualities of warmth, empathy, and trust expressed in others correspond (or not) to ours.

Participating fully in this step is vital, for it will constitute the foundation that the entire self-discovery process will build on, providing a basis for comparing and evaluating the self as perceived from within and as mirrored by others from without. Balancing these inner and outer perceptions will be the work of the final stage in which a third, neutral, space is carved out, a place of "common ground" as Jesse Jackson has passionately stated in many talks and speeches.

I believe that toward that end of the first step we begin to become conscious of the fact that racism, prejudice, stereotyping, and other "-isms" are central factors in the social and organizational process.

Our survival demands an intense determination to look searchingly at ourselves and our organizations before the carelessness of our relationships and interaction with others leads to unnecessary loss of opportunity and human potential. The only lasting answer to the challenge of diversity is to uncover the roots of who we are, including our hatred and rage, and through self knowledge move toward the process of change.

Step 2: Build and Bridge

During this phase those participating in the process actively interact. Armed with insights gained from having uncovered a wealth of information about their own values, beliefs, and attitudes and having clarified their perceptions of others' reality, participants are ready to actively build on that foundation and begin the process of bridging differences. The differences uncovered represent not only those between two human beings but also differences between the perceptions each side has held in the past, of themselves and others. In other words, having worked through the unmasking, participants are now able to detach somewhat from tenaciously held, albeit unexamined, beliefs about who they are and who others are and contemplate a new basis for relationship, one that does not rely on automatic labeling.

This is a critical period. At this stage, the individual is exposed and vulnerable, not unlike the hermit crab which, as it reaches milestones of growth and development, must crawl out of its outgrown shell and creep, alone and unprotected, toward the roomier shell it will call home for the next period of time. It is important that each side approach the other free of preconceived judgments, that they enter an active exchange in which listening with respect and sensitivity is a key requirement. Together, participants will enter the newly created relationship space between them and begin to clarify for each other who they truly are, separating past false perceptions from present realities as they exchange information with new trust and openness. [I have found the MYTO Diversity Exercise (Fig. 7-3) to be a useful technique for building and bridging across differences.]

The bridging phase is strongly interactive. It is a time when each person is asked to truly see and hear another and to recognize that the truth of any situation is not "my" truth or "your" truth but something that happens at the interface of their differences. Both sides need to be responsible for themselves and each other (friendship carries with it mutual responsibility) and to listen actively and without judgment. The responsibility in this phase becomes one of multicultural risk taking and cocommitment to the process. There is a move away from the

Objectives

To focus thinking on the diversity challenge.
To relax individuals and encourage them to participate.
To uncover existing knowledge, foundations, and backgrounds to the task or topic. To make sure you have a firm foundation on which to build. To help you to organize new ideas when you hear them later on. Understanding of new material and memory will be strengthened if a foundation exists on which to build.

Method

My   Get comfortable (lying down, sitting, and so on). Run though a quick relaxation exercise. As individuals, close your eyes and think of the issue at hand. Ask yourself how diversity (especially cross-cultural relationship) affects you at work. What are some of the key concerns in this area. Evaluate how you relate to other people and how significant others have in turn, related to you. Try to recall how different relationships are expressed by yourself and others of a different cultural group. If you wish, write down some of your ideas.

Your   Split into pairs, and find a person who is most *similar* to you in terms, culture, work experience, language, and so on. Exchange information on the diversity challenge and related issues. A facilitator should ask each pair to briefly report back to the group on the important issues that they talked about. Note these issues for use later in the session. Discuss how easy or how difficult it is to communicate with another individual from a very **similar background.**

Their   Again, split into pairs. This time, choose someone who is **very different** from yourself (for example, background, work experience, language, or someone you would not normally work or talk with). Repeat the same exercise, focusing on sharing your different world "views".

Our   Break into groups of four to six people. Each group should be composed of people with both similar (my and your) and different (their) backgrounds—ideally a group that would represent the diversity profile of the organization. These diverse groups exchange views, exploring similarities and differences. Participants report back on how easy or how difficult they found relating to a very diverse group of people. Most importantly, they try to find a common ground.

Figure 7-3 The MYTO (My, Your, Their, Our) diversity exercise.

earlier subjective inspection of self toward active exchange and dialogue, creating that "dynamic" space between.

A good facilitator can make an important difference in how smoothly this transition is made. Again, specific strategies are available to the facilitator to make this step a fruitful one for all (Fig. 7-4).

Figure 7-4 Activator sheet: Build and bridge. (*Continued*)

What	Think about *what* build and bridge means to you.
	Exchange what you and others know about yourselves and each other. Consciously link different sources of information and ideas.
	Ask each other all of the "what" questions that you can: for example, "Tell me what is your reality, and I will tell you mine."
Why	Think about *why* this step of the change process is necessary. Increase the basic body of knowledge as much as possible before adding new inputs. Decrease the shaky base and have a firmer foundation to build on. Check wrong assumptions by sharing with others. Create anticipation and direction for new information. Understand where others are coming from. Promote active listening and communication. Build enhancing relationships.
	Ask yourself "why" questions: for example, "Why are our values different?" "Why my reality, or why your reality?"
How	Think about *how* to facilitate the build and bridge aspect of this process. Make a conscious effort to relate to each other, asking questions, comparing perceptions and clarifying old perceptions. Consciously bridge and link information and knowledge. Go beyond pair discussions, and share ideas in a small group, or conduct an open forum discussion in the workplace or workshop.
	Ask yourself as many "how" questions as possible: for example, "How did our different realities develop?"

When and where	Think about *when and where* this step of the process can happen comfortably.
	Ask yourselves "when" and "where" questions. Share the discoveries you make in step 1.
Who	Think about *who* is responsible for building and bridging realities in and out of the workplace. The individual should always take personal responsibility as it is in the individual's interest to build and bridge. However, in today's workplace, cocommitment and shared responsibility are vital. Other key players in the sharing game are peers, buddies, coworkers, mentors, facilitators, instructors, coaches, and team members.
	Ask yourself as many "who" questions as possible: for example, "Who helped create our different realities?"

Figure 7-4 (*Continued*)

Step 3: Understanding

At this juncture, participants are likely to be in different places in terms of assessing themselves and reevaluating their relationship to others (Fig. 7-5). Each person's process and progress depends, obviously, on a multiplicity of factors. Nonetheless, the power of relationships first formed with coworkers or "buddies" and then with strangers, as well as a growing relationship taking place with the facilitator and the group as an entity unto itself, reflect important shifts being made.

The meaning of *empathy* is becoming more clear as participants learn to listen, without judgment, and to hear in the present rather than see through a prejudicial screen erected years ago. Slowly, one by one, each individual begins to understand not simply who he or she is, or even who the "other" is, but, on a more significant plane, what it means to be open to people of diverse backgrounds and value systems. Attitudes that were once polarized and judgmental are dissipating in the understanding that a new "playing field" has been opened and that the rules now have to do with expressing warmth, empathy, and trust.

The relationship space is more alive than it was when participants first entered the room. For some, this new space will feel shaky, unpredictable, chaotic, and even unwelcome. Change is simply like that, especially for those who cherish stability and don't deal comfort-

Figure 7-5 Activator sheet: Understanding. (*Continued*)

What	Think about *what* understanding means to you. Understanding takes place through a conscious connecting of ideas, making what is "out there" a part of what is "in here." There is active integration and consolidation of information.
	Ask yourself as many "what" questions as possible: for example, "What do you understand about your existing values?"
Why	Think about *why* this step of the process is important. Change tends to happen if there is an attempt to really understand views and seeing the relationship between views. After self-analysis and interpersonal interpretation, the point of understanding is close.
	Ask yourself as many why questions as possible: for example, "How do I get to understand myself and others?"
How	Think about *how* you can activate the understanding aspect of this process. Through thinking, discussion, spray patterns, writing brief summaries, outlining, clarifying and verbalizing insights, simulation, notes, visualizing main ideas, acting out, reciting ideas, projects, and so on.
	Ask yourself as many "how" questions as possible: for example, "How do I get to understand myself and others?"
When and where	Think about *when and where* this step of the process is most applicable. This step applies throughout the process of development, before and after new inputs of knowledge, ideas, values, and so on. It can take place inside and outside the workplace. Active participation should be strived for by the individual and encouraged by facilitators, buddies, peers, and coworkers.
	Ask yourself as many "where" and "when" questions as possible: for example "Where and when did you begin to acquire your values?"

Who	Think about *who* is responsible for understanding self and others. Individuals and team members or partners have the key responsibility. Unless the individuals or team understands, they are unlikely to be able to apply their information in a relevant context. It is also in the interest of others (supervisors, managers, coworkers) that the individual workers and team members understand self and others. These significant others can play a key mediator role, making the link between different realities or worlds of the multicultural workplace. Ask yourself as many "who" questions as possible: for example, "Who helped us understand each other's realities?"

Figure 7-5 (*Continued*)

ably with ambiguity. But, with a grasp, however tenuous, on understanding something more about human interaction generally and one's own in particular, there is excitement, as well.

Some consolidation of steps 1 and 2 is occurring as each person works to integrate what he or she has learned and try out new behaviors. At this stage, most are better able to see how, in the new dynamic created, it is possible to lower or eliminate conflict, to improve communication on a moment-to-moment basis, and to give up the kinds of labeling and polarized judgments that typified past thinking. We have moved toward a place of understanding when we can ask

- What is missing in our usual ways of thinking, feeling, perceiving, valuing, judging, behaving, and labeling?
- What more do we need if our ideas, emotions, actions, judgments, labels, values, and so on are to serve us well?

In focusing on the relationship space between diverse people and in trying to understand this space, we are actively searching for a way to "think" about this new-found space between us. The way to fully understand it is to regard it as "alive"—in process and constantly changing.

The reality between self and others is a multifaceted and dynamic movement of differences. The acceptance of the reality of this movement between differences (now my perspective, now yours, now a third perspective) offers a radically more useful, alive, and "opportunistic" way to understand ourselves and others. Such understanding lowers conflict, increases communication, and prepares the soil for a new kind of creativity in work teams and partnerships. Most important, it allows us to move away from polarization in the workplace and toward harmony and balance. It is important not to be put off by the dynamic quality of the "space" between differences, regarding it as confusing and messy; rather, we need to embrace the opportunity it presents.

Understanding implies that something's been firmly communicated and has been agreed upon and settled, that there is a fuller grasp of the information intended to be conveyed. At the end of this stage each person should have a clearer understanding of the other, capable of saying: "I understand your past memories; I am clearer about your present reality and your future expectations; I am aware of my own stereotypes, prejudices, my way of relating and my way of being; I am now able to put myself in your shoes." Understanding is the basis of empathy. During the build and bridge and understanding phases, the participants are naturally improving their relationship skills—their capacity for expressing empathy and nonpossessive warmth.

Step 4: Neutral Space, Negotiating New Ways

The old images will have become "looser" and "fuzzier" now. The form of the old stereotypes and assumptions may still be there, but there is a willingness to let them blur and float away. More open interactions with others now call into question the "absolute" quality we had formerly attached to our different world views. When old realities become fuzzy and ambiguous, then the subconscious mind can begin its search for something new—something much more useful and diverse than a single (often energy-depleting) label.

Having identified and moved toward a neutral space, participants are now ready to negotiate across their different backgrounds and dispositions to take in new information (Fig. 7-6). No longer relying solely on the kind of information that comes from assisting people to simply "be" with another, reading material, audiovisual aids, and various other "products" proven to be useful tools for advancing communication and cooperation can now be introduced.

Cultural, racial, ethnic, and other differences are no longer perceived as barriers, and participants can now proceed to negotiate some of the issues specific to their work environments. The person facilitating can be especially active at this juncture not only by bringing in tan-

What	Think about *what* new inputs and information are available in the diversity challenge. Once a foundation for learning and change has been created in the earlier steps, you are open to absorb more formal learning material in the diversity field. Your earlier explorations and preparation have enabled you to energetically participate in the formal learning process through critical evaluation and active integration of new inputs. A variety of diversity learning tools are available (audiovisual, written, print material, as well as experts).
Why	Think about *why* new inputs are necessary in the process of change. New perspectives and skills are needed to move ahead, develop, solve problems, communicate effectively, plan, and complete tasks in a cross-cultural situation. Old perspectives seldom meet the challenges of today but are part of an ongoing chain of knowledge building.
How	Think about *how* you or the facilitator can activate the new information aspect of the process, through active listening, active reading, active note taking, active research, and active analysis. When you are confronted with new information (by reading, listening, looking), make an active attempt to remember to be attentive and start organizing material as it comes in. Do not passively take in knowledge; actively search for answers.
When and where	Think about *when and where* is this step of the process most applicable. This is usually the most formal and structured part of the learning process. You can receive new information and inputs from a variety of sources once you have increased your awareness through self-discovery.
Who	Think about *who* is responsible for new inputs of knowledge in and out of the workplace. You are always responsible for learning and can actively search for new inputs. A facilitator may be responsible for providing new information in the classroom, but buddies, mentors, supervisors, and coworkers can also be active "inputters," or referral agents.

Figure 7-6 Activator sheet: Neutral space for new information and inputs.

gible products but by actively assisting each person to express genuine regard for others as they begin to negotiate a real or hypothetical issue within their organization. It may be an issue over which they were previously deadlocked or a larger organizational issue they had either not been entrusted with heretofore or had not felt capable of dealing with. This phase presents the first opportunity for participants to actively engage together and to test their new skills, use new information, and negotiate a "third way," or middle ground—that is, as Eastern philosophy states, "not one, not two."

Step 5: Transformation

This is the step during which the old is transformed into something new (Fig. 7-7). There has, until now, been a complete immersion in trying to understand self and others. The new facts out on diversity have also been looked at and a third way negotiated. There has been an intense focus. Then if one is successful during this transformation step, there is a kind of relaxation of this intense focus and information gathering, and the challenge is allowed to retreat to the back of the mind, to the subconscious. In some mysterious way our subconscious begins to work things out. Then suddenly, after an indefinite period of time a new complete way of being or idea presents itself to the conscious mind. There is a transformation—there is an "Aha!"

During this phase, the role of the facilitator is even more crucial, for it is the time when it has become obvious to most that "the old is no longer working" but that new attitudes, awareness, and skills have not been fully incorporated. Nevertheless, there is anticipation and a level of readiness that the facilitator is wise to build on.

Some participants will be disturbed by the disappearance of past ways of relating to others, and they will be more tentative in approaching specific, work-related tasks and trying out new relationship skills on neutral ground. Others will be eager to try out new ways of working together—without the defenses, barriers, and prejudgments that at one time filled the space between them and coworkers, between them and management, between managers and department heads, between men and women, and the various other diverse combinations in their workplaces.

The facilitator might suggest that teams work on specific assignments, such as revising performance appraisals or recruitment policies, or, where applicable, testing their skills on issues previously the exclusive province of management, often working behind closed doors. The challenge will be to transform the space once taken up by "my" truth and "your" truth into a third truth that is not preordained

What	Think about *what* transformation might mean in a particular diversity challenge. Old realities are transformed into something more relevant to the new realities in the multicultural workplace.
Why	Think about *why* this step should be activated. You mistakenly believe that if you understand something or know all about it, you will remember it or change your own position. This is not the case. We must actively transform new inputs or realities from short-term to long-term memory and behavior. A way to slow down forgetting is through active transformation of knowledge.
How	Think about *how*, as facilitator, you can activate the transformation aspect of the process. Commit to practice, role-play, simulation, deliberate recall, writing summaries, discussion, and pairing of learning over a period of time instead of trying to achieve mastery in one attempt.
When and where	Think about *when and where* this step of the process is most applicable. This step comes toward the end of the learning process. It begins to occur after new inputs and information have been explored. Practice can happen in the classroom, but the real goal is enacting new patterns in the actual work environment.
Who	Think about *who* is responsible for transforming knowledge. This step is an individual responsibility. Again, others (buddies, supervisors, mentors, parents) can facilitate change through overviews, reviews, feedback, incentives, and so on.

Figure 7-7 Activator sheet: Transformation.

but that emerges spontaneously, in the present, from a genuine coming together of formerly polarized sides.

This is also the time when participants will sense, and be able to accept, that there are some areas that simply cannot be bridged; but, unlike before, they will not be regarded as unresolvable obstacles or sources of conflict or struggle. Like so many other truths the culture learns, mimics, forgets, and periodically resurrects, the prescription lies in the familiar serenity prayer that tells us to have "the serenity to accept the things we cannot change, the courage to change the things we can, and the wisdom to know the difference." All Eastern philosophy has pointed us to a third or middle way, but until now, its contemplative stance has been regarded as having no place in the aggressively action-oriented society of the Western world. Indeed, in any fast-paced urban economy, one of the most difficult transformations to be effected, and one resisted by workers and management alike, is rethinking the way time has been traditionally allocated—that is, shifting from the entrenched belief that only upper management can make the important decisions and decide what, when, how, and who need to be involved. In the old way, decisive action is held in high esteem and, at a scarcely veiled level, responsibility for determining overall organizational actions is thought to be something rightly (and righteously) the bailiwick of those high up in management. When workers are made part of decision making, when their input is seriously and genuinely accepted as a vital contribution to the final "product," whether a tangible or intellectual product, then time must be allowed for each person to have a say and for their input to be carefully assessed and made part of the final decisions before giving the signal to start "production." For each person to be encouraged and empowered to take responsibility for his or her part of the whole, management needs to give up thinking that workers have value only when they are actively "producing" what has been decided by others and summarily assigned to them.

Those progressive organizations in the United States, in South Africa and other countries, that have established an organizational culture honoring inclusionary practices, valuing diversity, and empowering all workers not only have been rewarded by the increased loyalty that comes from worker satisfaction but also by a boost in creative input and bottom-line results that still stand as the measure of an organization's success.

Trust becomes the basis of a transformed relationship and is the foundation for creating an *ubuntu* aliveness among people that interact across differences. Although real people may feel real loss in that they may have to let go of some of what they have valued, believed, or experienced, there are real opportunities and returns for beginning the process of transformation. The old versions are formless and "fuzzy," and the new vision is more integrated and clear. The final step in the process is to utilize this "aha!" or transformed view, to put this new reality into practice in practical situations within the work context.

Step 6: Utilization

Patience, constant practice, and time are needed for any new behavior to be internalized. The rewards of what, for many, will have been a deeply moving experience of self-discovery and an uprooting of long-held beliefs are now ready to be enjoyed. Although some tentative steps will have been taken to apply what was learned while still in the

What	Think about *what* utilization and practice of your trans-formed reality means for you. Cultivate trying out your new body of knowledge, values, ideas, and relationship patterns in new and in old situations.
Why	Think about *why* this step of the process is important. There is only one way to know if you have understood and can apply your new awareness and skills: through successful utilization in a real work context. Utilization is also vital for long-term change.
How	Think about *how* you or the facilitator can activate the utilization aspect of the process. Create an overview of the learning you have accomplished. Set yourself goals to try outside the workshop. Use case studies in which to utilize new information. Practice with coworkers, take risks, and tackle real situations. Draw up a self-monitoring "Behavior Sheet," and check how well you are progressing. Introduce the concept of *ubuntu* to your work team.
When and where	Think about *when and where* this step of the process is most applicable. This step can happen in the workshop by utilizing or practicing new relationship patterns and diversity awareness in quality teams, different work for-mats, in management roles, with customers, and so on.
Who	Think about *who* is responsible for the utilization of knowledge. This can be an individual, group, or organi-zational responsibility. Significant others can play a large role in facilitating utilization of knowledge and values back in the workplace. A formal *ubuntu* change plan can be put into place by various interest groups.

Figure 7-8 Activator sheet: Utilization.

formal *ubuntu* change process group, most of the continuing implementation will happen when participants are back in their workplaces (Fig. 7-8). Once in their own places of business, most find it useful to generate agreement that what has been learned will, in fact, be put into practice on a continuing basis. A system for monitoring, receiving feedback, and assuring committed participation usually needs to be put in place right away. Indeed, working out formal systems for maintaining *ubuntu* principles, as individuals, groups, teams, and organizations as a whole, will constitute the first immediate task for those who have gone through the change process. With these structures in place, one or more key issues may be assigned as targets for renegotiating on common ground.

An *Ubuntu* Conversation

The following is a conversation between Lente-Louise Louw and Joe Ndlela, a senior black human resource manager in South Africa.

LENTE: I'm speaking to Joe Ndlela from Transnet, and we're discussing the whole concept of *ubuntu*. What does *ubuntu* mean to you, as well as to other traditional black Africans? In fact, anything you want to share.

JOE: *Ubuntu* is a term that we actually use in all the African languages in South Africa. In *Shangaan,* we say *munhu*, in Zulu we say *umtu*, in Xhoza, *umuntu*, in Se-Sotho, *motho*, in Venda, *muthu,* and in Tswana, *motho*. You can hear, from what I've said to you, that the word sounds the same, and it means "a person." There is commonality between all the tribes in Southern Africa in terms of a value. What it means is, "I am what I am through other people." In African languages, especially *nguni*, which is the predominate language in Southern Africa, it's *umuntu ngumuntu nga bantu*. Translated in terms of international language, "A person is a person through another person." People could argue and say, "When you say that a person is a person through other people, what do you mean?" I mean, you know, if you see a human being standing in front of you, he's a person. Yes, indeed, he is a person, but what we are actually saying is that your behavior, your attitudes, your actions, are different from other people. You have feelings toward other people. The way you form relationships with other people is in such a manner that you don't create hardships for other people. If one were to look at it in terms of Christian norms and values, you do unto others what you would like them to do unto you.

LL: In others words, the way you treat them is how you want to be treated. So if you treat people in a way that is depleting, negative, and, in the extreme, totally inhumane, what are you telling those people about themselves, and what are you telling them about yourself?

JN: If you behave in a manner that is highlighted and inhumane in our culture, *we regard you as no person. You are an animal.* Not an animal in the sense of animal in its meaning as a "living thing," having certain characteristics that distinguish it from plants. Animals are also humane. If one were to play with terms, we talk about a person being an animal, belonging to the animal kingdom, and you sometimes say a person is humane, and you say that an animal can also be humane because it's loving, it's caring. It's only when it's threatened that it will behave in a much crueler manner. You are saying to that person that you are an animal in that you are doing things as though you are reacting in self-defense to what is being done to you which is not positive. Therefore, you are creating a defensive mechanism which is unacceptable. Your behavior in that context would be regarded as animal which is basically vicious, brutish and inhuman. There are behaviors which are destructive to a person's nature. We then say, "He has lost his *ubuntu* or humanity." So when we talk about *ubuntu*, we talk about a person who reflects humanness, kindness, togetherness, oneness with other people. Being in a position that you say, "So Lente has a problem. How can I assist Lente so that Lente and I are in the same wavelength?"

LL: Does the Rogerian term, *a helping relationship*, help us understand the concept? Carl R. Rogers tried to understand and deal with the interactions between human beings who are trying to create helping relationships. He wrote (*On Becoming a Person*, Houghton Mifflin, Boston, Mass., 1961) about the optimal helping relationship and *"the degree to which I can create relationships which facilitate the growth of others as separate persons [as being] a measure of the growth I have achieved in myself"* (emphasis added).

JN: Also, it helps me grow and helps you realize that I appreciate you and that I am a person. What I want to highlight is that our culture as black people in this country has been negatively impacted upon and affected by the policies of apartheid. The humaneness within the black community has been taken away. In the traditional black community, the person who doesn't work hard, who is lazy, who doesn't associate with other persons, who has not been seen as neighborly, is always rejected. He'll be scorned by people as being *"not a person,"* as *hana botho*. You are not a person, and people argue, "What does it mean when you say he is not a person? This is a person, a human being." Apartheid has helped create behaviors, actions, attitudes, patterns, and personalities that would not be expected in terms of the norms and values of what constitutes human nature in traditional African culture.

LL: Do you believe in a kind of *interconnectedness between people?* That every individual is an integral part of the community? I believe life is interconnectedness. Nature is interconnected, and we are not apart from this community of nature. Western man has set himself apart, always trying to conquer other parts of nature. So, when I hear you speaking, I hear "advanced" man speaking. The tragedy of the West is that they have not recognized how advanced African and other cultures in the world have been and still are (when not exploited), especially spiritually and ecologically. So advanced that I can see parallels between traditional African values and insights and the realities and insights that modern science is only recently beginning to verbalize and understand. You are at the same level, ahead of science, while Western man, who has prided himself as being "scientifically," or more accurately, "technologically" advanced is, in fact, only now discovering what was always true, is behind. And, yet, because Africa, put very simply, isn't feeding itself (and we both understand the complexity of this challenge), the West has, at times, labeled Africa as inferior. I find it extremely frightening because, when I hear you and other Africans speak, your values and insights are very advanced. As someone once said, "Africa is like the roots of a tree, and if the roots die, so will the rest of the tree."

JN: Lente, I must say that we believe that one cannot argue the question that a person is an individual. But as one listens to people from a Western culture, one has to move beyond their notion of individuality and competitiveness that goes with "their economic theory of competitiveness." *We, as Africans, take note of that, and we appreciate that each individual person is different; however, we also believe in collectiveness.* We believe that in order for an individual to be effective, that individual should be part and parcel of a team and be in a position to be able to contribute, to ensure that the team operates effectively in terms of oneness.

LL: *Are we then talking about a balance?* And in some ways, aren't things out of balance? In the past, we've had people in more Western, as well as patriarchal cultures (including black culture), focus very much on the individual, neglecting the team, neglecting the essence of community cooperation. However, in other cultures, participation, cooperation, and community has, sometimes, been overemphasized. So the challenge seems to be how do we return to a dynamic balance where individualism and cooperation, community, collectivism, and so on are part of the same whole—part of a natural creative tension which I believe is the perquisite for change and growth. It is not this or that but, at the very least, this *and* that. Ideally, we want to go beyond *and* to a dynamic interaction and balance of, so-called, polar opposites. We all have lessons to learn from each other.

JN: Indeed. You know, we emphasize the whole concept of communalism where, despite our differences, you get together and focus on what is at hand for the good of the community. But being a member of the community, if things don't go well, they impact on you as an individual. So individualism is being recognized and is being respected and, hence, *the whole question of* ubuntu: *You are a person through another person.*

LL: If we look at organizations, particularly corporations which are still dominated by white males, they seem to work very much as individuals—individualism based on an individualistic economic theory. Yet, most white males clearly operate in a community. They have their networks and their "old school" ties. So, they seem to, also, have access to that support, that *ubuntu,* but within their own ranks and have fully excluded other people from this network. Other cultures enter this world with their differences and individualism, but they are not given access to this white corporate community. So it's become difficult to achieve their full potential, especially when your own community has been destroyed. So Africans operate in white-dominated organizations on their own as an individual. It must be a challenge to go very far on your own without access to that *ubuntu.*

JN: *You tend to find these double standards in organizations,* which is unacceptable in our culture, because of the fear of competition from blacks when, in fact, all blacks want is to participate in creating that business environment. I was born into the Ndhlela family. My dad is known for how he interacts with people in terms of his *ubuntu* personhood. If I, as his son, want to do things out there in the community which are not acceptable—robbing people, stabbing people, beating up people, molesting, whatever—people say, "You know, that chap Joe is behaving in a manner that is uncharacteristic of his family." That, in itself, would curse the Ndhlela family despite the good personhood or personality of my dad. That would destroy the whole family.

LL: So, in other words, the community would moderate your behavior. You don't need formal policing when the traditional values of the community are intact. What happens in a society like South Africa where the community is broken down? Where there are no natural moderators of behavior, and there is no informal recourse to what you do, only policing? All our humane behavior seems to have been interfered with.

JN: In actual fact, *each and every black child who comes from a traditional black family is supposed to uphold the name of the family.* The family guards against any behavior that might place it in an unfortunate position whereby the child would be perceived as an *un*-person (*ha se motho*).

LL: In South Africa we have destroyed family life, and in organization, we have stilled the qualities of *ubuntu.* Who is going to foster these qualities, especially in the youth?

JN: I think you've asked a very good question in terms of who's going to be responsible for that. I think, parents and families, especially Black families, must start refocusing on traditional values. *We need to bring forth the whole culture of ubuntu, of tolerance, of understanding that we are all different, and of the same humane community if we wish to contribute to a stable and progressive environment.* We need to respect one another's feelings. That has not been done.

LL: What are the key qualities of *ubuntu?* You've mentioned humaneness. I have just heard you mention respect.

JN: Trust.

LL: What do you mean by trust?

JN: *Trust is openness toward one another.* Being able to open up one's heart to the next person. Whatever you have discussed and agreed upon in a situation, there is no way that that person would do you under in this specific situation or any other situation you are engaged in. You know that once you have agreed upon what has to be done, it will be done in such a manner that the person that you've been engaged in, in terms of the specific formulation of the project or situation, will do that without your having to ask, "Will they do it in the manner we agreed to?" or "Are they doing something else that is beyond what we agreed to?"

LL: In other words, something behind your back.

JN: It has to be done in such a manner that you won't need to have sleepless nights about a specific project you're engaged in. If, for example, Joe is engaged in a specific project and Lente is also engaged in this project, and both of us have the same vision, we will support each other. There is no other way.

LL: I know what you are talking about.

JN: Whoever might have an ulterior motive in terms of sabotaging that process is behaving in a manner foreign to the values of *ubuntu*.

LL: I know exactly what you're talking about.

JN: Nevertheless, it happens. You enter the corporate world. These values don't exist, don't exist at all. People talk about honesty, but the things that they do once you leave their office are totally different from what has been discussed and agreed to. So, the whole question of trust is an issue that is creating a lot of problems in terms of organizational effectiveness. *I think we have to address this question of trust which, I believe, in the black community is the core and seed of our humaneness. It starts with your own trustworthiness.* You may not necessarily be expecting the other person to behave the same as you but trust that what you do will create a vision in that other person's mind that you are an individual who has respect and trust for that person as a person. That's what it is. It then becomes a process of mutually creating that trust.

LL: It is an investment that takes place over quite a long period of time. But once that trust is broken, what then?

JN: It becomes very difficult.

LL: How do you regain it?

JN: It's very difficult to regain trust. However, because of the humaneness in us as a people, especially blacks, we tend to forgive very easily, even if someone has done very negative, very hurtful things to you. But, you see, the trust would have been impacted. You will give that person an opportunity to rescue him or herself. Blacks are capable of being in oneness, because trust is oneness. *It is being you watching yourself in a mirror. That's what trust is.*

LL: That's excellent. Being yourself, watching yourself.

JN: Watching yourself in a mirror. So this is what you need to encourage people to be capable of doing.

LL: So, in a way, the way you treat other people is a reflection of who you are. If you are a person who lies, manipulates, you really are reflecting who you are.

JN: One could expect that to happen to you. And have the whole question of "You're an animal, you're not a person."

LL: You're sabotaging yourself, your own development, your own spirituality. So what better monitor has one got than yourself? Once you get that, what other way is there to behave? You're only damaging yourself, in the long term.

JN: Sure, and people don't realize that. We are people, we are human beings, and being a human being is being a living creature who is supposed to be above all else, who has been created in the image of God. With that, one needs to say, that if I happen to find myself in a situation where I put other people down, stab them in the back, as happens in many business transactions that people are involved in, or in the corporate world where you find that colleagues are quick to say negative things about their colleagues, that that, in itself, is something one can reflect on and say, "I'm doing this, but what guarantees do I have that what I'm saying about this individual won't be said about me?" So, one needs to constantly have these things at the back of the mind.

LL: Now, what would you say has God, in whatever way we understand Him, given man? What is the greatest gift he has given man?

JN: The greatest gift that God has given man is to be able to distinguish between right and wrong, to be able to live with other people in harmony—which man has not utilized effectively, because of greed.

LL: And that's a powerful gift. I would like to share with you what I think it is because I think we're saying the same thing: The greatest gift He has given us is the potential to work together, to cocreate. God creates, so He gives man the gift to cocreate in relationship with Him and other beings.

JN: Not for self, but for everybody.

LL: What's a child? How are children created?

JN: Through cocreation and *cooperation.*

LL: Now, that is one example of cocreation. How many other things can we cocreate together, if we are in harmony? Not competition, in harmony?

JN: A lot of things.

LL: You talked about competition earlier. I think competition is more primitive than cooperation. And I think people aren't going to survive if they don't move beyond productivity, beyond competition, and move toward self to cooperation and breakthrough. Creation is something creative and unique. Competition is just like "mine is better than yours." That's not enough. How can ours, together, produce a third thing which is unique?

JN: I think...I want to make one statement which I strongly believe in. *A problem which has impacted negatively on our humaneness, on our person, our* ubuntu, *is the whole question of greed.* Greed, doing things to ensure that you're more powerful than anybody else. That is a problem. We need to change greed to a-greed. We are all agreed. We are in agreement about how things are done. We agreed that as from today, Joe and Lente will work together in assuring that what they believe can benefit the people in terms of valuing and managing diversity.

8

Valuing Relationship®

The Heart of
Valuing Diversity®

Lewis Brown Griggs

*So relationship is one of the most, or rather
the most important thing in life....One sees
that if there is no relationship between two
human beings, then corruption begins—not
in the outward structure of society, in the
outer phenomenon of pollution—but in inner
pollution, corruption, destruction begins
when human beings have actually no relationship at all....*

KRISHNAMURTI (1895–1986)

If there is anything that prior chapters in this book have made clear, it must be that only by *understanding difference* can we ultimately *make a difference* as diverse individuals in a workplace. And if there is another point clearly made by this book, it must be that only by coming to a working relationship as fully empowered individuals in all our diversity can we possibly create working relationships that help to accom-

The quotes in this chapter are from interviews conducted as part of the *Valuing Relationship*® film/video series.

plish the organization's purpose. So even though diversity is more complex and difficult to manage than homogeneity—and, in fact, precisely because it is so—learning to value one's difference is the primary step in learning to build relationships at work.

In this chapter I want to look from another angle and see the way in which *valuing relationship* is the primary step in learning to value and manage diversity. Through the *Going International*® and *Valuing Diversity*® films, I have sought to create awareness of the need to gain knowledge about cross-cultural differences in order to value our diversity, and that will always remain an important first step in the valuing and managing diversity process. Yet, ironically, I'm the first to balk when, having convinced someone of the need for cross-cultural knowledge to replace ignorance, I hear that person say, in effect, "Okay, now I'm ready to learn all there is to learn about how to relate to [one of those]." Maybe when we are heading into a weeklong negotiation with a group of "those" overseas, we can benefit from such a categorical approach to cross-cultural diversity; but when we are trying to value and manage the diversity within our own organization on a daily, ongoing, and quite personal basis, then my response, increasingly, is that in addition to replacing our ignorance about others with knowledge about the groups from which they come, we must focus equally on learning *how to relate*.

From this perspective, then, "valuing relationship" is the how-to of valuing and managing diversity—the missing link in the diversity chain without which all the other good diversity work would be for naught, without which all the other links in the diversity chain, or at least the chain itself, would fail to hold. So a conscious look at relationship issues is not only critical to the valuing and managing diversity process, it may be the very future of the process, the next step for all those organizations wondering where to go with their diversity initiatives.

In focusing on relationship, I will be reminding you of the many challenges facing organizations today and discussing why relationship is a primary challenge for an organization's growth and development. I will try to define what relationship is, look at the barriers to relationship, suggest ways to break down those barriers and build relationships that work, and then come back to the cross-cultural issues that lie at the heart of the diversity process.

Although every organization is a systemic whole (or a "holistic system" if you prefer) in which it is impossible to separate organizational, personal, and interpersonal responsibilities and opportunities, I will nevertheless ask us to do just that as a way of deciding what steps can be taken at the organizational level, what each of us as individuals must see as our own responsibility and opportunity, and where two or more in relationship must accept coresponsibility and act out of cocommitment to resolve an issue or accomplish a task.

Challenges

Organizations are constantly faced with major challenges. Nothing is more constant than change, and change is always a challenge to every organization (to its systems, strategies, policies, practices), to every individual (to his or her goals, behaviors, feelings), and to every team of two or more individuals (to its objectives, boundaries, procedures). Major changes being felt at organizational, personal, and interpersonal levels today are many. I will mention some just to remind us of the scope, the depth, and the breadth of the challenges we face.

Improved worldwide communication and transportation have helped to break down barriers between formerly isolated areas rich in resources, labor supply, and/or market potential, and to increase global competition for all three, leading, naturally, to a redistribution of all three. This development, in turn, has led to mergers, downsizing, and a variety of changes in management structures, work formats, policies, procedures, and practices. The amount of information and speed with which it comes to us is ever increasing and challenging our ability to even process it, much less respond to it.

Political, economic, social, and technological changes have always created challenges, but the speed with which they happen requires speedier responses and shorter, if any, rest periods in between before new changes challenge us to respond again. We are all feeling more and more unsettled because there is less and less time for any response to satisfy us as "the solution" for any significant period of time.

Fritjof Capra isn't the first to use the words "turning point" (*The Turning Point*, Simon & Schuster, N.Y., 1982), but he helped us understand the words in a far more significant way than we had before. It's not just that we are always challenged to do things in new ways to be responsive to new realities. As the simple chart in Fig. 8-1 so clearly helps us to see, it is that, often, the new way not only may not yet be clear but may not yet even work as well as the old way. We may feel that the old way is on the way out and that a new way is evolving, but we may not yet be exactly sure what the new way is or at what moment we should turn from the old way to the new way.

Now if this change could happen slowly enough so that we could see clearly the best and safest point at which to make the change, we could adjust more easily. But when these "turning points" come at us

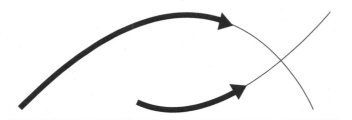

Figure 8-1 The new way of thinking and doing things does not always supplant the old way in a single abrupt change. (*From Fritjof Capra, The Turning Point.*)

so quickly, as they do now in so many areas of our life, we are doubly challenged to see clearly when to shift to avoid the increased cost of shifting too early or too late. The imminent arrival of the next turning point is unsettling, exhausting, and stressful; and it constitutes the greatest challenge facing every organization, every individual, and every interpersonal relationship today.

In responding to the question of what *relationship* has to do with the diversity challenge in the workplace, let's look more closely at what relationship entails in this setting. Together with changes occurring in competition, technology, organizational structure, information transfer, and demographics, relationships at all organizational levels are forced to change as well. Old ways of relating no longer suffice in the face of these profound external changes. Relationships between managers and employees, members of teams, men and women, as well as across foreign cultures, across national subcultures, with the public, with shareholders, with clients and customers, students, suppliers, subsidiaries, branches, regions, patients, leaders, peers, and so on are all affected in varying degrees. And these changing relationships, as indicated previously, oftentimes present as great a challenge as the very challenges that brought them about in the first place. And so, one wonders, how can we call on relationship to address the challenges facing the workplace today, especially the diversity challenge which, itself, makes relationship more difficult?

Why Relationship?

If relationships in the workplace are such a problem at best and are amplified in a diverse workforce, why then should organizations look to relationship as a place to begin the diversity journey? The answer is clear. Every initiative or program developed in response to any human resources challenge (quality, leadership, just-in-time, benchmarking, creativity, or even diversity), every effort to improve sales, management, recruitment, training, brainstorming, research, teaching, or productivity is completely and absolutely dependent upon the capacity of its workforce to form productive relationships. Accordingly, every organization's mandate is to create an environment that *enables* relationships to form and to work constructively toward common goals. Whatever your organization's bottom line (profit, quality of service, quantity of clients served), that bottom line and thus your organization's survival are directly served by assuring a workforce in which every individual feels free to be his or her fullest self, to allow those around him or her to do the same, and to willingly cocreate with those above them, beside them, or below them whether on tasks internal or external to the organization.

We've heard it said before that our human resources are our most important resource, and it is true. Or at least it is true that our human resources are *as* important as our financial, natural, and technological resources, and, as such, require no less attention. "No potential lost," a concept explained in Chapter 2, should be our goal in recruiting, training, retaining, promoting, and managing each "human resource." Remember, our unique differences are our greatest gift to each other and to our organization. From a management perspective, placing this emphasis on your human resources also means limiting organizational norms to those critical to accomplishing the organization's goals and recognizing that "normalizing" individual differences beyond that only limits the potential energy available to apply toward those goals. Most, in fact, would consider valuing and managing diversity work to be successful if each individual human (resource) were fully developed and fully valued. To some extent, this is true, but "valuing relationship" asks that we go a step further and recognize that it is the relationship *between* two or more "human resources" that is our most underutilized natural resource!

Until now, I have spoken generally about the challenges affecting the organization, the individual, and interpersonal relationships, as if the impact were the same at all levels. I have not made the case, for example, that these challenges affect the organization more than the individual or the individual more than the team. Throughout the rest of this chapter, then, I will focus on the organizational, personal, and interpersonal perspectives separately, first focusing on why dealing with relationships may be the key response organizations need to make to the challenges they face. I will then answer the question "What *is* relationship?" and continue on to explore the barriers to relationship, ways

to break through those barriers, and, finally, the cross-cultural consid-
erations involved in relationship issues in the workplace.

Organizational Energy

People—and the energy they bring—are key factors in creating systems (political, economic, social, and technological). And relationship
between workers is the enabling element that promises the extra
results, the unusual loyalty, and the often extraordinary output all
managers hope for. It is the element that can make the organizational
engine run smoothly or bring it to a grinding halt.

William Esrey, Chairman and CEO of Sprint, says in the *Valuing
Relationship*® films:

> Organizations today face enormous challenges. How do you
> attract, keep, and motivate exceptional people to really make the
> decisions and lead the organization through the unknown waters
> that we're all going to face tomorrow?

Although we cannot know all the challenges the future holds, we do
know that human energy is the most vital resource at the organization's
disposal and that all organizations must seek ways to release and direct
that energy effectively, that is, without overcontrolling or blocking it.
Organizations that do not recognize the value of people and relationship are shortsighted. The diversity of networks and interactions (relationships) among humans and the overall quality of their interactions
(the relationship) comprise the human energy that drives the organization. Given the national and increasingly global integration of markets
and customers—and employees to serve both—diversity and quality
interaction in the workforce become the greatest assets an organization
has for managing change. As Margaret Wheatley says in *Leadership and
the New Science* (Bernett-Koehler, San Francisco, Cal., 1992):

> It is the participation process that generates the reality to which
> (employees) make their commitment....We need a broad distribu-
> tion of information, viewpoints, interpretation, if we are to make
> sense of the world....A quantum universe is enacted only in an envi-
> ronment rich in relationships....Nothing happens in the quantum
> world without something encountering something else...Nothing is
> independent of the relationships that occur.

Relationships are the information and communication networks of
the organization, creating its real structure and its texture. Whatever
the organizational chart may look like, it is these relationship net-

works and partnerships that either facilitate the growth and development of employees and, by extension, the organization, or produce stagnation. Similarly, various "subcultures" that naturally emerge on the basis of job functions, operating units, or social and cultural groupings, can support or undermine the organization's overall mission. Just as strife between individuals and subcultures hinders productivity, relationship building and teamwork can get groups working together—breaking down the "us-versus-them" mentality that prevails at different levels within so many organizations.

Relationship is also the vehicle for turning inputs (human energy, partnerships, teams) into positive organizational outputs (productivity, cooperative, trusting and satisfied employees, retention of skilled talent, a healthy workforce, low absenteeism, and so on). The quality of the relationship determines the potential for synergy, where the "sum is equal to more than the parts" (for example, $3 \times 4 = 12$ instead of $3 + 4 = 7$), and organizations need this synergy if they are to be creative, to encourage breakthrough thinking, or even to simply remain competitive and responsive to the multiple challenges coming at us so quickly.

The quality and type of relationships within an organization define its culture which, in turn, influences the level of human energy potentially available to it. Individuals and teams do not give of themselves in organizations whose culture is characterized by rigidly controlling, judgmental, suspicious, or narrow-minded management. Furthermore, all human relationships are the basis of learning, change, growth, and maturation, and the same is true at the organizational level. All organizations must continually renew themselves. Every organization must be a *learning* organization to survive.

Personal Patterns

Personal relationship—relationship with self—is the key to developing and realizing personal, interpersonal, and organizational energy. According to Virginia Rebata of Marriott Management Services,

> Having a positive relationship with yourself absolutely enables you to have a positive relationship with others. It starts with self.

The quality of my relationship with myself (my integrity, character, and competence) directly affects my relationships with (diverse) others, my ability to take personal responsibility for getting the job done with others (teamwork), my ability to take personal responsibility for organizing others to get the job done (manage), and my relationship with my customers. The quality of my relationship with myself enhances my self-esteem and my self-confidence and is a source of personal empowerment. By understanding and knowing who I am and what I can do to be more competent, I can be more trustworthy, and I must be trustworthy before I can trust others or expect others to trust me.

Relationship with self is the real first step of valuing and managing diversity. By looking at my own internal responsibilities, I can come to understand that the prejudices I hold are just a form of denial (*I'm* not responsible for the discomfort I feel with *your* difference) and projection (so *you* must be responsible for my discomfort). I can come to see that my past experiences and learned prejudices are having an impact on my present and are, in fact, keeping me from "being present" in all relationships.

Knowing myself is what allows me to know, understand, and value the diversity of others so that I can build trust with them. With more trust comes the ability to communicate more clearly, to problem solve and network more effectively, and to realize the value of synergistic relationships and productive interdependency. Investing in my relationship with self and thus enhancing my relationships with others is therefore an important insurance policy against lost opportunities.

Interpersonal Synergy

Why are interpersonal relationships a vehicle for transforming personal and organizational energy in a way that helps us to meet new challenges? Even though, in the ideal sense, one enters a relationship as full and integrated a human being as possible, it is really a network of relationships (with family, friends, and the larger community) that forms us in the first place, and it is through these continuing, expanding relationships that we learn to become more. (See Chapter 7 on the *ubuntu* philosophy in Africa.)

According to Andrew Hughey of San José State University:

> I need relationships to cocreate. If I'm by myself, the only thing I bring to the table is what I have. It can be meager or bountiful, but it's only what I have. Only through relationship, only through interacting with you, can we transform that bounty into something that's bigger than both of us.

Relationship facilitates increased participation and thereby greater opportunity for synergy (3×4 instead of $3 + 4$). It also enables something new and unpredictable to take place. While it is true that having a diversity of perspectives available provides us with different options for problem solving, it is only with synergistic relationship that the contributions of each party can result in something way beyond what any individuals could dream of producing alone. The end result is pure magic. True breakthroughs can come out of such interactions—ideas and solutions not directly attributable or traceable to any one participant but, rather, reflecting the contributions of all the participants.

Participation at this level brings with it a sense of strong connection and belonging, both of which are vital to the health and well-being of the individual, those with whom one works, and the organization as a whole. Holistic health professionals emphasize that our physical and emotional health is affected by the extent to which we "see" and "are seen" by others—that is, the extent to which we feel acknowledged and understood. With feelings of connection and belonging with others in the organization, we can participate fully, cocreate with others in healthy, synergetic relationships, and contribute more productively to the organization. With some, perhaps only a few, the connection will be very close; with some, it will be close enough, and with an even larger group it will be cordial, but in all cases there will be feelings of mutual trust.

In summarizing this section explaining the centrality of relationship in our organizational lives, it should be clear now that what we can hope to be on our own is limited and limiting. Developing relationship is the key to maximizing our human resources, enhancing our personal creativity and our cocreativity, and successfully meeting personal, interpersonal, and organizational goals. Everything is related. Every action we take (and don't take) affects those around us.

What Is *Relationship?*

In the previous section my intent was to respond to the question Why—for what reasons and in what ways—is relationship the key vehicle for responding to the array of challenges faced by organizations that want and need to grow? In this section I will explore the fundamental question: What *is* this thing called *relationship?* You will notice that I chose to define it only after establishing its relevance. Most of us, in my view, want to see the relevance of a concept before we care enough to examine it at the close range necessary for intervention and implementation of programs, for example.

In working to define *relationship,* we at Griggs Productions came to the conclusion that it is not enough to see it as the "connection between" or even the "space between" two people. If two gases "meet" and "mix" with each other through a conduit, the conduit is not the relationship; and if there is no rigid conduit but just air between, then the air, the space between, is also not the relationship. But the relationship does take place *somewhere* in the space between. And so we asked, does it take place only at the point of "meeting"? No, it seems to begin ahead of the actual meeting of "matter" and to continue after the separation of physical matter. So what, then, is relationship?

Regardless of whether the relationship is in a homogeneous or a heterogeneous population, it always involves a bridging between differences. And so we perceive relationship as being that which goes on, that movement of energy, in the dynamic space between individuals. This "space between" is not empty; it is filled with energy waves transmitted by individuals as they interact. These "here-and-now" interacting energies move within an already existing energy field created by past interactions with a host of others. This existing energy field, then, has a life of its own; its "memory" of past relationship interactions produces invisible patterns in our minds, and they have a strong impact on all new interactions. In that sense, no relationship is fixed or limited to the parties immediately involved. Rather, it is in a constant state of being what it is and becoming what it might be.

Given, then, that relationship involves movement between differences, you can see how we came to the realization that valuing and managing relationship is the how-to of valuing and managing diversity. The following narration excerpted from our *Valuing Relationship*® films constitutes a useful introduction to the ideas I shall present next as I examine, one by one, the inseparable organizational, personal, and interpersonal aspects of The Relationship System© designed by Griggs Productions.

> Our world, with all the power and energy of its natural resources, is an interconnected, living system, a vast web of dynamic relationships.
> All relationships are a continuous movement between differences, part of an underlying pattern connecting us all, and all of nature's patterns are constantly changing.

Our focus is no longer only on the individual parts, but more on the synergistic relationship between the parts, that cooperative process of creation and cocreation which leads to growth, change, and unpredictable breakthrough.

The participation of human energy, in all its diversity, is an essential part of this web of life. And our capacity for relationship provides us and our organizations with the most flexible resource for responding to the complex challenges of today.

Relationship patterns in organizations are like a unique "ecological system," a living network of dynamic energies, in which no one part is as important as the whole and the relationship between the parts.

Neither the organizational, personal, nor interpersonal aspects of the "relationship system" is solely or independently responsible for the breakdown or the recovery of an organizational culture. As is the nature of any "system," each component is inseparable from the other; they are interdependent. But for purposes of discussion, I will deal with each in turn and rely on you to realize that they must exist in dynamic unity if an organization is to recover from past underutilization and transform itself to deal with present and future realities.

Organizational Energy

Over time, personal and interpersonal relationship patterns create a dynamic organizational energy field with potential for enhancing or depleting human productivity.

An organization's culture is shaped by the diverse interactions that create its own "energy field" over time. Increasingly diverse relationships now characterize today's organizations. Within the organization are: cross-functional relationships, manager-employee relationships, mentor-apprentice relationships, staff-patient relationships, and rela-

tionships within and between teams. In addition are relationships between an organization and its customers or clients and with the community. All other factors being equal, it is the *quality* of these relationships that creates opportunities for competitive advantage.

Nothing that goes on in an organization is independent of the relationships within it. Every interaction is potentially important to the organization if it is to create an "energizing" culture and environment.

The organization, like the individuals in its workforce, is a living system, and like a family system, nature's ecological system, or our body's systems, the behavioral dynamics that take place in that system can be depleting and/or enhancing—that is, closed versus open, controlling versus enabling, rigid versus flexible. The dynamics that typify the organizational culture affect the extent to which the potential human energy of its workforce is available to the organization. An organization can be regarded as *inclusionary*—that is, encouraging open, trusting, and participatory relationships among its people—or it can be seen as *exclusionary*—that is, establishing divisions and hierarchies that separate one from another.

In either case, a "relationship field" is created, and it affects all employees, old and new, and stakeholders. When depleting patterns of relating persist and are picked up by new employees, there is usually something in the organizational culture that is triggering the pattern. Significant action is required for deeply entrenched patterns to be transformed.

It is the organization's responsibility (and opportunity), through its systems, policies, and role models, to foster relationships that work by creating a culture in which individuals feel safe and empowered to be their fullest selves expressing all of their diversity. In these efforts, leaders and other individuals in the organization can make as much or more of a difference than any system or policy they enact. Author Steven Covey even stresses that "there is no such thing as organizational behavior—there is only individual behavior—everything else flows out of that" (*Principle Centered Leadership*, Summit Books, N.Y., 1990/91).

Personal Energy

Each person is a natural source of available energy with unique personal patterns and the choice to act in depleting or enhancing ways.

Each of us is a powerful resource, an almost endless source of energy potentially available to apply to every situation and relationship to which we are exposed. For many, however, that energy has become blocked or misdirected by past experiences and memories, future expectations or fears, and present conditions within and around us— much of which we may not know at a conscious level.

As Marilyn Zuckerman of AT&T puts it in the *Valuing Relationship®* films:

> There are structures and patterns that exist within each person, within ourselves, and very often these structures and patterns are things that we're not consciously aware of; but they're influencing how we behave, they're influencing the decisions we make, and they very often get in the way of our relationships [with others].

And so, as has been emphasized throughout this book, knowing ourselves is the foundation for any contributions we can hope to make to others, whether to other individuals, to our work teams, or to the organization as a whole. We must become conscious of the energy patterns rooted in our genetic inheritance, our history, our culture, and so forth. We must become conscious of our own attributes, skills, talents, blocks, shortcomings, and inabilities. Self-awareness is a process that happens over time and continues throughout life. It is built step by step, interaction after interaction, relationship by relationship. If it is sometimes a struggle, it is also a key vehicle for liberating ourselves from past tyrannies that have, unwittingly in many instances, driven our actions in the present.

Paradoxically, while the intense inner work of increasing our self-awareness can be accomplished only by ourselves at a very personal level, it cannot be done alone. "Everywhere I go I find myself" is true for everyone. Our relationships with others illuminate our relationship with ourselves. The degree to which we are able to form relationships with others is a measure of the growth we have achieved within ourselves. We can become our fullest selves only through relationship and through reflecting on our responses to relationships we form. In the self-discovery process, we need to give ourselves permission to make mistakes and learn from our experiences. It helps to regard one's self as a dynamic, changing, energy force that "dances" with another's energy force from which both may enter into an unanticipated and unpredictable relationship pattern, sometimes creating between you a third pattern—manifested in a product, concept, or approach neither of you saw before.

So in looking at *personal* aspects, responsibilities, and opportunities in relationship, we are focusing the camera, so to speak, on *my* relationship with self, *my* relationship with others, *my* contribution to the dynamic, *my* responsibility to get the job done with others, *my* responsibility to organize and to facilitate others. And it becomes obvious that all of this has a ripple effect that extends far beyond our personal arena.

As Carl Rogers states in *On Becoming a Person* (Houghton Mifflin, Boston, Mass., 1961), "If I can provide a certain type of relationship, the other person will discover within himself the capacity to use that relationship for growth, and change and personal development will occur."

Interpersonal Energy

Diverse individuals have an opportunity to cooperate, cocreating unique and unpredictable outcomes.

As Willis Harman of the World Business Academy says in the *Valuing Relationship*® films,

> We are individuals, [but] we're also part of a whole, and the process through which we come to understand is through relationships. Relationships can be with other people; they can be with other events; but all of those relationships, together, form the web with which we come to understand.

And as Jeanne Guillot of Sprint adds in the same film,

> There's an energy that goes on between people; it's almost like it's an electrical current; and it's that current that carries the message of who we are or what we want to say to the other person.

In other words, relationship is not something static or fixed (although it may sometimes seem so); it is a fluid and ever-changing energy pattern between and among individuals. The overall quality of the relationship is determined by how the individuals behave in relation to one another. No matter how entrenched one's behavior is or how strong one's personality, each individual is influenced by the other on an ongoing basis. Once you recognize the interdependent nature of relationship, you can consciously plan to change your behavior, knowing that in doing so you will influence the other person and the relationship.

Because relationship is constantly evolving, it requires constant practice and skills-building efforts to safeguard it. But because relationship is a dynamic entity, once you focus on it, it starts shifting. Relationships, as organic entities, have the potential for self-correction, but, to ensure the desired results, both parties need to consciously focus on the dynamics of the relationship.

Although much has been said about communication in connection with relationship, there is much more involved than "good" or "bad" communication. You can have productive communication as you are making sexist or racist remarks and still, obviously, find that you have no enhancing energy or trust between you. Meaning and intention are as important as the verbal or written messages we deliver. The quality of our interpersonal relationships determines whether the outcome will be merely additive ($3 + 4 = 7$) or synergistic ($3 \times 4 = 12$). In a numerical sense, relationship also has the potential for subtracting from each individual—depleting energy and arriving at negative results.

As indicated previously, relationships are formed over time, and re-forming them also must be done over time. Our communications with others tend to settle into patterns. When negative relationships have been allowed to endure, out of neglect or, most often, out of our feelings of inadequacy in "fixing" them, it is time to learn new patterns of relating that will renew or even transform the "energy potential" of the relationship. In every interaction there is an opportunity for the individuals involved to consciously invest in that interaction, whether destructively by lodging a "mistrust" brick in the wall of the relationship or constructively by lodging a "trust" brick. The number and quality of our interactions eventually shape the interpersonal relationship. Once the *quality* of the relationship—enhancing or depleting—has been established, only a significant event will change it.

In the following sections, I will first label those recurring patterns that are known to create difficulties in our relationships and then offer some remedies or behaviors that we have found to facilitate communication, restore constructive interactions, and lead to synergistic solutions.

What Are the Barriers to Relationship?

It has been well established in the previous chapters that once diversity has been acknowledged as an asset, valuing diversity must become an integral part of overall organizational strategies and not left to chance. The same must be said of relationship. I hope it is now evident that relationship represents the most untapped natural resource available, whatever the context. In that sense, relationship, also, must become the focus of conscious organizational strategies. The process might start with looking at what *prevents* cooperative and enhancing relationships within the organization, within each of us as individuals (the personal level), between us in our partnerships and teams (the interpersonal level), and in the operations of the organization as a systemic whole (organizational). Again, let's take these on one by one even though they function dynamically in all organizations.

Organizational Barriers to Relationship

Past history, traditions, rules, policies, procedures, and standards often prevent enhancing relationships from developing in organizations. "We've always done it this way." "If it ain't broke, don't fix it." But the truth is that what worked before usually worked in another time with another set of external realities and another group of employees and/or customers. And while it is true that you don't want to "throw out the baby with the bathwater," it is also true that the bathwater can't be used and reused forever; it has to be changed and replaced with fresh water. So although historical traditions are valuable and should be maintained if they still serve those involved, rules and policies and standards work best when they are periodically questioned and rewritten to be made applicable to today's employees, customers, clients, students, and so on.

The structure of an organization can also be a barrier to effective relationships in the workplace. As Beatriz Vidal of Xerox has said,

> Organizations have a lot of barriers in terms of developing relationships. Hierarchy is one of them. The more hierarchical the organization, the less it tends for relationships to develop.

What she says makes sense. Vertical relationships within a highly structured organization dependent on maintaining authority and power over others can create only those relationships responsive to such dynamics.

Lack of safety is another barrier to relationship. If the organization is punitive, if relationships are defined by stress, fear, and mistrust, then the organization depletes the energy of its employees because they must use what energy they have to survive; they can't afford the "risk" of putting energy into creative pursuits. If the cost of relating is too great, employees will "stay but leave"—stay employed by doing just enough but leave emotionally by not bringing their real energy to work. The other solution for them is to leave completely.

Connected to safety is trust, inside and outside the organization. If the organization is concerned only with its own growth and profits at the expense of the employees—or the clients, the community, and the environment—then it will be a struggle to develop trusting relationships at any level. Yvonne Alverio of Aetna has said,

> Oftentimes, when there isn't trust in an organization and something goes wrong, then you start pointing the finger at who did it and what happened, and because there's no trust, you start saying, "I didn't do it, you did it." And before you know it, you're not able to get the task done.

Lack of leadership constitutes another barrier. Without role models demonstrating how to relate vertically, horizontally, in teams, in all our diversity and cross-culturally, how can employees feel safe to practice new ways that might work with new realities?

Organizational energy patterns and relationship patterns can be very depleting. Remember that the organization is a living system that is characterized at any given time by patterns of interacting that have developed over time. If these patterns are energy depleting (controlling, closed, indecisive, blaming, prejudiced, risk averse, or conformist), then there is literally less human energy available to apply to the organization's goals and objectives. And if relationship patterns have become institutionalized, then it becomes increasingly difficult and sometimes impossible for any individual to act differently and survive.

Let's look at control as an example. Obviously, balance is everything, and each specific situation calls for a different balance. A military attack requires more control than an architectural brainstorming session. But too much control is as frequent a barrier to relationship as is chaos—too little control. So I want to use control as an example of how imbalance (too much control or too little control) creates an environment that depletes the amount of energy available for relationship and therefore for creativity. Stephen Covey, you will recall, said that all behavior is ultimately personal, not organizational. While it is true that in each moment each of us chooses to behave as we do, it is also true that certain organizational cultures are so dominant that they attract people of similar style and/or mold them to their style. The control-chaos spectrum is one of these "personal" behaviors that I believe can become an "organizational" behavior and which therefore lends itself to being looked at from an organizational perspective.

Overcontrol starts at the top. If the leader in the organization or the senior management team is overcontrolling, then the behavior is likely to spread out and down the hierarchy. It may look like "take-charge" behavior, but it is the sort of take-charge behavior that inhibits the participation and input of others. An overcontrolling organizational culture is one in which leaders, managers, and supervisors are dogmatic, perfectionist, rigid, and overly demanding. They impose on others their way of doing things, as though it were the only way—the "right" way. And to ensure conformity, they create and enforce a lot of rules for others to follow.

Controlled cultures do not respond well to change. In fact, they do not intend to respond to change. Where control is appropriate (in the military, in a laboratory, or in a bottling plants, perhaps), the flexibility provided by relationship may be less an asset than the certainty provided by control. But where change does affect an organization and therefore when an organization does need to respond to change—the assumption throughout this book—overcontrol is deadly precisely because it stifles the diversity of responses necessary to create the "best" response for the new situation.

What does "controlling organizational behavior" look like, feel like, sound like? When is there an imbalance of control that depletes the energy otherwise available to respond to change? It is when too many of the leaders and managers are behaving in too many of the following ways.

Values, Beliefs, and Assumptions

Need to look perfect outside to cover lack of substance within

Belief that world and/or other people are basically unsafe and unreliable

Mistrust in others' competence

Belief that everything must be controlled

Characteristics and/or Traits That Might Appear

Manipulation

Repression

Prejudice

Perfectionism

Dogmatism

Polarized thinking

Narcissism

Stereotyping

Judgmentalism

Righteousness

Invasiveness

Inflexibility

Self-centeredness

Obstinacy

Defensiveness

Overfocus on Peripheral Aspects of Production

Efficiency

Responsibility

Predictability

Orderliness

Consistency

Timeliness

Actions (Things We Might See)

Doors always open, closed, or 3 inches ajar

Lots of policies instituted

Constant check of time cards and/or punitive response to lateness

Lists, lists, lists

Obsessive behaviors (rechecking memos again and again)

Doing it all oneself (not leaving to "chance" lest others fail to do it, or to do it "right")

Desk and office in complete order always (everything in "its place")

Verbals (Things We Might Hear)

Interrupting to correct others (managing their conversations for them, finishing their sentences for them, or stressing their own point of view)

Constantly checking for approval on every small step

Using language in overly careful, overly conscious ways

Using vocabulary to intimidate others, to make them feel inferior, to distance self from others

Nonverbal Body Language

Hypervigilance

Tight jaw, shoulders, body

Invasive eye contact

Arms across chest

Ignoring others' boundaries

Restlessness (tapping, and so on)

Leaving early or coming late

No space or time for others

Looking at watch when someone else is talking

Their tension (as if they are entering a mine field)

Your tension (as if they will punish you for every "wrong" word or action)

And what does a chaotic, undercontrolled environment look and feel like? Obviously, just the opposite in most cases but sometimes too much of the opposite: indecision, equal weight or attention to all perspectives, no accountability, no direction, no leadership, no respect for schedules, no rules, and so on. I don't want to give equal space or time to a long list of those behaviors, but I do want to make it clear that too much of either extreme (control or lack of control) can be equally depleting to the human energy available and necessary for meeting challenges and responding to change.

Among all the interviews we did in the developmental phase of the *Valuing Relationship*® films, the following personal stories stood out as good examples of leaders who were too controlling (in the first case) or too lacking in control (in the second case) and whose behavior caused many other adaptive and maladaptive behaviors that wasted employee energy.

First, the story of a creative genius whose controlling personality inhibited the creativity of his employees:

He had designed a product more clever, more practical, and more cost-effective than anything available at the time. But his ego was such that his desire for the success of his product was sabotaged by his desire to be famous, to be recognized as having made it on his own.

He crushed our creativity by denying anyone the responsibility to make decisions without his approval, thereby destroying our incentive to perform well and our pride in our own contributions. He took away the carrot and instead hung weights of expectation over our heads. Then his response to our work was always critical of what was imperfect about it rather than supportive and encouraging about what was useful. And he constantly burst into our offices to see exactly what we were doing and if we were doing it "right."

He denied to the marketing department and to the creative software department the money necessary to get the product off the ground so that he could spend it on new inventions to make himself famous, all the while expecting us to make his first invention an immediate market success and then criticizing us when it didn't happen and when we didn't do it the way he told us to do it, which was usually either unfeasible or unethical.

He tended to see mistakes only as failures to do things the "right" way and was more concerned with finding someone to blame than with helping us learn something from our mistakes. His judgments were usually a premature yes or no when there should have been further exploration of alternatives. Furthermore, he was so concerned with being dominant that he made every situation a contest, preventing the emergence of new ideas. And he could neither accept help from, nor appropriately help, us.

Perhaps even more depleting than all of the above was his tendency to gossip about and conspire with employees, somehow imagining that each of us was more loyal to him than to each other. He literally talked with each of us about the errors and faults of others in the company, behind their backs.

Of course, we tried talking him out of his ways and into understanding our needs and concerns, but his response was just as neurotic as his original behavior. He pouted and fumed and made more demands, finally wanting to approve of every decision made in production, marketing, and the art department. His behavior completely destroyed any desire to create, or at least to create for him. We all remained committed to the success of the product, and we all saw how possible real success was if we could all cooperate with each other (as we were inclined to do) without his overbearance. But his presence and his demands were too much to overcome, and we all stopped creating and producing, slowly but surely, and irreversibly, until several of us could take it no more and left the company.

We could not have worked with a more intelligent and creative individual, but his own emotional problems were so great that they crushed our creativity and spirit.

The next story is of a manager whose lack of control or leadership failed to take advantage of the available energy in his department:

I found myself in an organization with lead or cement on its feet. Nobody was killing our creativity from above; it was more like our seeds of creativity were just never watered. There were no goals, no interest, no energy, no incentive, no leadership. There was always a reason not to do something, because it wouldn't work or it wouldn't sell.

The manager of our small group seldom initiated anything or even had a creative idea. He sort of slid in and out of his office and spent the day in useless meetings and out to lunch and hoping nothing very challenging would develop. If one of us had an idea he approved of, he would say to do it and let him know how it went, offering no creative input or support or even constructive criticism. His meetings with our group were "safely" shallow and trite, mentioning only what we all knew.

His reports to senior management were exaggerated and often patently false. And the greater the trouble he was in, the greater would be the fabrication he used to try to extricate himself.

This manager was so indecisive and afraid of risk that he couldn't even see a more effective way when it was presented to him, and he certainly didn't look for new ways. He had a need to work only on problems included in his job description and to have his responsibilities well defined so he couldn't be held accountable for more. He was afraid of making mistakes, and afraid of making any waves that might disturb the status quo. He even feared admitting that no solution had been found and would either use delaying tactics or report invented actions that had really not been taken.

This manager was pathetic in his lack of control, and the effect was like an insidious poison that slowly began to affect everyone around him. Since none of his neurotic behavior was aimed at us, none of us had the desire to strike back or score. We just went about our business, but we wasted energy tiptoeing around him, meeting on our own in secret, and working with top management to accomplish what he should have been accomplishing. We had tried to deal with him directly, but he was unable to do so, and we had no other choice. We eventually got good at it and made much progress working together as a team should, but the time and energy consumed working around him could have been spent on more creative activities (or at least more productive activities—I must admit our tactics for running the department around him were quite creative). Eventually he was fired, but not soon enough.

Control or chaos is only one aspect of leadership behavior that if not in dynamic balance can become dysfunctional "organizational" behavior. Obviously, there are many others. In fact, *any* other depleting personal or interpersonal behavior can affect "organizational" behavior.

Personal Barriers to Relationship

What are the personal issues that shape the type and quality of relationship each of us has with ourself and with others? Personal history, childhood experiences, family or country-of-origin issues, work experiences, and so on, if not resolved, can all feel like baggage we carry with us and into our work. They are part of who we are, but if we don't understand it consciously and take responsibility for it, then it can keep us from being fully *present* in our lives, at home and at work.

I'll never forget my amazement at discovering the extent to which we each subconsciously look for a workplace, or try to re-create it if it isn't already so, that replicates most of the primary relationships with which we grew up. You can determine whether that is true for you by creating your own "organizational chart" and filling in the roles of your siblings, parents, aunts, uncles, and grandparents, and any "significant others" in your life. On the lines between, make notes about the relationship (deaths and divorces, traits, such as abusive, loving, alcoholic, cooperative, trusting, mistrusting, codependent) whatever is descriptive of your family. Then create another organizational chart of your actual workplace and look specifically for any parallels. Don't make too much of it—take what you can use and leave the rest—but notice what stands out for you, and then reflect on whether any of the barriers you are experiencing in your working relationships are similar to those you have uncovered in your family constellation. Sometimes, this increased awareness enables a person to break through relationship problems that previously seemed insurmountable.

Just as living with our feet in the past keeps us from living fully in the present, so does living with our eyes on the future. Goals and objectives and other appropriate focusing on outcomes is generally constructive, but, again, a dynamic balance is required. Being constantly dissatisfied with the present is not the way to use your time most fully, to be your fullest self, or to achieve even your short-term ends.

When we have not integrated our strengths and weaknesses, our "light" and our "dark" aspects, or if we haven't achieved a balance between our intellectual, emotional, physical, and spiritual selves, then our relationships with others suffer. We "act out" one or more of these behaviors inappropriately and thereby deplete our own energy and the energy of those with whom we are in a working relationship.

Another barrier to effective relationship is hiding behind a mask, something that may have served you when you were young and you found that you got certain things only if you presented yourself in a certain way. As Ronita Johnson of Pacific Gas and Electric has said,

> We feel that we have to take on the same body language, gestures, styles of presentation as the dominant culture. That's very costly for us on a personal basis. Think of all the energy that I have to spend to be somebody else.

Sometimes we don't even know that we are hiding. For some, it is a lifelong pattern, but for others it is a behavior they use and discard as they perceive the need. Family, friends, and coworkers may see it, but, by not calling attention to it, they tacitly support this behavior. The truth is that we cannot be 100 percent ourselves when we are masking. We may "think" we are meeting what others "think" their needs to be, but when we hide behind a false self, no one's needs are being met.

Some other personal barriers that deplete the energy available for meeting personal, interpersonal, and organizational challenges are noted below. We may not recognize all of them as part of our own behavior, but most of us have used some of them some of the time. I express them in "we" form because doing is helps us be more conscious of when we do them than when others do them to us:

Control.   When we need to be right and make another person wrong, a power struggle ensues that leads to polarization and to the feeling that even more control is necessary.

Prejudice and -isms.   We often seem to be reacting to someone based on generalizations, stereotypes, or assumptions rather than facts. We "pigeonhole" people based on what they look like (race, gender, culture) rather than see them for who they are and what they are capable of.

I remember a white-male corporate director of human resources who began a diversity seminar by acknowledging that several years earlier he had discriminated against the (black) man most qualified for a new job. His open and tearful apology to the man (in the room!) was a powerful way to begin diversity training, but more importantly we could all feel the huge loss of potential and energy wasted (with endless ripple effects) by that one action several years ago.

Manipulation.   We sometimes try to orchestrate or twist another's efforts and behaviors and opinions to meet our own self-serving needs, usually to create the impression that it is in the other's best interest.

The following story came out of our valuing relationship research and illustrates how such manipulations play out.

A coworker took an idea of mine and tried to make it his own. This individual is extremely bright but has no self-confidence. He can never really say what's on his mind, so he twists other people's words and ideas to make them look like his own. He is a fence-sitter on everything, is extremely manipulating, and has a way of starting fights between others and then backing away when things get hot, leaving others holding the bag.

Another story we heard frequently was of a team organized for a specific purpose and encouraged to present ideas and plans to a manager, only to find that the manager was determined to do it his own way. Most people with this story felt they were used as puppets to serve the manager's self-interest and that the manager had a "hidden agenda" or "something up his sleeve."

Lying.   We sometimes say something that isn't true to protect ourselves from the shame or guilt we might feel if we were to tell the truth. Often we claim that our lie is actually to protect the other person from the truth (the feelings and anger and pain they would feel, we say, if they knew the truth).

We created a scene in the *Valuing Relationship®* film series to reenact the best (worst) example of lying that we had gathered in our research. In it, two partners in sales steal each other's best leads and then lie about it to each other. Not only are the immediate leads and opportunities lost to each and not only do they each feel justified in lying to the other but, most important, the trust is gone. Such depletion of energy from loss of trust is devastating to any relationship and any organization.

Withholding.   For self-serving reasons, we hold back information, blocking others from access to information or to resources they need to clarify or complete tasks. We can withhold information or truth by being closed-mouthed, deflective, vague, or evasive.

Often, withholding information, or the truth, is intended to keep someone off balance, keep the power of knowledge to oneself, so that we have time to operate behind the other's back. (Notice, in fact, how these depleting behaviors overlap: that is, withholding is a form of lying, and lying is both manipulative and controlling.)

Withdrawing.   We sometimes stop participating with others by "going away" physically, intellectually, or emotionally. We may get very quiet or appear to be "spaced out" or "confused." We may appear to be passive, disinterested, "somewhere else," and generally difficult for others to reach.

In my experience, when we withdraw, it is because we feel "right" and can't stand others being "wrong" and not acknowledging us, or we feel "wrong" and unable to face it at the moment or unable to tolerate the other's righteousness about whatever is at issue. It is usually the child in us making the familiar decision to "take our toys and go home." Obviously, no cooperative teamwork or even resolution can take place when we act out by withdrawing.

Doubting. Sometimes we treat others as potential threats rather than as potential supports. We view others with caution or suspicion and may even believe they are operating from hidden and undesirable motives. Or we might simply doubt their competence and fail to give them the "benefit of the doubt" (before we judge them) and the opportunity to risk or learn from their own experiences.

The "benefit of the doubt" is something we all ask for and expect, at least until we have had a chance to explain ourselves or our actions further; but it is difficult to really give someone the benefit of the doubt—especially when we think we know better already. It is really more a test of our ability to give than a test of the other's ability to earn it.

Judging or Righteousness. We are at times highly and inappropriately critical of others, even openly deriding or talking negatively about them. When we are being judgmental, we tend to look and act as if we feel superior to others, and we can be quite argumentative and polarizing.

It may not be necessary to add that when we are that judgmental, we might be feeling inadequate and uncertain of our position and thus overcompensating for our ultimate need to have our perspective heard, even if not agreed with.

Blaming. We sometimes seem unable to "see" or "own" our contribution to a situation and, instead, see another as the sole problem. "I am not the problem, you are." The problem is "out there," we want to say, justifying ourselves and rationalizing our behavior, often by intellectualizing.

In my experience, looking at my own behavior and that of others, blaming always follows a "denial" of responsibility within ourselves. Rather than own up, we project, or falsely attribute, our feelings or thoughts about which we are in denial on to others.

Sabotage. When feeling threatened by another's ideas or achievements or insecure about our own, we sometimes do or say something to discredit or harm the other or act in a way that makes others disapprove of us (especially if we are used to disapproval).

Any of these listed behaviors can be used to sabotage others indirectly, but sometimes people sabotage others directly. They will put someone down in front of others, for example, or openly ridicule and/or criticize someone in a way that forces the object of their attack to have to fight back from a deficit position to regain balance.

Victim or Martyr. We often feel that someone or some outside force or event has done something to us, that circumstances are something uncontrollable (events that "happen to us") rather than recognize the extent to which we create (or at least contribute to) the circumstances in which we find ourselves.

As hard as it is to believe, even though we moan and complain, sometimes justifiably, about the way someone has treated us, sometimes we seem to prefer the discomfort of being the victim more than the discomfort of facing our own contribution to the situation. Sometimes we even act in a way that gets the other to act in a worse way so we can accurately blame him or her and keep the focus "out there" on his or her bad behavior instead of owning our own behaviors.

It is important to notice all these personal patterns so that we can become conscious of the extent to which we may be acting in any of these ways. If we can detect them, we can sometimes avoid or correct them, if not right on the spot then shortly thereafter or at least "next time." And we can, sometimes even while it is happening, notice that the way we are behaving is having a depleting effect on our own energy, or on our own and other's energy, or on those not directly involved—even in the whole physical space in which we are operating. Such consciousness will go a long way toward our learning first-hand how our personal behaviors can be a barrier to interpersonal relationship.

Interpersonal Barriers to Relationship

What are the interpersonal barriers to relationship, as distinct from the personal barriers? That's a good question, particularly since we have already established that all behavior is personal. But just as we showed that a personal behavior can be reflected in organizational behavior, so it is also possible for each personal behavior described to become an interpersonal behavior—something actually going on between two people in which both parties contribute to the dynamic. Whereas in the personal barriers section I spoke of focusing a camera lens on only the personal contribution and/or reactions to a relationship, here, in the interpersonal barriers section I am suggesting we focus the camera lens on the space between two people. Even if we focus on both individuals in a transaction, we would still be looking at personal behavioral patterns, albeit of each of two or more people. To really see the *interpersonal* barriers in our relationships, we have to feel the energy moving within the space between us, for these energy patterns are something we undeniably cocreated, regardless of who did what first (which one of us was the chicken and which one of us was the egg).

Let's start by returning to the list of frequently encountered personal barriers to see how easily they can be seen as describing *interpersonal* barriers we both had a hand in creating. Together, that is, we can fill the space between us with behaviors and/or attitudes that are

Controlling

Lying

Judging

Doubting

Manipulative

Withholding

Blaming

Prejudicial

Sabotaging

Victimizing

It's easy to see how there could be *mutual* lying or even how one of us could act in a controlling way *because* the other is withholding, or one us becomes manipulative because the other is lying, or, to be fair, one of us is withholding because the other is controlling, or one of us is lying because the other is manipulating. We each believe that we are doing what we are doing only *in response* to the other. But even if our blaming is accurately placed, justifying ourselves and putting the blame on others can spiral onward forever, and, again, we have the familiar chicken-and-egg competition which, like most competition, constitutes a real interpersonal barrier to relationship. It takes two to play, and whenever it is happening, all parties are engaged in it, and all parties to it are "equally" responsible.

Does "equally" responsible mean 50/50? Sometimes, but not always. Sometimes the 25 percent one party contributes is all it takes for the other party's 75 percent to come out. Given that the dynamic wouldn't have taken place at all without the contributions from both sides, then, yes, we are "equally" responsible. To get around this debate over whether the responsibility for an interpersonal dynamic is 10/90, 50/50, or 90/10, some prefer language that says we are each 100 percent responsible—again, not simply to describe our precise contribution but to apply to the whole dynamic.

At the very least, we should be able to see that, together, we are 100 percent responsible for cocreating every interpersonal pattern. If it is a depleting one, both are depleted by it. Unless we take mutual responsibility for the dynamic we created, we cannot take the next step: accepting mutual responsibility for fixing the dynamic. We are then faced with another interpersonal barrier to relationship. To repair a relationship requires first noticing and then acknowledging what is in need of repair. It is this mutual recognition that allows us to grasp a vision of what can be. A lack of willingness to "see" together what is so or to name it or accept responsibility for it is to conclude that change is not possible. What could be more energy depleting?

Similarly, lack of trust is clearly a barrier to interpersonal relationship; in fact, it is one of the most common traits we see in people. As Ronita Johnson of Pacific Gas and Electric has said,

> Often it has to do with the fact that I don't trust you...and you may not trust me...so there is a wall between the two of us, and we have not developed a way to get through that wall and really interact with each other.

When the lack of trust is mutual, it is often used as a reason for acting in all of the depleting ways we've discussed—and the reverse is certainly true: that by acting this way we create a lack of trust. And, as with the other behaviors, it starts with self. It's not possible to trust another if one is not trustworthy oneself.

Another interpersonal barrier to relationship may be the history of that relationship, the past experiences people have already shared. As Dr. Robert Hayles of Pillsbury (Grand Metropolitan) has said,

> Honesty and trust are very fragile entities. If I tell you 99 things that are true and 1 lie, that lie will taint the 99 things I said that were true.

That is just one example, but any past experience of a depleting nature makes us at least a little uncertain about what to expect in the present or the future. And when we are feeling unsafe to trust, for whatever reason, our energy is depleted.

And finally, differences (unless they are complementary) are a barrier to relationship. One difference alone is not a problem, but it is a reality that any two differences might do more than trigger feelings of discomfort in one another; they might inhibit the possibility of our developing an enhancing relationship at all. When I speak of differences in this context, I speak not only of differences in culture and language, as you might expect, but also of differences in job function, personality, communication styles, motivation, values, needs, intentions, and even differences in the *degree of expression* of some of the behaviors we have been discussing.

Let's say, for example, that two individuals who have a need to be in control (within the "normal" range) might not be able to relate as effectively together as two individuals whose personal needs are complementary—that is, one needs control and the other cooperation (even if outside the "normal" range). This is how lack of "compatibility" can act as an interpersonal barrier to relationship between two people, although each one might be able to form very effective relationships with another, more compatible person.

Skills and Tools for Building Relationship

Relationship-enhancing patterns increase the "working" energy available to individuals in their interpersonal and organizational relationships. The following are some examples of perceived relationship-enhancing patterns across many cultures:

Commitment	Participation
Trust	Consciousness
Facilitation	Personal responsibility
Warmth	Empathy
Understanding	Openness
Honesty	Effective communication
Being present	Acceptance

Again acknowledging that "there are no organizational behaviors, there are only individual behaviors," we still need to ask, What can be done by organizations, by individual persons, and by partnerships and teams to build energy-enhancing relationship patterns in our organizations?

Organizational Energy

Organizations need to take responsibility for maximizing organizational energy by encouraging synergistic relationship patterns. Dr. Robert Hayles, again, says,

> The role of leadership is walking their talk around relationships. It means role modeling, building relationships with others, honesty, candor, giving feedback when it is most difficult to give feedback (and receiving feedback) without shooting the messenger.

And as William Esrey continues in the same film,

> There is one thing that we have that no one else has, and that is our employees. I think the key is to create an environment in which employees feel that they are wanted, that their contributions are eagerly sought after, that you want to listen to what they say, and that you want what they have to contribute.

The organizational culture, remember, is an accumulation of all the relationship patterns that went before, and it has an enormous effect on the individuals currently operating within that culture and on the relationships they form. But ongoing relationship patterns of employees, and especially of leaders, can change the culture from one that is closed to one that is open, understanding, and flexible, and establishing a culture of trust can change the quality of relationship between and among individuals throughout the organization.

The organization's leadership need only recognize that human energy is the most flexible and responsive resource available to them. Once they do so, leaders can be instrumental in building relationship by committing time and resources to creating a "trusting relationship field" into which employees enter. Effective leadership today is characterized by individuals who can relate to, understand, and value differences. The bases for effective leadership are trustworthiness (going on that inner journey), trusting others (by building relationships), making the effort to understand differences, and looking for the "common" human element.

Understanding and respecting the diversity of people's gifts is the first crucial step toward trusting each other and building relationship. For each of us, the "inner journey" is the key not only to our personal maturational process and to our capacity for good interpersonal relationships but also to the overall health and renewal of the organization.

As for the organization, it has at its disposal various ways of transforming relationship(s) and the organization:

- Culture (valuing differences, values of respect, and so on)
- Policies (EEO, AA, Valuing Diversity®)
- Structures (flatter, more communicative of participatory)
- Organizational forms for how the work gets done (There is a trend toward using teams, group problem solving, and partnerships.)
- People development and training (experiences to facilitate relationship between diverse employees and personal empowerment training)
- Role models, especially leadership and management that walks its talk (establishing a climate in which relationships flourish, actively building trust by being congruent and making a committed effort to understand and respect the gift of diversity offered by each employee)

- Reward systems (rewarding teamwork and communicative relationships)

- Informal activities (Outward Bound, picnics, parties, ethnic potluck meals)

Clearly, the organization has many ways in which it can bring into being a culture conducive to developing and sustaining energy-enhancing relationships. But as Ben Tong of the University of California, Berkeley, says,

> For sure, the organization has responsibility to create and sustain a climate that would encourage genuine personal expression, but the individual has just as much responsibility to be truthful to herself or himself regardless of the climate.

Personal Patterns

So what are the personal skills needed to build relationship? Since they are the key to building energy-enhancing interpersonal relationships, let's list them as we did the depleting patterns. Again, I will speak as "we" as a way of our "owning" these enhancing behaviors just as we needed to own the depleting ones. It is time to give ourselves credit for the fact that we do often behave in these positive and constructive ways. We might even visualize that behavior as a way of manifesting it more often in our daily lives.

Trust. We are willing to rely on the integrity, strength, and abilities of ourselves and others. We give ourselves and others the benefit of the doubt, believing and understanding that people are responsible and can contribute in diverse ways. We have faith in others and allow them to be responsible for the tasks they've been assigned. We are available to others as a resource but do not feel the need to interfere with or control the way others approach tasks. We convey (both verbal and nonverbal) confidence in others.

Remember that trusting others is dependent upon our being trustworthy ourselves first. That means we need to be deserving of someone else's giving us the benefit of the doubt. And it means that others can count on us to tell the truth, to do what we say and say what we do. It also means that others can count on us to "own" and accept responsibility for our energy-depleting behaviors when they do occur and to "buy into" and try our best to behave in these energy-enhancing ways that we are now listing.

Personal Responsibility. This is when we actively "own" and express thoughts, feelings, needs, and intuitions we've become aware of in a way that indicates how we've contributed to or cocreated, a particular situation. We demonstrate a willingness to hold ourselves accountable for our "side of the street." We have an accurate awareness of who we are (separate from others) that is shared with integrity. We tend to use "I" statements instead of "you" statements.

It is important to remember that we cannot continue to change others, that we can only change ourselves. In fact, for others to feel we are trustworthy and safe, we must consistently be willing to keep the focus on our "side of the street." "I must have misunderstood, I'm sorry" is better than "You misled me," but only if we mean it. If we don't mean it, our tone of voice or body language will convey our real feelings.

Honesty and Congruency. Our words are congruent with our feelings and actions. We give out clear messages, and they are transparently real. Honest people are aware of their thoughts, motives, and feelings and risk sharing them. We communicate in an effort to be true to ourselves instead of trying to "change" or convince others. We value the "microscopic" truth over withholding or lying. We tend to be direct about what we want.

Telling the truth really does avoid distance in relationship. No matter what the truth is, a good relationship can survive the truth better than it can survive the distance created by anything less than the truth. We need to have the underlying willingness to lose something in front of others (such as "losing face," feeling embarrassment or shame) in order to maintain a sense of harmony within ourself and in the relationship, and if we are not willing to make that trade, then we have made a choice (which is worth knowing) about which is more important to us.

Consciousness. We are in touch with, and try to integrate, all of the sources of information available to us (feelings, thoughts, and intuitions), and we are open to receiving the feelings, thoughts, and intuitions of others. This may extend beyond personal and interpersonal awareness to an awareness of the dynamics of the whole system in which we are functioning.

It is really only in knowing ourselves that we are capable of truly "seeing" and knowing others, and only by knowing ourselves can we adjust to the ever-changing space around us. In fact, the only person we have any real control over is ourself, so to survive in a rapidly changing organization, the person we have to know most about is ourself.

Acceptance. Acceptance happens when we really "see" another person for who they are without trying to change them. Value is placed on allowing another space to have feelings or thoughts that are different.

Acceptance is a state of grace. It's a moment of clarity in which "who the person is" is valued over who you need them to be.

There is a great value (as painful as it sometimes is) in uncovering what is so, and letting that be, rather than constantly striving to make things other than they are. Truth and real understanding are more important than maintaining an image or fantasy and are better for everyone in the long run. We must let others air their feelings or beliefs on a particular topic rather than block them. In doing so, we might even learn something we can use. Everyone's "truth" can be understood to fit into the "overall truth" and need not be threatening to us.

Understanding. We are able to let go of biases, expectations, or assumptions long enough to safely perceive what is actually intended by another person. There is commitment to listening to and valuing others rather than manipulating outcomes. An understanding person actively asks questions in an effort to link incoming information with personal experience. We actively try to understand the "experience" of others and are willing to change.

Just as our own reality has validity, so does another's. Different perspectives need to be seen by each of us as clarifying and adding to our knowledge base. Life is about learning more, not about already knowing all there is to know.

Openness. An open person tends to share information freely and he or she values and is receptive to the input to and feedback from others. We are flexible, able to integrate and incorporate diverse ideas in a way that adds to our current understanding. New input is not resisted or guarded against; it is used. We are comfortable testing perceptions and assumptions, and we are not afraid to ask questions. Open exchange of ideas and energy is perceived to be of mutual benefit. We are open to change.

We need to be sure we are operating from an assumption of abundance rather than scarcity and an assumption that we benefit rather than lose by being open to diverse perceptions and diverse experiences.

Facilitative. We encourage, nurture, and empower others in a way that helps them to connect with and build on their own experience and competence. We use ourselves as an instrument to draw out, highlight, and expand the expertise that already exists. We support people in their process of "becoming" and view mistakes as experiences from which we can learn (rather than as "failures").

We need to trust that everyone is an "expert" at something and a "resource" with something of unique value to contribute. Only by facilitating, rather than blocking, their expression can we find out whether this contribution is something we can use personally or in our organization.

Being Present.   Our past experiences or future expectations do not affect or interfere with the relationship opportunities presented in the moment. We are aware of ourselves, the other person, the relationship dynamics, and the external environment.

We need not forget the past; we must remember and keep with us lessons learned from the past without reliving the past. We need not ignore the future; we must have some sense of where we intend to go if we hope to be able to get there, but we are not so fixed on future expectations that we can't change our direction. Each moment is the only moment in which we live; we must live each moment as fully as we can.

Commitment.   We make a conscious decision to see a process or relationship through to its agreed upon or intended conclusion.

There is recognition that commitment requires continual conscious choice to act in ways consistent with the goal. There is a tendency to show up, follow through, and persist. We need to keep appointments, do what is necessary to accomplish our goal, call when we say we will, and work late if necessary to get something accomplished. We need to face, not avoid, challenges and uncomfortable issues, and we need to convey that we will still be around and still committed even during and after tough times.

Effective Communication.   Our communications are clear. We are conscious and tolerant of different styles, language, accents, and so on. Our verbal and nonverbal messages match. Our intention, always, is to reach, relate, and achieve a mutual understanding rather than to simply pass on information.

Since communication is two-way, not one-way, we must let others complete their thought without our interrupting, abruptly ending or changing the subject, or completing their sentences for them. We must be sure we are involved in the communication to understand or to connect—not to get power over another.

Participation and Cocreation.   We consciously participate and value the participation of others. We work willingly with others to achieve mutually beneficial results. We value the contributions, inputs, and suggestions of others. We recognize that productivity and creativity, as a synergistic process between people, yields more than what either could have achieved in isolation.

Personally, we must believe that what we have to contribute is of value to others, and we must share our direct experience, feelings, and intuitions. We must "show up," be present, tell the truth, and then let go and trust the process.

Valuing Diversity. We respect and appreciate the "differences" (cultural, ethnic, racial, and so on.) that affect life experiences, values, beliefs, and styles of communicating rather than just "tolerating" them. We acknowledge and examine our stereotypes and assumptions so that balanced, mutual exchanges can take place. We treat people equitably—not uniformly. We see rewards and advancements as being available to everyone. We place emphasis on including and integrating the strengths and world views of everyone concerned.

I have intentionally listed "valuing diversity" as a personal relationship-enhancing behavior, even within the chapter stating that "valuing relationship" is the "how-to" of valuing and managing diversity. Each value and behavior facilitates other values and behaviors. There is no conflict or competition between them; not only are they compatible and complementary, they are impossible to achieve without one another. Both are personal values and behaviors that become interpersonal and organizational behaviors as soon as they are practiced and expressed.

Interpersonal Synergy

What interpersonal skills are needed to build relationship? Diverse relationships are the vehicles for capturing and enhancing the most valuable and flexible resource on this planet (perhaps fourth only to air, water, and food), yet we relate with others all the time without the benefit of conscious thought about what is going on. Our interactions are often automatic and occur, for the most part, outside of our awareness. Consequently, we often address this most important part of our private and working lives, this most important asset of the organization in which we work, in an extremely haphazard and unconscious way.

When working in pairs or teams, we need to recognize that each of the "personal" behaviors just discussed must become "interpersonal" behaviors to which we subscribe, making only minor adjustments as needed to reflect that both or all of us are required to "buy in" if we are to succeed in any joint undertaking.

Even though every relationship we enter—in the workplace, every partnership or group or team—would be safest and most synergistic if all the personal behaviors listed above were mutually agreed upon and committed to, it is probably acceptable "enough" if we each just "personally" agreed to do our best on our own as far as

- Being present
- Being open
- Being accepting of differences
- Remaining conscious
- Taking personal responsibility
- Being facilitative and empowering

Even "valuing diversity" can be considered a personal goal and commitment, rather than an "interpersonal" contract. The ideal of using each human resource to its fullest potential and achieving synergistic interpersonal and team relationships cannot possibly be realized without our personal, interpersonal, and organizational commitment to valuing diversity. That statement, alone, must be made clear, for it is the foundation of this book as it is of all my work. If, however, as we journey on the road to fully valuing diversity we find ourselves merely tolerating, allowing, enabling, and supporting diversity, then we must forgive ourselves and keep striving.

With regard to the other personal behaviors, however—honesty, understanding, trust, communication, participation, and commitment—I really believe that not even a safe, much less an ideal, relationship can happen unless these behaviors are mutually agreed upon. Communication must, at the least, be understood to be a mutual two-way phenomenon. Both verbal and nonverbal communication define, maintain, and alter the relationship through the language we use and the tone (for example, subservient, aggressive, victim) we take, and our communication skills allow us to make appropriate changes and accommodations as we see the need. But we must establish rules for various situations and either maintain those rules or change them based on whether they are enhancing or depleting to the "energy" field between us and others. In every communication between individuals in a relationship, the opportunity exists to either maintain the status quo or redefine our relationship.

Understanding, itself, must be a mutual, two-way phenomenon. We must each be willing to make a commitment to understand the other person before even making our self understood. We should then use that understanding to change our own behavior in a way likely to be most helpful to the relationship. When people speak to us, we have to make an attempt to listen actively and to make sense of what they are trying to convey, instead of comparing their gestures, tone of voice, facial expressions, and ideas to beliefs and attitudes we hold and to perceptions we have already formed (based on assumptions, stereotypes, and past experiences).

Honesty must be mutually assumed, assured, or agreed upon if there is to be the safety required for any synergistic growth. If one of us lies or withholds any relevant truth from the other, the break created in the energy flow may be so serious that the other feels constantly uncertain about what is true and what is not. If one of us manipulates the other to serve our own needs, that is also dishonest and leaves the other uncertain about whether what happens is motivated by the "right reasons" or by less trustworthy reasons. With any dishonesty, the "other" is left feeling "crazy" or uncertain about his or her feelings and instincts. Dishonesty of any kind is a real projection of one's own discomfort onto another; it is cowardly and cruel. Relationship can be enhanced only by total and mutual honesty—appropriate to the nature of the relationship and the circumstances, of course.

That trust is vital to interpersonal relationships is understandable. As I have already indicated, mutual trust requires mutual trustworthiness. It is only possible for me to trust you if I am trustworthy myself, and I can ask you to trust me only if I am trustworthy myself. Similarly, you must be trustworthy to ask me to trust you or to be able to trust me. While ultimately there are no guarantees—all each of us can do is let go and be trustworthy and trust—it remains that when we are in relationships where there is a commonality of goals or purposes and our stake in the relationship is a significant one, we need to have an understanding about what each party needs, expects, and wants; we need to set up some boundaries and rules so that each party can agree or not agree at the outset to behave in a trustworthy manner. As Shirley Dong of Avon has said,

> If you don't have trust in a relationship, it seems that it's built on nothing, and it's very easy to either blame or have the relationship come to an end. When you have trust in a relationship, you learn to rely on the person, you learn to be able to count on them in any situation. I think in a team situation, it's extremely, extremely important because in a team, you're working together, and when you're working together synergistically, then you know you're working properly, and it is the most efficient way to work.

Participation must be mutual, as must be the recognition that everything going on synergistically in the space between us is cocreated. Therefore, if there are problems, if there is an energy-depleting aspect to the relationship, it is somehow and to some extent cocreated. Ideally, then, each party must examine his or her contribution to the problem instead of automatically blaming the other. Furthermore, again ideally, there must be a real attempt to move beyond the additive (3 + 4) value of each other toward a multiplicative (3 × 4) synergy between parties.

And for collaborative cocreation to take place, commitment must become cocommitment, and responsibility must be felt to be 100/100, not 60/40 or even 50/50. There is nothing more critical to a relationship's chances than cocommitment. With it, the highest level of self-fulfillment and the highest level of synergy can be achieved simultaneously.

In addition to arriving at these six elements of personal behavior requiring mutuality in order for "no potential lost" to be attained in relationship, the following might serve as useful pointers in building effective relationships in the workplace:

- Be aware or conscious of the "realness" of relationship as a flexible "transformation or change vehicle," as well as the barriers that deplete relationship. This awareness enables us to plan our efforts to help the relationship achieve its greatest purpose—collaborative cocreativity.

- Identify commonalities (shared visions, values, goals, interests, objectives).

- Consider what is happening now between you and "the other" and how the pattern can be changed. What is causing the conflict could be any number of factors including obvious differences, but it is sel-dom fruitful to pinpoint blame. The key is to acknowledge the dis-comfort, to find a way to build a bridge, and to change the patterns.

- Make deposits and/or investments in the relationship over time, as each interaction builds trust and "meaning" in the relationship.

- Build trusting, cocommitted, and conscious relationships by creat-ing ground rules and establishing boundaries. We have the capabili-ty to change the rules and boundaries as needed.

- Take personal responsibility for one's own mistakes and take mutu-al responsibility for getting the job done.

- Decrease energy-depleting patterns (control, manipulation, lying) and increase energy-enhancing patterns (honesty, understanding, commitment).

- "Manage conflict" by consciously facilitating participation, that is, the me *and* you within a situation of acceptance, warmth, and safety as opposed to the me *then* you relationship or the me *or* you survival situation characterized by fear, win-lose, survival feelings.

- Identify a facilitator or leader to enhance the relationship process in teams. Even in self-directed work teams, individuals can play a facilitation role, and it can be rotated.

- Accept that the relationship is a struggle and in the process of becom-ing. Postpone evaluations and judgments and check assumptions. Value and facilitate the diverse contributions of diverse persons.

How Does Diversity Affect Relationship?

In this final section I am not going to distinguish between the personal, interpersonal, and organizational. In fact, I could also have chosen to address this issue at each stage throughout the chapter rather than address it once at the end, but I chose to address it once because it really comes down to one question: "Do real cultural differences affect each of these values and behaviors I've suggested as *the way* to build effective personal, interpersonal, and organizational relationships?" And the answer is clear: "Very much so."

That's why we have joined to write this book. That's why we have produced the *Valuing Relationship*® and the *Valuing Diversity*® and the *Going International*® video series. That's why there are so many diversity and cross-cultural consultants at work around the world addressing these issues. It is a complex, nonlinear issue. Different cultures build relationships differently, even though the basis of enhancing relationships across all cultures comes down to trust, respect, and shared goals. Sometimes in the workplace we have to build a relationship with people whose difference from us makes us uncomfortable. There is often a common goal that can facilitate the relationship, but we must remember that one does not build intimacy overnight, especially across cultures.

The way people build trust is different from one culture to another. The way people express their comfort or discomfort in interactions will also vary across cultures. The way an African-American male masks or projects or denies his emotions (fear, anger) may be different from the way an Asian-American female expresses the same emotions. Conversely, the way culturally diverse people express enhancing patterns may be different. If we accept that honesty (congruency, authenticity) is universally a relationship-enhancing interaction, then the question we are grappling with is: Do people with differences express their honesty, openness, and congruency differently? The answer is yes.

Paul Pedersen of Syracuse University said it best when he addressed cross-cultural differences in the following way:

> You need to have a perspective that looks at similarities and differences at the very same time. You need to become cross-eyed in terms of one eye focused clearly on similarities and at the very same time the other eye focused on differences.
>
> The way to change bad conflict into good conflict is to focus on the expectations. Focus on the common ground, focus on the extent to which both people want the same thing, want respect, want sharing, want efficiency, want kindness, want caring. If you focus on this shared common ground expectation, then you can pull that

conflict out of the personal self and create enough trust so that people can behave differently and still get along.

This whole book is filled with examples of differences, how to address them, and how to value and manage them. The intent of this concluding chapter is essentially to make the point that in any culture of the world, in any organization, and within any working relationship of two or more, learning to value the relationship process and become conscious of the energy-depleting and energy-enhancing impact of our behaviors is as critical as valuing our differences and becoming conscious of the impact of our culturally different behaviors.

The systemic nature of The Relationship System of which we are each an integral part is best summarized by Willis Harman of the World Business Academy in the *Valuing Relationship®* films as follows:

> It may seem totally unreasonable that we should set out to learn to trust, to learn to trust the total environment, because there have always seemed to be elements out there that it was foolhardy to trust. But this is another part, and a very profound part, of the holistic thinking that if there really is one whole, and we're part of that whole, the discovery that that whole is trustworthy is an important part, and essential part, of human growth and development.
>
> There probably is an interim period in organizations where the manager may have to work at encouraging the development of cooperative attitudes. This is probably temporary. We're probably coming into a period in which that's going to be more and more natural for all of us, because once you really know yourself to be a part of a larger organism, what other way is there to behave?

In summary, the relationship process with its potential for creativity, is the lifeblood of every organization. In this world in which challenge and change are the only constants, effective personal, interpersonal, and organizational relationships are the most critical tools available for our survival, and the vehicles for our success. Valuing diversity is the how-to of valuing and managing relationship and valuing relationship is the heart and how-to of valuing and managing diversity. We can't do one without the other. It is that simple. It is that complex.

Epilogue

A Conversation
among the Authors

The following spontaneous, unrehearsed, and unscripted conversation took place among the contributing authors of this book. The exchange was facilitated by Shelley Lieberman of Griggs Productions. We at Griggs Productions thought that it would be interesting for you, the reader, to hear an energetic, free-flowing conversation among the diversity experts who wrote this book. Perhaps it will offer you a glimpse of a successful diversity process, one that combines the specifics of diversity training with the creative process necessary for innovation. We hope also that this dialogue will give you some insight to how diversity training and the creative process must work together to help organizations move toward greater efficiency, more effective human resources programming, and full employee participation. Finally, all of us at Griggs Productions hope that this discussion provides fertile ground for you to grow your own diversity and organizational ideas and visions.

Because participants are identified by their initials only, we provide you with the following key. (Shelley Lieberman's questions and remarks as moderator are italicized.)

LBG	Lewis Brown Griggs
	Griggs Productions
LLL	Lente-Louise Louw
	Griggs Productions and
	C.A.R.D.S. International
SL	Shelley Lieberman
	Griggs Productions
PT	Percy Thomas
	Success Behavior Institute

RG   Rafael Gonzalez
           Rafael Gonzalez Enterprises
FK   Dr. Frances Kendall
           Frances Kendall and Associates
SH   Steve Hanamura
           Hanamura Consulting

A Dialogue about Diversity

sL: *What do you generally experience as common pitfalls and basic problems in diversity training?*

PT: Well, one of the pitfalls I find is that participants perceive diversity training as being EEO training, and it takes them a while to shift that paradigm and really understand what *diversity* means.

RG: In addition to that, what I experience a lot is that there has not been any kind of a plan for follow-up activities after training. There is a lack of communication about what the session is about, how it's tied into the goals of the organization, or what senior-level commitment is, and so it's often treated as an isolated issue in a vacuum instead of a business issue.

LLL: I tend to agree with that. There seems to be no sort of internal mechanism or structure to really monitor the process and keep it going as a natural part of the business.

sL: *To what extent is top management to blame for not seeing the diversity process as a strategic organizational issue?*

PT: They don't see how it is in the organization's interest. They see it as a "deficit model" more than a "benefit model."

sL: *Can you explain what you mean by a "deficit model"?*

PT: Well, they see diversity and "people of differences" as taking away from the organization rather than adding to it or bringing something to it.

LLL: They don't really see the opportunity that diversity presents to the organization.

LBG: In addition, they fail to perceive that it is in their self-interest, not only their organizational self-interest but even personal self-interest.

RG: Then there is the whole issue around backlash.

PT: Well, part of the pitfall is that top management has a big phobia about diversity and diversity training. Many have a fear that when you stop talking about benchmarking and you finish doing your cultural audits, that something deep and dark and nasty is going to surface about their organization.

FK: Right, and it's more complicated, I think, than just having to do with top management. I think the backlash is also happening in the culture. White men are continually being told by films, by articles, that they are being replaced and that they are not useful anymore. They walk into the organization, of course, with that fear, that input, and somebody comes in and says, "Either we are going to have a grievance on our hands, or we really need to begin to recognize that we are becoming more and more diverse." When they hear this, it means, "I am out of here—that's what I'm being told in the culture." Naturally, that makes them even more frightened and less willing to embrace and see the positive benefit of diversity.

sh: Another pitfall has to do with the sophistication of the audience. There are some people who are dangerous because they know a little bit about it and think they know it all, and they start telling you how you ought to do the training. I'd rather take someone who knows nothing about it and work with that.

rg: And that gets played out with people's special agendas—when you have special interest groups coming in and you walk in to do a training session, all of a sudden you get arguments and issues coming up, and you don't know where they are coming from. What it is is that people have come in trying to work their own agenda so they wind up having to have a limited conversation that is related to their personal group. It's not organization-wide.

fk: I think we can think of it as people coming in and having the agendas for their own group, but I also think that, often, there are also organizational personal agendas that get played out in those sessions. I think it's really important to understand both of those pieces of reality.

rg: Yes, I think an example could be the Hispanic support group, the gay-lesbian support group, all of those support groups—to increase the hiring of their specific groups, that's the primary agenda that they are going to come in with, and from an organizational perspective, too. Then there're all kinds of issues that go on that have to do with even what function is valued or not valued. People are saying, "I'm now an hourly employee, and I am working in manufacturing, and I'm being treated like dirt. That's how it is working here and so I'm having a hard time hearing anything about 'valuing diversity' when every day this is how I get treated." I know this is an organizational norm.

pt: One of the things that I'm finding recently is that a lot of organizations are now looking toward diversity training as a mechanism for resolving EEO issues or when their organizations have been besieged by complaints of racism or there has been some sort of demonstration. Then people say, "Well, we have to look at diversity." When you bring diversity in with that backdrop, it makes it very difficult, early on in a training, to get people to separate and make those distinctions.

sh: It's almost like they see it as a "fix-it"—that once it is done, they should move on. What they don't understand is that it's an *ongoing* process.

PT: This is triggering something else in my mind when it comes to pitfalls. I don't know if any of you have experienced this, but I have experienced, several times, a company calling me up saying, "It's urgent! Come help us out," and then when I get there and explain what the diversity process means to them, then they want to try to get you to modify it or tone it down. "Can you let us have a piece of it? Can you dilute it?" You start the process, and they will abort it. I find that to be a real pitfall.

SL: *Why would an organization commit to a diversity process and then back down from that commitment?*

LBG: All too often, it's really a denial system; they are willing to touch certain things but not others, so they draw boundaries around the stuff they are in denial about.

PT: One of the things that the training does is foster relationship, and in many organizations they really don't want others to know what they are doing. So when you come in and start talking about valuing diversity and fostering relationships across ethnic, cultural, and organizational divisions and departments, and you get people to talk, this stuff becomes so effective that they don't want you to do it.

FK: I worked with an organization where the CEO depended on people not talking to one another, depended on the chaos, depended on people being nervous about him and not speaking up to him. I worked with the vice presidents, directors, and mangers, and they all began to talk to one another, and the CEO did exactly what Percy said—he aborted the process.

SL: *So what do you all see as the cost incurred in that kind of lack of interaction and commitment to the process?*

PT: I think it's a lot of in-fighting, a lot of slowdown in the organization, in terms of productivity.

RG: Bad decision making—-it costs millions of dollars.

LLL: It impacts totally on their ability to be creative and innovative.

PT: My fear about this is, and this is a real fear, is that when you have companies reacting this way, eventually these disagreements will get down to a one-on-one situation and become personal. We'll begin to see more violent behavior in organizations because the relationship base won't be there for anything else.

SL: *So if I'm a person who is going to be doing this kind of training and I see and hear all of these potential difficulties, how do I get my organization to move in the direction that you are all advocating?*

FK: I think the first thing you have to do is be real clear about intention, delivery, and follow-through. With the CEO, for example, I pulled out. When the CEO says, "We're done with this training now," we don't have very many options. But I do think that people who are left there will either leave or they will push their company to be something different. They are different than they were before. They have been changed by the process, and they will be less likely, if they are going to stay there, to shut up. And they are going to be more likely to speak up.

LBG: Once the door is open, it is hard to close.

RG: One of the interventions that is important is that a conversation be had about "Why do training now?" "What is the organization ready for?" "How is this going to help us achieve our goals?" The cultural audit and all of that other stuff come in, but they really need to first think about the process. I think a lot of people simply start training, and they end training. They don't think about it as a process.

LLL: Also this area is so very systemic that one needs to look at what door one can enter for that particular organization. It might be leadership, quality, or teamwork. It is very likely that they are already in the diversity or relationship area. They may not perceive it as such, but it's all very much interlinked.

SL: *As you talk about pitfalls, is there any advice or suggestions you can give for moving from pitfalls toward positive solutions and active programming?*

SH: In thinking about solutions to the pitfalls of training, I think we have to frame ourselves, put ourselves in an organizational context, and then we can address the organizational issues.

RG: I just want to say that I think that is really important—the way we are talking about training. I don't even sell myself as a trainer, that's just the way I package myself.

SL: *Can you speak a little more about that—"I don't sell myself as a trainer?"*

RG: Yes. I believe that what I do is consultation, and training is just a piece of it. It's a lot of development work and a lot of transformational work. It's a lot more than training. Training is just an element of it. I think often a lot of folks are selling just a program.

LLL: Exactly. We are dealing with a change process here, and a program may just be one aspect of that change process. But if one looks at this area of purely needing training programs, I think that one is not going to move very far, and next year, there is going to be something else they need.

SH: So Shelley, we're really answering your question, "What are the pitfalls," "How do you get past the pitfalls of training" with a different paradigm response, which is to address the issue of "organizational change."

SL: *How would you help individuals who are caught in the "revolving door" about diversity to see it as a larger strategic issue? And how does the diversity issue help shape other organizational issues?*

RG: For me it's that first conversation again. You look at the different goals that organizations have, you look at the initiatives that they have. For example, most organizations are having "reengineering" or "customer service" or "quality" efforts. An organization cannot do a good job in those areas if it does not have diversity somehow included in it. Or if you are looking at new markets or products or services, you start looking at what starts or what drives the initiative, the measurements for success, what is important for getting the products and services out—and then you see the role diversity has in each one of those.

LLL: Make organizations and employees see that what we are dealing with is interaction between people and that every one of those areas involves some kind of interaction, and interaction across differences, whether we like it or not.

PT: That is so important—that people begin to perceive "new organization" and the new mix of people from a new reality base. My recommendation is that companies need to start looking at anthropological models within their organization so that they can truly look at the behavior. They want to go to a quantitative model; they want to collect hard quantifiable data. Well, when you start looking at different people coming from different perspectives in your organization, different units operating from different perspectives, some of that behavior is not readily quantifiable because you haven't identified it. So you need someone who is skilled there, someone who can do some observational work and draw some conclusions or some hypotheses from which to then collect some hard data. The second thing is that the more diverse your population is, the more you will need someone in there facilitating those relationships—the human dynamics—to bring about understanding.

LLL: I also think the organization will have to be very conscious about from what perspective they are going to be looking at this thing. At the moment, many are pretty confused. They are not sure whether they are looking at things from an organizational, interpersonal, or personal perspective.

SL: *Where do you see diversity going? What I am hearing from everyone is that diversity is taking on a larger organizational role, that "diversity" may not even be the right name for it anymore.*

FK: This is really about organizational change.

PT: It's about world change.

LLL: I think there is a danger here of saying it's just "organizational change." Organizational change is such a dynamic and complex issue, one can get lost in that. Even though we really need to recognize that it is dynamic and complex, we still need very specific and decisive action in certain diversity or relationship areas. We need to value these areas within the context of the bigger picture.

SL: *What do the specifics of this look like?*

FK: Our challenge is to frame organizational change around the needs of individuals who are different by race or age or gender or sexual orientation. We can't drop that out. And when we talk about looking at organizations, we must look at all of those dynamics of the systemic, the personal, and the interpersonal. But the future of diversity is not going to be just: "We are all in it together."

LLL: I think it also involves some kind of decision about the process, where you are going to start, and taking some kind of responsibility, whether it be personal, interpersonal, or organizational. Otherwise, one gets overwhelmed by the extent of the task. Practical actions need to happen every day, and sometimes at the personal employee level.

SH: That reminds me of when I was standing outside waiting to vote for the presidential election; I had already found out who had won. I was standing in line waiting to vote for Carter or Reagan or whoever it was who was running, and they said, "Well, Reagan won." So I thought, "What's the difference? I don't make any difference in this world." So what you're saying is that a person sometimes feels overwhelmed, and we need to break it out into some kind of increments where a person can feel like they can do something—they can make a difference.

SL: *How does the idea of relationship impact on diversity?*

LBG: It's critical. In the future it's going to come down to a "relationship" issue. Each individual or pair of individuals is not just an isolated human resource, to be valued in their separateness. But in addition to valuing each individual's separate difference, which is a part of the process, we've got to recognize that none of us has spoken today without using the word *relationship*. Every two human resources must relate to one another in order to generate the kind of energy, creativity, and productivity that makes organizations work. That means in addition to focusing on our *differences*, we have to focus on the process of *relating* and understanding that it's in one's personal self-interest to do so, so that I can be me, you can be you, and together we can create something new.

LLL: And I also see it, to some extent, as *relationship* within the organization, relationship between different functions, for example, that is changing; that's kind of a structural thing, but it's still a relationship issue although it's not necessarily human relationship. It's, in essence, got to do with how the organization is relating to its different parts, and it needs to do so in a new way.

LBG: Right. The word *relationship* still applies, and in a group and a team there are relationships, there is a group relationship.

LLL: Boundaries are changing, really.

LBG: And organizationally on a systemic level all those different functions are related to one another.

FK: But I think this is a risk. Often what we think is, "If we can just get people communicating better with each other." I often hear, "Well, really it's just a matter of common courtesy. We'll just all like one another." The fact is, if we sprinkled pixie dust on everybody and we all loved each other, nothing would change because the systems would still be the same. So we have to be really clear that what we are talking about is changing systems, where it is not just about me and Rafael or me and Rafael and Steve liking one another or even communicating well with one another....

LBG: That's correct. That is why it has to be the personal, interpersonal, and organizational. We have to look at each level. Each of us must be conscious about the whole—the parts—how they interrelate.

PT: I agree with you. In this whole business of diversity, we are trying to get people to move, and we are trying to get people to accept a new language and get these people on the same wavelength because we're not going to move this business of diversity forward and we are not going to get people in sync with this if we don't change the language; because the language that's pretty consistent in organizations today, and the understanding of many people in the organization, is *competition*, being aggressive. Well, we have new people coming into the workforce who don't understand that language and who, to some extent, will have a lot to do with the reshaping of the organization. A part of the message we must teach people that control and right now have a say in how the organization will be shaped is that you have a whole mix of people coming in that don't respond to the old paradigm, and there must be some guidance from us, as leaders in the diversity field, to shape this new language.

LLL: And it is a new language because I also hear the old people resisting the kind of new language that is brought in by new people. That's not the total direction either; there is a balance that is needed.

SH: People are worried about being politically correct, but they'll do that just to not change the language.

SL: *So what is the process to help people to understand and accept and embrace this new language?*

PT: Well, part of it is writing books and getting the word out there and going into the organizations and having people hear it over and over again.

LLL: I also think part of it is trying to create safety in organizations so that the old and the new can really dialogue and talk to each other and together, participatively, create a kind a language that works for them in that organization. So you might have a national language that emerges in this area, but I also think it's a matter of finding that balance that works for the organization, with the changing culture.

SL: *OK, I'm a diversity professional, picking up this book, and I think I am going to get a book about diversity. It took me a long time to move from EEO and Affirmative Action to diversity in my organization, and now you are asking me to move from diversity to relationship. How do I do this? How do I digest and synthesize all of this information to be effective in what I am trying to do in my diversity efforts?*

SH: I think the real question is, "Where can I start?" This book gives the reader some place to start.

LLL: I think you start where you have already had some progress and basically build on existing success.

SL: *The other thing that I am hearing as a diversity reader is that I am no longer focusing on issue-specific areas. Are you are telling me I have to move to a process orientation?*

FK: My experience is that many organizations don't have the luxury of deciding where to start. They wait until something is presented to them front and center. One of my clients has 12 people of color who are presenting grievances. A class-action suit is exactly what it is. Well, they didn't stop to say, "Four years ago, we needed to pay attention to the fact that all of the people who run our organization are white and male." I think it's not so much a question of where I start. I think the harder question is, once we've dealt with that specific, once we have opened the door, how do we then broaden that to be something that is organization-wide. And that to me is the real challenge. It goes back to what Percy said of looking at the organization anthropologically. What is the context of the organization that allowed a class-action suit to be the only answer? Lawsuits are really the last answer. How can we step back from this experience to get a broader picture of what is going on so that we don't keep putting out fires, so that we really move to change the organization, as opposed to dealing with the fires?

SL: *If you take an anthropological approach, you could be doing your surveys and your studies forever. I'm somebody who has got limited time and limited budget; how do I get my organization to get it? Can you give a list, not a quick-fix list, but a list of active steps that my organization can take to get the process moving along?*

LLL: Well, you have to have role models in the organization; that has to be in place. I think that they have the most authority in the organization, and I would say that is the easiest place to start.

LBG: Also, I think that when we present, when we train, when we consult, we are modeling the behaviors we are trying to teach by being our fully different selves.

SL: *But how do you do this in an organization that is having trouble right now? Do you get the CEO to really "get it" in whatever way he can and then he plays that role model? Do you go to the lowest common denominator, at the bottom of the organization, and look for change agents?*

LBG: Most people agree that the ideal is when it starts at the top, but the reality is that anywhere it starts is sufficient. If you have individuals who are able and willing to model this kind of behavior, then it can spread. I remember once being introduced for a speech by a human resources person. It was going to be an unimportant moment. This person chose to admit that five years before, he had allowed a certain job to go to X individual instead of Y individual, who deserved it, and Y individual was sitting there in the audience as this man, right then and there, apologized with tears in his eyes. They didn't even need the rest of the seminar—the point had been made.

SL: *I'm looking for action-oriented steps. My organization is downsizing, for example, and I am looking for action steps beyond modeling behavior.*

FK: Even though you're in a hurry and your organization is downsizing, and so on, if you are not clear about how your organization makes decisions, if you are not clear about how power is manifested in your organization, if you are not clear about all that, you are not going to be able to make changes that are going to last. So if I am looking at my organization, I'm in a hurry because we're downsizing, and we are firing all of the people of color (which is one of the ways of course that downsizing affects organizations that aren't serious about being diverse), then I first of all need to bring that to somebody's attention. That is what, as an individual, I need to do. But I also need to be clear about how that organization makes decisions because what I am going to want to do is change the way they make decisions. So I need to know that. Even if I am in a hurry, I have to stop—and this is not an ongoing anthropological study until we are dead—but I have to stop and really study what the organization is doing, or I will never be able to make changes.

LLL: Yes, we need to know, "Where am I now?" "Where do we want to be?" We need some kind of stopping somewhere and some kind of energy exerted. The solution just doesn't fall out of the sky.

SL: *I'm hearing leadership, I'm hearing assessment, I'm hearing vision.*

LLL: If one can get some kind of groundswell movement going in the organization, that can have impact.

SL: *What do you mean by that?*

LLL: People from the bottom, if they are facilitated to create awareness in this area, can help change the top culture in the organization. Now who leads that group can be a problem, but usually the human resource people, who are middle management, need to give the group some credibility, whereas in the past middle management has really served senior management. I think middle managers today are becoming more aware of their role as being facilitators between the two, and they need to legitimize the lower levels in the organization and get a groundswell going of people who are really drawing attention to inequities in this area.

SH: The people at the bottom of the organization can achieve this groundswell in the form of networking. The term *networking* has been used rather loosely, but in the book, *Entrepreneuring,* the author talks about how, if I'm on the bottom, I network—not with my direct manager, but if I know somebody who is my manager's counterpart, I seek out that kind of mentoring relationship. You can do some real conscientious things about networking. It is very systematic and very strategic. We do it politically when we want to get an agenda set up, and we also do it in positioning ourselves at work to understand the political realities of the organization.

LLL: Let's assume that there is one person who is serious about this area, who has seen the light in this area, a human resource or diversity person in an organization. I think it's important to identify pockets of energy that they can work with very quickly, and increase their support in this area. It's a groundswell process—I don't think that it is anything else, and I don't think it happens immediately. It really is a process, and one needs to get more support in the areas where it is moving. It's a "gentle rain over time" rather than a "thunderstorm on barren land."

SL: *So keeping all that in mind, a question that comes up time and time and time again for people who are trying to make this happen is: "We are trying to convince the organization to get this, but how do we measure effectiveness? What kinds of things are we looking for?*

LLL: I think every organization needs to define that itself. What are their quantitative and qualitative measures? I think the worst thing to do is to use some kind of external or unknown criteria. Then you fail. I think that even before you start the process, people must be very clear about what changes they are going to be looking for and then set their program to address those criteria.

About the Facilitator

Shelley Lieberman is a professional in the field of multicultural and international education. She has worked with renowned organizations such as the Institute for International Education, the California Institute for Integral Studies, the American and Foreign Fulbright Exchange Programs, and the American Institute for Foreign Study. During her 17-year career, she has helped countless corporations, educational institutions, and government agencies understand how to more effectively value and manage their culturally diverse workforce. As a diversity professional with Griggs Productions since 1984, she has contributed to a national awareness of cultural diversity not only by providing consultation, intervention, and multicultural awareness sessions to client groups but in directing international distribution of Griggs' award-winning *Going International®*, *Valuing Diversity®*, and *Valuing Relationship®* training materials.

About the Authors

Lewis Brown Griggs

I'm pleased that we have chosen to have all contributors to this book provide a personal biography explaining, among other things, their self-interest in doing diversity work. I feel strongly that each of us must begin this work with consciousness of our own differences and a clear sense of our personal motivation for being a part of the diversity movement. Only with both can we hope to contribute anything "different" and model for others ways of valuing diversity from which they might benefit.

Professionally, I have worked in the government, nonprofit and profit sectors, in all cases communicating in whatever ways I could to get ideas heard, products sold, and/or services used. After graduating from Amherst College in 1970 with a B.A. degree in political science, I worked in the federal government for two years in Washington, D.C. In 1972 I moved to Boston and spent two years helping an entrepreneur start a small company targeting educational learning aids for elementary classrooms. In 1974 I began two years at Boston's public broadcasting station WGBH, soliciting grants from corporations to underwrite its national programming. In 1976 I moved to San Francisco and spent two years doing personal, foundation, and corporate fund-raising for San Francisco's public broadcasting station KQED. Then in 1978 I began two years at Stanford University's Graduate School of Business focusing on new enterprise management, earning my M.B.A. degree in 1980. For two years after business school, I consulted to various small organizations, two of which were start-up genetic engineering firms.

It was with one of those organizations that I had a "turning-point" experience. I was in a meeting with Japanese pharmaceutical executives and found myself totally, inexplicably lost. That experience was one of the catalysts for my coproducing the cross-cultural film series entitled *Going International®* as well as coauthoring a book by the same title. After four years of speeches around the country, I began to grasp clearly that cultural differences don't start at the border. Also, the Hudson Institute report, *Workforce 2000,* much cited throughout this volume, helped us all to see the scope of changing demographics. I coproduced the *Valuing Diversity®* video series to redirect attention from the practice at the time of smoothing over or ignoring differences among individuals to advocating open acceptance and valuing of our individual differences. In a new partnership with South African Lente-Louise Louw, Griggs Productions has recently published the *Valuing Diversity® Training System©* and released the *Valuing Relationship®* video series, which we regard as an important piece of the diversity work we must all address, now and in the future.

It is for very personal reasons, however, that I have embarked upon the professional diversity journey in which I find myself actively engaged. My work is complemented but not driven by my 1960s' experiences and values, which certainly include an understanding of the reasons for affirmative action, equal opportunity, and similar programs. However, I am driven by my own personal self-interest in reducing the personal costs of my own ethnocentrism, my own ignorance, my own nåiveté and discomfort with cultural, ethnic, racial, gender—you name it—differences. I was raised in Minneapolis-St. Paul, born into an upper-middle-class, 12-generation-old founding family, and I am white, Anglo, Episcopalian, and privately educated. I am heterosexual, father of a girl and a boy, and stepfather of two girls. I play tennis and ski, drive a Volvo station wagon and a BMW convertible, have two golden retrievers, and dress in clothes from Brooks Brothers, Land's End, L.L. Bean, or The Gap. It's OK to laugh, and all of this I mention for two reasons: First, with regard to the issue of stereotyping, it is important for us to notice how much or how little we actually know about someone from such a brief introduction. It is my opinion that we need to know *more,* not less, about the cultures and groups from which we each evolve and that, of course, as with all knowledge, we need to use such information responsibly; we need to hold it in a neutral, nonjudgmental place as we get to know someone and, in particular, as we discover the ways in which our knowledge of the groups and cultures from which one comes does and does not help us to know the individual at hand.

Second, and more important, I am clear that in addition to all the wonderful aspects of my upbringing, for which I am grateful, it is only from such roots that I can bring to the diversity field some consciousness of my own deep ethnocentrism. Since I am not an anthropologist, a trainer, a consultant, an academic, or a civil rights leader, and since I am not a person of color, female, homosexual, disabled, foreign, or even bilingual, it may be that my only gift to this field is to help others understand ways in which each of us benefits by discovering, owning, and then recovering (constantly) from our own ignorance of and/or discomfort with difference, our own racism, sexism, classism, able-bodied-ism, heterosexism, and whatever *-ism* prevents us from fully *seeing* another human being and even from *being* our own fully human being.

Without the experience of "seeing" and "being seen by" others, our relationships cannot work, and without effective relationships we can neither grow to our fullest potential as individuals, in all our difference, nor can we work in pairs or teams to help the organizations in which we work successfully create and deliver their products and services.

Lente-Louise Louw

My awareness of cross-cultural differences has been with me as long as I can remember. Born a white female in the province of the Orange Free State, one of the most rural provinces in South Africa, I lived with my Afrikaner parents and grandparents on our family farm. My family, Boers of French Huguenot descent, fought against British oppression in the Boer War alongside their black farmworkers.

The farm was called "Opstal," which means "homestead," and together with some surrounding farms, Opstal has been in our family for nearly 200 years. The dwelling itself was an isolated, stone farmhouse filled with the history of the past—tangible evidence in the form of artillery damage and burned spots on the walls floors and intangible evidence in the form of memories of family members who had been interned in British concentration camps.

From infancy, then, I grew up with black farmworkers and their children. Although it is not that unusual in South Africa for white children to play with black children, I and my sister and brother were nurtured by black people; we looked up to our black "grandparents" and other parental figures who told us stories about the Boer War, about the foolish British manner of marching over the hills, about their practice of raising dust to alert the Boer freedom fighters, and other such tales, which we devoured.

And as we played in the dust with our black friends, we envied their ease and competence in building fires, making dwellings out of mud and dung, and playing all sorts of games—using stones, drawings in the dust, and toys fashioned of grass and bones. In adulation, we copied the way they dressed and often ran around naked, except for short skirts made of beads and string.

Beyond these strong, binding relationships with the black community, we were also isolated from white society by reason of our "politics." My grandfather, for example, refused to vote or join the White Dutch Reformed Church because to do either would implicitly support the status quo. He became, in effect, an isolationist and was thought of as a *draadsitter*, a "fence-sitter." If I grew up knowing that our family was referred to scornfully as *Kaffir Boeties* ("nigger lovers"), it is also true that I grew up calling the "British enemy" *Roei nekke* (rednecks). Other than visits to the cafés or occasional trips to town for necessities, we had little contact with white society. Because my grandmother was a teacher, she taught us at home for the first few years of schooling, but, later on, I attended seg-regated white schools. Although our home language was Afrikaans and we were taught English at school, as a child I had spoken fluent *Sotho* (one of the seven main black lan-guages in South Africa), and I and my sister and brother had been given Sotho birth names: mine is *Puleng* (Rain), my broth-er's is *Rastuna* (Son of the Gun), and my sister's is *Malitsatsi* (Mother of the Sun). We spoke *Sotho* so fluently that my moth-er sometimes needed an interpreter to understand us.

I regard these early relationships with my extended black family as the foundation of my being. Despite my white skin and my French ancestry, I know I am African. I *feel* African. And I will always have a deep sense of connection with black Africans. It was only as I grew up and had to stay away from our farm for longer and longer periods of time that I began to fully understand the racial prejudice embedded in the society I had been born into.

It should be no surprise, then, that in adulthood my career path became totally intertwined with the black community. Once I qualified as a clinical psychologist, I focused my efforts on assisting disadvantaged students (mostly black South Africans), applying equal opportunity strategies in white South African organizations, developing a variety of educa-tional and training programs to advance the careers of young people here and in South Africa, and, finally, came to my pre-sent work on valuing and managing diversity in organization-al settings.

Over time, I learned to link my formal Western psychologi-cal training to the less formal but invaluable learning experi-ences that came out of my childhood in South Africa. A major outcome of my effort to formalize what I knew to be valuable linkages between these two world views has been the develop-ment of an *ubuntu* model—a strategy for applying the lessons of the rich African philosophy I grew up with to an apartheid-driven workplace. This change strategy, called "Building on *ubuntu*," has been used effectively over the past six years by organizations and individuals committed to reactivating a "human-friendly" culture in the workplace and in educational settings. Indeed, *ubuntu* philosophy is at the heart of all my work in the broad area of diversity.

Steve Hanamura

My introduction to the world was that I was born blind and of Japanese-American descent at a time when the United States was at war with Japan. Many Japanese-Americans were interned because our country was afraid of what damage might occur to them from any Japanese person. Growing up, little did I realize how being blind and Japanese-American would influence the way others treated me or how I would

respond to them. There were times when I believed that my
ethnic background and blindness were the only way people
thought of me as a person. As an adult, I was constantly being
asked to talk to groups about what it was like to be Japanese
and blind. I soon learned that those two attributes alone did
not make me an expert on either subject.

Another dimension of my life that had a significant impact
on me was that I was a single parent for seven years with cus-
todial responsibilities for my two sons. Though less visible,
single parenting added an interesting sidelight to my other
unique characteristics of being blind and Japanese. Again, my
personal experience as a single parent did not make me an
expert on the subject, but it did provide me with a perspective
of how issues of *diversity* come up on the job. For the single
parent, an often unspoken question is, "Can you be committed
to the job and still take care of your children?"

All three of these dimensions, I found, played a major role in
how I contributed to others and in how, generally, one can
value people who are different and still meet the bottom-line
needs of a company. But, as I indicated before, it is important
to emphasize that having expertise does not come from just
being a certain way. You have to work hard to develop skills,
knowledge, and expertise before you can present yourself as a
consultant or trainer in the field of cultural diversity.

Personally and professionally, I work from the mission
"Celebrating Oneness," which means, simply, that I strive to
empower individuals and organizations to develop themselves
to their fullest potential. A measure of success can be said to
occur when both individuals and systems are working in harmony with each other. This situation creates a sense of belonging for the people involved and a sense of ownership for their
work with each other.

Frances E. Kendall, Ph.D.

I feel as though I have been studying racism and organizations
for most of my life. I was born in 1947 and raised in Waco,
Texas; my family is in the cotton business. As a white Southern
woman, I learned early that skin color is a major determinant
in one's access to privileges and resources: I was able to sit
anywhere on a bus, eat at any restaurant, go to any theater,
and move freely and with relative safety in any part of town.
None of those things was true for any of my contemporaries
whose skin was a different color from mine.

My formal work on issues of difference and organizational
change began in 1966 with my involvement in the National
Student YWCA. There I learned two lessons that continue to
affect the ways I consult with organizations: First, as individuals we are able to change our attitudes—even those we have
held for most of our lives. And second, it is possible to make

fundamental changes in organizations when colleagues who
are committed to long-term change work together.

I prepared myself for life in academia, getting my master's
degree at the Bank Street College of Education in New York
and my doctorate at the University of North Carolina at
Chapel Hill. In 1980 I began what I thought would be my lifelong career at Tufts University. While I enjoyed teaching, it
quickly became clear that my real passion was working on
diversity concerns. In 1982 I moved to the San Francisco Bay
Area and created my own consulting firm. The focus of my
work is organizational and personal change. I consult with
institutions and organizations of all kinds as they strive to
become more hospitable to all people.

I have been incredibly lucky to be able to carve out a career
that I love. One of the prerequisites to my being successful is
that I continue to examine my own prejudices and my own
racism (and classism, and heterosexism, and anti-Semitism,
and sexism, and able-bodied-ism, and so on). My approach to
this work is greatly affected by my belief that none of us is ever
finished with our own personal journey. This is the good news
and the bad news—the bad news being that we are never
done. But the good news is that, knowing we always have
more work to do, our expectations of the changes we are able
to make are likely to be more realistic.

Another reason the work I have chosen is so perfect for me is
that I am fascinated by organizations and the ways in which
each one works (or doesn't, as the case may be). When I begin to
work with a new client, my first step in studying the organization is to talk with employees at all levels. Only through understanding a system can we change it, so my initial task is to find
out as much as I can in order to be able to design the most effective plan for change. The combination of working with people
on personal stereotypes and prejudices and helping organizations become more effective workplaces for all employees is a
perfect marriage of my interests and commitments.

Rafael Gonzalez and
Tamara Payne

Rafael Gonzalez

Rafael's commitment to assist groups, work teams, communities, and organizations create high-performing, productive environments using diversity as a catalyst for change is deeply rooted in his life experiences. Rafael Gonzalez spent his early years
in Puerto Rico surrounded by generations of family, culture, and
history. As a child moving to the mainland United States, Rafael
had many experiences balancing accommodation and assimilation of cultures. These experiences compelled him to work with
diverse communities throughout the United States and interna-

tionally as a community organizer, educator, mental health therapist, administrator, organizational consultant, and trainer.

Although he has spent most of the past three decades of his life in California, his experiences in Puerto Rico and abroad have been instrumental in shaping his view of belonging to a global community. His multiracial, multilingual, and multicultural background has provided him with an abundance of experiences that have helped to shape his view of diversity; he believes it is important for people, teams, and organizations to recognize, value, and use their difference and similarities for common goals. Rafael believes that work environments that value diversity will foster individual and organizational growth, development, and productivity and make the workplace a place where a diversity of people can contribute and participate fully.

Rafael Gonzalez has been the president of Rafael Gonzalez Enterprises, a successful consulting and training firm, for 16 years. Rafael works with a community of highly skilled diverse multilingual and multicultural associates, all contributing a wide range of talents and experience. Their clear commitment to their values of mutual support and personal growth enhances their work, inspiring creativity and sustaining energy and vision.

Rafael has worked with an impressive list of Fortune 500 companies including Levi-Strauss & Co., AT&T, and General Electric. A number of newspaper and broadcasting companies such as Gannett Co., Tribune Co., Knight-Ridder, Inc., and McClatchy Newspapers count themselves among Rafael's clients. In the public sector, Rafael has worked with hundreds of cities, school districts, and community agencies as well as federal, state, and local governments and libraries. He has been instrumental in creating and implementing bilingual mental health and youth leadership programs.

Rafael continues to contribute his considerable talent and expertise to supporting community projects and mentoring young people. In addition to consulting at numerous colleges, universities and executive management programs, Rafael is presently director of Diversity Programs at Northwestern University's Kellogg's School of Business Newspaper Management Center.

Rafael and Stella, his wife of 20 years, live in San José, California, along with their twin daughters, Tara and Erica, their teenaged son, Carlos; and Rafael's mother, Norah.

Tamara Payne

Growing up in America with both African and European ancestry gave Tamara an early understanding of the complexity of diversity issues in the United States. The frequently blurred lines between race and culture created an intriguing and sometimes challenging backdrop for learning about what it meant to be biracial.

Tamara spent her earliest years growing up in the military and benefited from being surrounded by the diversity within the armed services. Memories of the direct and immediate impact of war on that community instilled in Tamara a sense of interconnectedness and interdependence of people and an awareness of global issues.

Tamara built on the foundation of her own experiences for her studies in social psychology, concentrating on the areas of gender and race relations. She went on to research management and leadership styles and creativity and policy development, with a special emphasis on diversity. She continues her research in this area through organizational assessments and audits.

Using her educational and research background, her extensive business experience, as well as her own intimate knowledge of the challenges and barriers to bridging diverse communities, Tamara has consulted, lectured, and created and implemented custom-designed training and development programs in both the public and private sectors. She has worked with such companies as Chevron Corporation, Gannett Co., and AT&T, consulting in over 20 states throughout the United States.

Tamara's current focus as executive consultant for Rafael Gonzalez Enterprises is on working with senior executive groups and diversity committees to develop practical systemic strategic plans in the area of diversity.

Tamara is committed to the development of people, creating and maintaining successful and diverse organizations, and enabling organizations to recognize and use their human resources most effectively.

Tamara currently lives on the East Coast, happily balancing a hectic work and travel schedule and family life with her partner, Mike.

Percy W. Thomas, Sc.D.

I am a long-time freedom fighter and an advocate of civil and human rights for all people. I introduce myself to you as an advocate for understanding and valuing human diversity.

The journey toward understanding and valuing human diversity began for me at an early age. I am the youngest of two children born to Percy and Lillian Thomas. My mother started her work career as a beautician and ended it, after 25 years of service, as a laboratory technician. My father, Percy Thomas, was a career soldier in the U.S. Army. My sister, Evelyn Thomas Labode, and I are the products of a broken home; my mother and father separated when we were still very young children.

Mother and father were reared in the rural South. The Baptist Church was the dominant religious influence in their lives. My parents taught me Christian principles, which the pastor reinforced on Sundays. Thus, the Baptist Church has played a significant role in shaping my perceptions of the world. My father's career in the army caused the family to move frequently from military base to military base. We met lots of people, most of whom were black.

Before entering Johns Hopkins University in 1972, my entire education had been in all-black institutions. In fact, my entire cultural exposure for more than 27 years had been predominantly black environments. I thought only in terms of a black and white culture; I was isolated from other cultures cognitively and physically.

Despite this isolation, I grew up exposed to diversity: I lived on a farm, I was the son of an army sergeant, I was of divorced parents, I was reared by a single parent, I lived in an urban, inner city, I was religiously oriented in the Baptist Church and sprinkled with Catholicism, and I was educated in both the public and Catholic school system. So for me, dealing with diversity has been a lifelong learning experience. (I define *cultural diversity* as the differences in people of different ethnic, racial, and cultural origins.)

My formal education continued to reflect my early experience as a person who is comfortable with differences. I received a bachelor of science degree in health and physical education from the University of Maryland, Eastern Shore, a master's degree in special education (with a concentration in the psychology of the emotionally disturbed child) from Coppin State College, and a doctorate from Johns Hopkins University, with a concentration in mental health administration.

Most of my formal education is relevant to the subject of diversity. My experiences in completing the requirements for the doctorate of science degree at Johns Hopkins University remain one of the most memorable and influential cultural diversity episodes in my life. The title of my dissertation was *Black Adolescent Males and the Decision to Work: A Study in Stressful Transition.* It is out of this study that I developed skills and techniques for working in the area of diversity. Working with members of different street gangs, for example, helped me sharpen my observation techniques and recognize the value of people who are perceived in society as being different. Moreover, it is through this study that I learned the fundamentals of qualitative research methodology, which is an important and necessary tool in benchmarking diversity issues within organizations and society. Further, my work with young people on a personal and interpersonal level has resulted in my developing the idea of *cultural rapport,* the focus of my contribution to this volume.